FREE VIDEO  FREE VIDEO

ASTB Essential Test Tips Video from Trivium Test Prep!

Dear Customer,

Thank you for purchasing from Trivium Test Prep! We're honored to help you prepare for your ASTB exam.

To show our appreciation, we're offering a **FREE *ASTB Essential Test Tips* Video by Trivium Test Prep.*** Our video includes 35 test preparation strategies that will make you successful on the ASTB. All we ask is that you email us your feedback and describe your experience with our product. Amazing, awful, or just so-so: we want to hear what you have to say!

To receive your **FREE *ASTB Essential Test Tips* Video**, please email us at 5star@ triviumtestprep.com. Include "Free 5 Star" in the subject line and the following information in your email:

1. The title of the product you purchased.
2. Your rating from 1 – 5 (with 5 being the best).
3. Your feedback about the product, including how our materials helped you meet your goals and ways in which we can improve our products.
4. Your full name and shipping address so we can send your **FREE *ASTB Essential Test Tips* Video**.

If you have any questions or concerns please feel free to contact us directly at 5star@trivium-testprep.com.

Thank you!

- Trivium Test Prep Team

*To get access to the free video please email us at 5star@triviumtestprep.com, and please follow the instructions above.

ASTB Study Guide:

2 Practice Tests and ASTB-E Exam Prep

5th Edition

Elissa Simon

TABLE OF CONTENTS

ONLINE RESOURCES

To help you fully prepare for the ASTB, Trivium Test Prep includes online resources with the purchase of this study guide.

Practice Test

In addition to the practice test included in this book, we also offer an online exam. Since many exams today are computer-based, getting to practice your test-taking skills on the computer is a great way to prepare.

Flashcards

A convenient supplement to this study guide, Trivium's e-flashcards enable you to review important terms easily on your computer or smartphone.

Cheat Sheets

Review the core skills you need to master with easy-to-read Cheat Sheets. Topics covered include Numbers and Operations, Algebra, Geometry, Statistics and Probability, and Grammar.

From Stress to Success

Watch *From Stress to Success*, a brief but insightful YouTube video that offers the tips, tricks, and secrets experts use to score higher on the exam.

Reviews

Leave a review, send us helpful feedback, or sign up for Trivium's promotions—including free books!

To access these materials, please enter the following URL into your browser:

www.triviumtestprep.com/astb-online-resources

INTRODUCTION

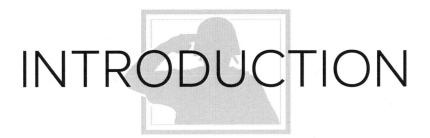

Congratulations on choosing to take the Aviation Selection Test Battery (ASTB-E)! By purchasing this book, you've taken an important step on your path to joining the military.

This guide will provide you with a detailed overview of the ASTB-E, so you know exactly what to expect on exam day. We'll take you through all the concepts covered on the exam and give you the opportunity to test your knowledge with practice questions. Even if it's been a while since you last took a major exam, don't worry; we'll make sure you're more than ready!

WHAT IS THE ASTB-E?

The ASTB-E is an exam to measure a candidate's verbal and quantitative ability, spatial awareness, and knowledge of general aviation concepts. The ASTB-E is an indicator used to determine eligibility of college graduates desiring to become an aviation officer (pilot and first officer) in the US Navy, Marine Corps, or Coast Guard. The result from this exam is also used to determine eligibility as a nonaviation officer in the US Navy and Coast Guard commissioning programs. These commissioning programs include appointment into the US Navy and Coast Guard military academies, Naval Reserve Officer Training Corps (NROTC), and Officer Candidate School (OCS).

The ASTB-E is developed and monitored by the Naval Operational Medicine Institute (NOMI). The Educational Testing Service collaborated with NOMI to produce the exam in paper and computer adaptive test formats. The Naval Personnel Command and Commandant of the Marine Corps establish eligibility requirements.

The ASTB-E is administered at Navy Recruiting Districts (NRDs), Navy ROTC units at selected universities, and Marine Corps Officer Selection Offices (OSOs). High school candidates applying for the navy and coast guard military academies or NROTC and college graduates with a bachelor's degree are eligible academically to take the exam.

COMPUTER ADAPTIVE TESTING

Computer adaptive testing (CAT) allows the test administrators to get a more complete view of your skills in less time and with fewer questions. These tests start with a question of average difficulty. If you answer this question correctly, the next question will be harder; if you answer it incorrectly, the next question will be easier. This continues as you go through the section, with questions getting harder or easier based on how well you perform. Once you've answered enough questions for the computer to determine your score, that section of the test will end.

Often you will be able to immediately see your score after taking a CAT exam. You will also probably answer fewer questions than if you'd taken a paper-and-pencil test, and each section will take less time. However, you will not be able to go back and check or change your answers.

The ASTB-E is offered in both CAT and paper-and-pencil form.

WHAT'S ON THE ASTB-E?

The ASTB-E, revised in 2013, has three versions—Form 6, Form 7, and Form 8. Previous versions (Form 1 through Form 5) are no longer being used, although test scores are still valid provided the applicant has not retaken the exam with Form 6 through Form 8.

The current ASTB-E has seven subtest components. Candidates seeking nonaviation positions are only required to take the Math, Reading, and Mechanical Tests to obtain an Officer Aptitude Rating (OAR). Candidates seeking aviation officer positions must take the entire exam to obtain their specific rating.

A list of the individual ASTB-E subtests follows:

- Math Skills Test (MST)*
- Reading Skills Test (RST)*
- Mechanical Comprehension Test (MCT)*
- Aviation and Nautical Information Test (ANIT)
- Naval Aviation Trait Facet Inventory (NATFI)
- Performance-Based Measures Battery (PBM)
- Biographic Inventory with Response Validation (BI-RV)

*Scores from these subtest components are used to determine an OAR.

The BI-RV component is designed for candidates to take on their own time prior to arriving at the test location. This component is web based and requires between forty-five minutes and two hours for candidates to complete.

The OAR portion of the ASTB-E requires one and a half to two hours to complete, and the remaining subtest components require anywhere from two to three hours and fifteen minutes to complete.

The ASTB-E is offered in paper format and CAT format. The paper format requires strict time limits for subtests, whereas the time taken for each subtest in the CAT format may be shortened. Since, the computer automatically provides harder or easier questions depending on the correctness of the candidate's answers, actual test-taking time is adjusted on the CAT.

What's on the ASTB-E?

SUBTEST	APPROXIMATE NUMBER OF QUESTIONS	TIME LIMIT
Math Skills Test	30	40 minutes
Reading Skills Test	20	30 minutes
Mechanical Comprehension Test	30	15 minutes
Aviation and Nautical Information Test	30	15 minutes
Naval Aviation Trait Facet Inventory	88 – 99	35 minutes

SUBTEST	APPROXIMATE NUMBER OF QUESTIONS	TIME LIMIT
Performance-Based Measures Battery	scenario-based modules	45 minutes
Biographic Inventory with Response Validation	110	No time limit
Total	319 multiple-choice questions + scenarios	Up to 3 hours, 15 minutes

Breakdown of the Subtests

Math Skills Test (MST): requires you to solve for algebraic, arithmetic, and geometric equations and word problems. Questions may include formulas, probability, fractions, ratios, and time and distance estimations.

Reading Skills Test (RST): evaluates your reading comprehension by interpreting word passages.

Mechanical Comprehension Test (MCT): measures your understanding of high school-level physics problems. These problems may include questions about gases and liquids, pulleys, fulcrums, pressure, volume, velocity, principles of electricity, weight distribution, and performance of engines.

Aviation and Nautical Information Test (ANIT): tests your knowledge of aviation history, navigation terminology, Federal Aviation Administration (FAA) flight rules and procedures, basic navigation rules, and aerodynamic principles.

Naval Aviation Trait Facet Inventory (NATFI): measures how you may react to or think through situations using a personality test.

Performance-Based Measures Battery (PBM): assesses your three-dimensional thinking and physical dexterity through flight simulation modules with relevant scenarios. Nicknamed the *stick-and-throttle set*, this subtest measures your hand-eye coordination to recreate aircraft control input and response.

Biographic Inventory with Response Validation (BI-RV): enquires about your academic career and participation in school activities or sports. This unscored subtest is done on your own time prior to sitting for the ASTB-E exam.

HOW IS THE ASTB-E SCORED?

The ASTB-E paper exam is sent back to NOMI for scoring. Unlike other military aptitude tests, recruiters must wait for the official score. They are not provided an unofficial score for the ASTB-E. The ASTB-E CAT exam is scored immediately after completing the exam.

Nonaviation candidates who only take the OAR portion of the ASTB-E will receive one rating as the OAR. Aviation candidates and those nonaviation candidates who take the entire ASTB-E receive ASTB-E scores in the form of four ratings as described next.

Aviation Qualifications Rating (AQR)

The AQR is used to predetermine an aviation candidate's prospective success in preflight instruction and the primary phase of ground school. Although all subtests are used to compile this rating, the score received on the MST is heavily weighted. This rating will be a 1 – 9, where 1 is equivalent to

1 – 4 percent, 5 equals 40 – 60 percent, and 9 equals 96 – 99 percent. The percentage represents how your scores compare to those of other candidates who took the exam.

Pilot Flight Aptitude Rating (PFAR)
The PFAR is indicative of expected success for flight performance tasks during flight training for Student Naval Aviators (SNAs). Although all subtests are used to compile this rating, the score received on the ANIT subtest is heavily weighted. This rating will be a 1 – 9 similar to the AQR stanine.

Flight Officer Flight Aptitude Rating (FOFAR)
The FOFAR identifies the probable achievement for position as a student naval flight officer (SNFO). Although all subtests are used to compile this rating, the score received on the MST subtest is heavily weighted. This rating will be a 1 – 9 similar to the AQR stanine.

Officer Aptitude Rating (OAR)
All candidates receive this rating, regardless of desired officer specialty. OAR scores are ranked from 20 to 80 based on three subtests (MST, RST, and MCT).

Ratings used for positions:
- OCS—OAR
- SNA—AQR and PFAR
- SNFO—AQR and FOFAR

For current minimum score eligibility requirements, contact your recruiter or refer to the Navy Personnel Command Program Authorizations 106 and 107 and Marine Corps Order 1542.11.

RETAKING THE ASTB-E

There is a three-time lifetime limit to attempt the ASTB-E. If a candidate wishes to retest, the date of retest must be no earlier than thirty-one days after the date the initial exam was taken. If a second retest is desired, the candidate may retest not earlier than ninety-one days after first retest.

Exam results of candidates who previously took the ASTB-E (Form 1 through Form 5) do not count toward the three-time lifetime limit; however, those results remain valid until another ASTB-E is taken.

Individuals who took the ASTB-E for an OAR only may return within thirty days of the initial test to complete the ASTB-E by taking the remaining subtests. This is called a *test merge*. In this case, candidates must wait until the OAR score is received prior to taking the remaining subtests. Additionally, even if the OAR portion was taken by paper format, the remaining test must be conducted using the CAT format. The date the candidate completes the remaining subtests is considered the official test date toward the three-time lifetime limit.

For example, Candidate Doe takes an initial ASTB-E for an OAR on March 1. He decides to take the remaining subtests for eligibility toward an aviation position. He has until March 31 of the same year to finish the complete ASTB-E. His first official test date toward his three-time lifetime limit is now March 31 (or any date beforehand) when he completed all subtests of the ASTB-E. If Candidate Doe never returned before March 31 to take the remaining subtests, his first official test date remains as March 1 and counts toward his three-time lifetime limit.

How is the ASTB-E Administered?

If you are ready to take the ASTB-E, contact your local recruiter. Your recruiter will determine your initial qualifications and schedule you to take the ASTB-E. The location where you take the ASTB-E will be decided when a test seat is available. Possible testing locations include Navy recruiting stations, NROTC units at selected universities, Marine Corps officer selection offices, and military institutes. Prior to the ASTB-E test date, complete the BI-RV subtest on your own. This will require a computer with an internet connection.

On the day of the exam, you will need to bring an identification card and your Social Security card to verify your identity. Testing materials are provided by the test proctor. Calculators are not allowed. If your recruiter drives you to the testing location, the recruiter cannot be in the testing room. Personal breaks are scheduled by the proctor, so be prepared to remain in the testing seat until dismissed.

Getting to Know the United States Military

The US Navy is tasked with missions to maintain freedom on the seas and in the sky above the seas. The US Navy has enlisted personnel, warrant officers, and commissioned officers among its ranks. Navy officers are listed in three categories:

- junior officer (includes ranks of O-1 to O-4)—ensign, lieutenant junior grade, lieutenant, and lieutenant commander
- senior officer (includes ranks of O-5 and O-6)—commander and captain
- flag officer (includes ranks of O-7 to O-10)—rear admiral lower half, rear admiral, vice admiral, and admiral

The US Navy offers officer career fields in surface warfare, submarine, aerospace maintenance, chaplaincy, healthcare, supply, logistics, and transportation as well as aviation positions as a naval aviator and flight officer.

The US Coast Guard's role is to protect the public, environment, and US economic interests at the nation's ports, waterways, international waters, and maritime regions necessary to protect national security. The Coast Guard's officer ranks match those of the US Navy. They also have enlisted personnel and warrant officers. The Coast Guard offers commissioning career fields in law; the US Public Health Service; aviation; engineering; command, control, and communications; computer technologies; and intelligence.

The US Marine Corps is designed and trained for offensive amphibious employments and as an expeditionary force in readiness for multinational military operations. The Marine Corps officer ranks match those of the US Army:

- company-grade officer—second lieutenant, first lieutenant, and captain
- field-grade officer—major, lieutenant colonel, and colonel
- general officer—brigadier general, major general, lieutenant general, and general

The Marine Corps offers officer career fields in personnel, administration, intelligence, infantry, Marine Air-Ground Task Force plans, communications, field artillery, and training.

THE MILITARY RECRUITMENT PROCESS

As stated before, the ASTB-E is just one requirement toward qualification for military service as an officer in the US Navy, Marine Corps, or Coast Guard. You may contact your local recruiter through your high school counselor or college adviser, or visit your local military recruitment center.

Once you contact your local recruiter, he or she will meet with you at the recruiting office, your school, or your home. During this meeting, the recruiter will conduct an interview to initiate the recruitment process. This process begins with the recruiter determining if you meet the basic qualification requirements. Expect a review of your education level, financial record, background investigation, interests, criminal record or drug history, height and weight, age, and citizenship. Once basic qualifications have been established, the recruiter refers you to an officer recruiter who will schedule you to take the ASTB-E. Once receiving your official scores, your recruiter will schedule you for a physical exam. You will meet with your officer recruiter to discuss your ASTB-E scores and any medical issue that may preclude your entrance to an officer commissioning school leading to an appointment as an officer. During this meeting, the officer recruiter will discuss which branch(es) of service you qualify for and possible career options for you to choose from. Your recruiter can answer any concerns or questions you have along the way.

ABOUT THIS GUIDE

This guide will help you master the most important test topics and also develop critical test-taking skills. We have built features into our books to prepare you for your tests and increase your score. Along with a detailed summary of the test's format, content, and scoring, we offer an in-depth overview of the content knowledge required to pass the test. In the review you'll find sidebars that provide interesting information, highlight key concepts, and review content so that you can solidify your understanding of the exam's concepts. You can also test your knowledge with sample questions throughout the text and practice questions that reflect the content and format of the ASTB-E. We're pleased you've chosen Trivium Test Prep to be a part of your military journey!

MATH SKILLS

The Math Skills test includes questions that cover concepts taught in high school-level math classes. Topics covered include percentages, proportions, properties of shapes, and algebraic expressions and equations. The paper test will have 30 questions, and the computer adaptive test will have between 20 and 30 questions.

TYPES OF NUMBERS

Numbers are placed in categories based on their properties.

- A **NATURAL NUMBER** is greater than 0 and has no decimal or fraction attached. These are also sometimes called counting numbers {1, 2, 3, 4, ...}.

- **WHOLE NUMBERS** are natural numbers and the number 0 {0, 1, 2, 3, 4, ...}.

- **INTEGERS** include positive and negative natural numbers and 0 {..., –4, –3, –2, –1, 0, 1, 2, 3, 4, ...}.

- A **RATIONAL NUMBER** can be represented as a fraction. Any decimal part must terminate or resolve into a repeating pattern. Examples include –12, $-\frac{4}{5}$, 0.36, $7.\overline{7}$, $26\frac{1}{2}$, etc.

- An **IRRATIONAL NUMBER** cannot be represented as a fraction. An irrational decimal number never ends and never resolves into a repeating pattern. Examples include $-\sqrt{7}$, π, and 0.34567989135...

- A **REAL NUMBER** is a number that can be represented by a point on a number line. Real numbers include all the rational and irrational numbers.

- An **IMAGINARY NUMBER** includes the imaginary unit i, where $i = \sqrt{-1}$ Because $i^2 = -1$, imaginary numbers produce a negative value when squared. Examples of imaginary numbers include $-4i$, $0.75i$, $i\sqrt{2}$ and $\frac{8}{3}i$.

- A **COMPLEX NUMBER** is in the form $a + bi$, where a and b are real numbers. Examples of complex numbers include $3 + 2i$, $-4 + i$, $\sqrt{3} - i\sqrt[3]{5}$ and $\frac{5}{8} - \frac{7i}{8}$. All imaginary numbers are also complex.

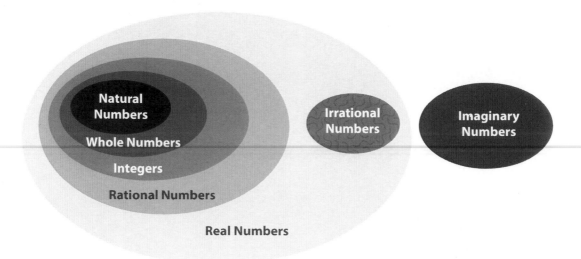

Figure 6.1. Types of Numbers

The **FACTORS** of a natural number are all the numbers that can multiply together to make the number. For example, the factors of 24 are 1, 2, 3, 4, 6, 8, 12, and 24. Every natural number is either prime or composite. A **PRIME NUMBER** is a number that is only divisible by itself and 1. (The number 1 is not considered prime.) Examples of prime numbers are 2, 3, 7, and 29. The number 2 is the only even prime number. A **COMPOSITE NUMBER** has more than two factors. For example, 6 is composite because its factors are 1, 6, 2, and 3. Every composite number can be written as a unique product of prime numbers, called the **PRIME FACTORIZATION** of the number. For example, the prime factorization of 90 is $90 = 2 \times 3^2 \times 5$. All integers are either even or odd. An even number is divisible by 2; an odd number is not.

> ⚠️
>
> If a real number is a natural number (e.g., 50), then it is also a whole number, an integer, and a rational number.

Examples

1. Classify the following numbers as natural, whole, integer, rational, or irrational. (The numbers may have more than one classification.)

   (A) 72

   (B) $-\frac{2}{3}$

   (C) $\sqrt{5}$

   Answers:

   (A) The number is **natural**, **whole**, an **integer**, and **rational**.

   (B) The fraction is **rational**.

   (C) The number is **irrational**. (It cannot be written as a fraction, and written as a decimal is approximately 2.2360679...)

2. Determine the real and imaginary parts of the following complex numbers.

   (A) 20

   (B) $10 - i$

   (C) $15i$

POSITIVE AND NEGATIVE NUMBERS

POSITIVE NUMBERS are greater than 0, and NEGATIVE NUMBERS are less than 0. Both positive and negative numbers can be shown on a NUMBER LINE.

Figure 6.2. Number Line

The ABSOLUTE VALUE of a number is the distance the number is from 0. Since distance is always positive, the absolute value of a number is always positive. The absolute value of a is denoted $|a|$. For example, $|-2| = 2$ since -2 is two units away from 0.

Positive and negative numbers can be added, subtracted, multiplied, and divided. The sign of the resulting number is governed by a specific set of rules shown in the table below.

Table 6.1. Operations with Positive and Negative Numbers

ADDING REAL NUMBERS		SUBTRACTING REAL NUMBERS*	
Positive + Positive = Positive	$7 + 8 = 15$	Negative – Positive = Negative	$-7 - 8 =$ $-7 + (-8) =$ -15
Negative + Negative = Negative	$-7 + (-8) =$ -15	Positive – Negative = Positive	$7 - (-8) =$ $7 + 8 = 15$

ADDING REAL NUMBERS		SUBTRACTING REAL NUMBERS*	
Negative + Positive OR Positive + Negative = Keep the sign of the number with larger absolute value	$-7 + 8 = 1$ $7 + -8 = -1$	Negative – Negative = Keep the sign of the number with larger absolute value	$-7 - (-8) =$ $-7 + 8 = 1$ $-8 - (-7) = -8$ $+ 7 = -1$

MULTIPLYING REAL NUMBERS		DIVIDING REAL NUMBERS	
Positive × Positive = Positive	$8 \times 4 = 32$	Positive ÷ Positive = Positive	$8 \div 4 = 2$
Negative × Negative = Positive	$-8 \times (-4) = 32$	Negative ÷ Negative = Positive	$-8 \div (-4) = 2$
Positive × Negative OR Negative × Positive = Negative	$8 \times (-4) = -32$ $-8 \times 4 = -32$	Positive ÷ Negative OR Negative ÷ Positive = Negative	$8 \div (-4) = -2$ $-8 \div 4 = -2$

*Always change the subtraction to addition and change the sign of the second number; then use addition rules.

Examples

1. Add or subtract the following real numbers:

(**A**) −18 + 12

(**B**) −3.64 + (−2.18)

(**C**) 9.37 − 4.25

(**D**) 86 − (−20)

Answers:

(A) Since |−18| > |12|, the answer is negative: |−18| − |12| = 6. So the answer is **−6**.

(B) Adding two negative numbers results in a negative number. Add the values: **−5.82**.

(C) The first number is larger than the second, so the final answer is positive: **5.12**.

(D) Change the subtraction to addition, change the sign of the second number, and then add: 86 − (−20) = 86 + (+20) = **106**.

2. Multiply or divide the following real numbers:

(**A**) $\left(\frac{10}{3}\right)\left(-\frac{9}{5}\right)$

(**B**) $\frac{-64}{-10}$

(**C**) (2.2)(3.3)

(**D**) −52 ÷ 13

Answers:

(A) Multiply the numerators, multiply the denominators, and simplify: $\frac{-90}{15} = $ **−6**.

(B) A negative divided by a negative is a positive number: **6.4**.

(C) Multiplying positive numbers gives a positive answer: **7.26**.

(D) Dividing a negative by a positive number gives a negative answer: **−4**.

ORDER OF OPERATIONS

The ORDER OF OPERATIONS is simply the order in which operations are performed. **PEMDAS** is a common way to remember the order of operations:

1.	**P**arentheses	**4.**	**D**ivision
2.	**E**xponents	**5.**	**A**ddition
3.	**M**ultiplication	**6.**	**S**ubtraction

Multiplication and division, and addition and subtraction, are performed together from left to right. So, performing multiple operations on a set of numbers is a four-step process:

1. P: Calculate expressions inside parentheses, brackets, braces, etc.

2. E: Calculate exponents and square roots.

3. MD: Calculate any remaining multiplication and division in order from left to right.

4. AS: Calculate any remaining addition and subtraction in order from left to right.

Always work from left to right within each step when simplifying expressions.

Examples

1. Simplify: $2(21 - 14) + 6 \div (-2) \times 3 - 10$

   Answer:

$2(21 - 14) \times 6 \div (-2) \times 3 - 10$	
$= 2(7) + 6 \div (-2) \times 3 - 10$	Calculate expressions inside parentheses.
$= 14 + 6 \div (-2) \times 3 - 10$ $= 14 + (-3) \times 3 - 10$ $= 14 + (-9) - 10$	There are no exponents or radicals, so perform multiplication and division from left to right.
$= 5 - 10$ $= \mathbf{-5}$	Perform addition and subtraction from left to right.

2. Simplify: $-(3)^2 + 4(5) + (5 - 6)^2 - 8$

   Answer:

$-(3)^2 + 4(5) + (5 - 6)^2 - 8$	
$= -(3)^2 + 4(5) + (-1)^2 - 8$	Calculate expressions inside parentheses.
$= -9 + 4(5) + 1 - 8$	Simplify exponents and radicals.
$= -9 + 20 + 1 - 8$	Perform multiplication and division from left to right.
$= 11 + 1 - 8$ $= 12 - 8$ $= \mathbf{4}$	Perform addition and subtraction from left to right.

3. Simplify: $\dfrac{(7 - 9)^3 + 8(10 - 12)}{4^2 - 5^2}$

   Answer:

$\dfrac{(7 - 9)^3 + 8(10 - 12)}{4^2 - 5^2}$	
$= \dfrac{(-2)^3 + 8(-2)}{4^2 - 5^2}$	Calculate expressions inside parentheses.
$= \dfrac{-8 + (-16)}{16 - 25}$	Simplify exponents and radicals.
$= \dfrac{-24}{-9}$	Perform addition and subtraction from left to right.
$= \dfrac{\mathbf{8}}{\mathbf{3}}$	Simplify.

UNITS OF MEASUREMENT

The standard units for the metric and American systems are shown below, along with the prefixes used to express metric units.

Table 6.2. Units and Conversion Factors

DIMENSION	AMERICAN	SI
length	inch/foot/yard/mile	meter
mass	ounce/pound/ton	gram
volume	cup/pint/quart/gallon	liter
force	pound-force	newton
pressure	pound-force per square inch	pascal
work and energy	cal/British thermal unit	joule
temperature	Fahrenheit	kelvin
charge	faraday	coulomb

Table 6.3. Metric Prefixes

PREFIX	SYMBOL	MULTIPLICATION FACTOR
tera	T	1,000,000,000,000
giga	G	1,000,000,000
mega	M	1,000,000
kilo	k	1,000
hecto	h	100
deca	da	10
base unit	--	--
deci	d	0.1
centi	c	0.01
milli	m	0.001
micro	µ	0.0000001
nano	n	0.0000000001
pico	p	0.0000000000001

A mnemonic device to help remember the metric system is *King Henry Drinks Under Dark Chocolate Moon* (KHDUDCM).

Units can be converted within a single system or between systems. When converting from one unit to another unit, a conversion factor (a numeric multiplier used to convert a value with a unit to another unit) is used. The process of converting between units using a conversion factor is sometimes known as dimensional analysis.

Table 6.4. Conversion Factors

1 in. = 2.54 cm	1 lb. = 0.454 kg
1 yd. = 0.914 m	1 cal = 4.19 J
1 mi. = 1.61 km	$1\ ^{\circ}F = \frac{5}{9}(^{\circ}F - 32^{\circ}C)$
1 gal. = 3.785 L	$1\ cm^3 = 1\ mL$
1 oz. = 28.35 g	1 hr = 3600 s

Examples

1. Convert the following measurements in the metric system.

   (A) 4.25 kilometers to meters

   (B) $8\ m^2$ to mm^2

   Answers:

   (A) $4.25\ km\left(\frac{1000\ m}{1\ km}\right) = \mathbf{4250\ m}$

   (B) $\frac{8\ m^2}{1} \times \frac{1000\ mm}{1\ m} \times \frac{1000\ mm}{1\ m} = \mathbf{8{,}000{,}000\ mm^2}$

   Since the units are square units (m^2), multiply by the conversion factor twice, so that both meters cancel.

2. Convert the following measurements in the American system.

   (A) 12 feet to inches

   (B) $7\ yd^2$ to ft^2

   Answers:

   (A) $12\ ft\left(\frac{12\ in}{1\ ft}\right) = \mathbf{144\ in}$

   (B) $7\ yd^2\left(\frac{3ft}{1yd}\right)\left(\frac{3ft}{1yd}\right) = \mathbf{63\ ft^2}$

   Since the units are square units (yd^2), multiply by the conversion factor twice.

3. Convert the following measurements in the metric system to the American system.

   (A) 23 meters to feet

   (B) $10\ m^2$ to yd^2

   Answers:

   (A) $23\ m\left(\frac{3.28\ ft}{1\ m}\right) = \mathbf{75.44\ ft}$

   (B) $\frac{10\ m^2}{1} \times \frac{1.094\ yd}{1\ m} \times \frac{1.094\ yd}{1\ m} = \mathbf{11.97\ yd^2}$

4. Convert the following measurements in the American system to the metric system.

   (A) $8\ in^3$ to milliliters

   (B) 16 kilograms to pounds

DECIMALS AND FRACTIONS

Decimals

A DECIMAL is a number that contains a decimal point. A decimal number is an alternative way of writing a fraction. The place value for a decimal includes TENTHS (one place after the decimal), HUNDREDTHS (two places after the decimal), THOUSANDTHS (three places after the decimal), etc.

Table 6.5. Place Values

1,000,000	10^6	millions
100,000	10^5	hundred thousands
10,000	10^4	ten thousands
1,000	10^3	thousands
100	10^2	hundreds
10	10^1	tens
1	10^0	ones
.		decimal
$\frac{1}{10}$	10^{-1}	tenths
$\frac{1}{100}$	10^{-2}	hundredths
$\frac{1}{1000}$	10^{-3}	thousandths

Decimals can be added, subtracted, multiplied, and divided:

- To add or subtract decimals, line up the decimal point and perform the operation, keeping the decimal point in the same place in the answer.
- To multiply decimals, first multiply the numbers without the decimal points. Then, sum the number of decimal places to the right of the decimal point in the original numbers and place the decimal point in the answer so that there are that many places to the right of the decimal.
- When dividing decimals move the decimal point to the right in order to make the divisor a whole number and move the decimal the same number of places in the dividend. Divide the numbers without regard to the decimal. Then, place the decimal point of the quotient directly above the decimal point of the dividend.

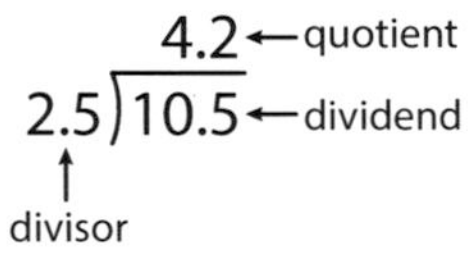

$$\overset{\text{4.2} \leftarrow \text{quotient}}{2.5 \overline{)10.5}} \leftarrow \text{dividend}$$
$$\uparrow$$
$$\text{divisor}$$

Figure 6.3. Division Terms

Examples

1. Simplify: 24.38 + 16.51 − 29.87

Answer:

24.38 + 16.51 − 29.87	
24.38 + 16.51 = 40.89	Align the decimals and apply the order of operations left to right.
40.89 − 29.87 = **11.02**	

2. Simplify: (10.4)(18.2)

Answer:

(10.4)(18.2)	
$104 \times 182 = 18{,}928$	Multiply the numbers ignoring the decimals.
$18{,}928 \rightarrow 189.28$	The original problem includes two decimal places (one in each number), so move the decimal point in the answer so that there are two places after the decimal point.

Estimating is a good way to check the answer: $10.4 \approx 10$, $18.2 \approx 18$, and $10 \times 18 = 180$.

3. Simplify: 80 ÷ 2.5

Answer:

80 ÷ 2.5	
$80 \rightarrow 800$ $2.5 \rightarrow 25$	Move both decimals one place to the right (multiply by 10) so that the divisor is a whole number.
$800 \div 25 = 32$	Divide normally.

Fractions

A **FRACTION** is a number that can be written in the form $\frac{a}{b}$, where b is not equal to 0. The a part of the fraction is the **NUMERATOR** (top number) and the b part of the fraction is the **DENOMINATOR** (bottom number).

If the denominator of a fraction is greater than the numerator, the value of the fraction is less than 1 and it is called a **PROPER FRACTION** (for example, $\frac{3}{5}$ is a proper fraction). In an **IMPROPER FRACTION**, the denominator is less than the numerator and the value of the fraction is greater than 1 ($\frac{8}{3}$ is an improper fraction). An improper fraction can be written as a **MIXED NUMBER**, which has a whole number part and a proper fraction part. Improper fractions can be converted to mixed numbers by dividing the numerator by the denominator, which gives the whole number part, and the remainder becomes the numerator of the proper fraction part. (For example, the improper fraction $\frac{25}{9}$ is equal to mixed number $2\frac{7}{9}$ because 9 divides into 25 two times, with a remainder of 7.)

Conversely, mixed numbers can be converted to improper fractions. To do so, determine the numerator of the improper fraction by multiplying the denominator by the whole number, and then adding the numerator. The final number is written as the (now larger) numerator over the original denominator.

To convert mixed numbers to improper fractions:
$$a\frac{m}{n} = \frac{n \times a + m}{n}$$

Fractions with the same denominator can be added or subtracted by simply adding or subtracting the numerators; the denominator will remain unchanged. To add or subtract fractions with different denominators, find the **LEAST COMMON DENOMINATOR** (**LCD**) of all the fractions. The LCD is the smallest number exactly divisible by each denominator. (For example, the least common denominator of the numbers 2, 3, and 8 is 24.) Once the LCD has been found, each fraction should be written in an equivalent form with the LCD as the denominator.

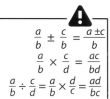

$$\frac{a}{b} \pm \frac{c}{b} = \frac{a \pm c}{b}$$
$$\frac{a}{b} \times \frac{c}{d} = \frac{ac}{bd}$$
$$\frac{a}{b} \div \frac{c}{d} = \frac{a}{b} \times \frac{d}{c} = \frac{ad}{bc}$$

To multiply fractions, the numerators are multiplied together and denominators are multiplied together. If there are any mixed numbers, they should first be changed to improper fractions. Then, the numerators are multiplied together and the denominators are multiplied together. The fraction can then be reduced if necessary. To divide fractions, multiply the first fraction by the reciprocal of the second.

Any common denominator can be used to add or subtract fractions. The quickest way to find a common denominator of a set of values is simply to multiply all the values together. The result might not be the least common denominator, but it will allow the problem to be worked.

Examples

1. Simplify: $2\frac{3}{5} + 3\frac{1}{4} - 1\frac{1}{2}$

Answer:

$2\frac{3}{5} + 3\frac{1}{4} - 1\frac{1}{2}$	
$= 2\frac{12}{20} + 3\frac{5}{20} - 1\frac{10}{20}$	Change each fraction so it has a denominator of 20, which is the LCD of 5, 4, and 2.
$2 + 3 - 1 = 4$ $\frac{12}{20} + \frac{5}{20} - \frac{10}{20} = \frac{7}{20}$	Add and subtract the whole numbers together and the fractions together.
$4\frac{7}{20}$	Combine to get the final answer (a mixed number).

2. Simplify: $\frac{7}{8} \times 3\frac{1}{3}$

Answer:

$\frac{7}{8} \times 3\frac{1}{3}$

$3\frac{1}{3} = \frac{10}{3}$	Change the mixed number to an improper fraction.
$\frac{7}{8}\left(\frac{10}{3}\right) = \frac{7 \times 10}{8 \times 3}$ $= \frac{70}{24}$	Multiply the numerators together and the denominators together.
$= \frac{35}{12}$ $= 2\frac{11}{12}$	Reduce the fraction.

3. Simplify: $4\frac{1}{2} \div \frac{2}{3}$

Answer:

$4\frac{1}{2} \div \frac{2}{3}$	
$4\frac{1}{2} = \frac{9}{2}$	Change the mixed number to an improper fraction.
$\frac{9}{2} \div \frac{2}{3}$ $= \frac{9}{2} \times \frac{3}{2}$ $= \frac{27}{4}$	Multiply the first fraction by the reciprocal of the second fraction.
$= 6\frac{3}{4}$	Simplify.

Converting Between Fractions and Decimals

A fraction is converted to a decimal by using long division until there is no remainder and no pattern of repeating numbers occurs.

A decimal is converted to a fraction using the following steps:

- Place the decimal value as the numerator in a fraction with a denominator of 1.
- Multiply the fraction by $\frac{10}{10}$ for every digit in the decimal value, so that there is no longer a decimal in the numerator.
- Reduce the fraction.

Examples

1. Write the fraction $\frac{7}{8}$ as a decimal.

Answer:

| $\begin{array}{r} 0.875 \\ 8\overline{)7000} \\ -64 \\ \hline 60 \\ -56 \\ \hline 40 \end{array}$ | Divide the denominator into the numerator using long division. |

2. Write the fraction $\frac{5}{11}$ as a decimal.

Answer:

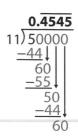

| Dividing using long division yields a repeating decimal.

3. Write the decimal 0.125 as a fraction.

Answer:

0.125

$$= \frac{0.125}{1}$$
Create a fraction with 0.125 as the numerator and 1 as the denominator.

$$\frac{0.125}{1} \times \frac{10}{10} \times \frac{10}{10} \times \frac{10}{10} = \frac{125}{1000}$$
Multiply by $\frac{10}{10}$ three times (one for each numeral after the decimal).

$$= \frac{1}{8}$$
Simplify.

Alternatively, recognize that 0.125 is read "one hundred twenty-five thousandths" and can therefore be written in fraction form as $\frac{125}{1000}$.

RATIOS

A **RATIO** is a comparison of two numbers and can be represented as $\frac{a}{b}$, $a:b$, or a to b. The two numbers represent a constant relationship, not a specific value: for every a number of items in the first group, there will be b number of items in the second. For example, if the ratio of blue to red candies in a bag is 3:5, the bag will contain 3 blue candies for every 5 red candies. So, the bag might contain 3 blue candies and 5 red candies, or it might contain 30 blue candies and 50 red candies, or 36 blue candies and 60 red candies. All of these values are representative of the ratio 3:5 (which is the ratio in its lowest, or simplest, terms).

To find the "whole" when working with ratios, simply add the values in the ratio. For example, if the ratio of boys to girls in a class is 2:3, the "whole" is five: 2 out of every 5 students are boys, and 3 out of every 5 students are girls.

Examples

1. There are 10 boys and 12 girls in a first-grade class. What is the ratio of boys to the total number of students? What is the ratio of girls to boys?

Answer:

number of boys: 10
number of girls: 12 | Identify the variables.
number of students: 22

number of boys : number of students $= 10 : 22$ $= \frac{10}{22}$ $= \frac{5}{11}$	Write out and simplify the ratio of boys to total students.
number of girls : number of boys $= 12 : 10$ $= \frac{12}{10}$ $= \frac{6}{5}$	Write out and simplify the ratio of girls to boys.

2. A family spends $600 a month on rent, $400 on utilities, $750 on groceries, and $550 on miscellaneous expenses. What is the ratio of the family's rent to their total expenses?

Answer:

rent $= 600$ utilities $= 400$ groceries $= 750$ miscellaneous $= 550$ total expenses $= 600 + 400 + 750 + 550$ $= 2300$	Identify the variables.
rent : total expenses $= 600 : 2300$ $= \frac{600}{2300}$ $= \frac{6}{23}$	Write out and simplify the ratio of rent to total expenses.

PROPORTIONS

A PROPORTION is an equation which states that two ratios are equal. A proportion is given in the form $\frac{a}{b} = \frac{c}{d}$, where the a and d terms are the extremes and the b and c terms are the means. A proportion is solved using cross-multiplication ($ad = bc$) to create an equation with no fractional components. A proportion must have the same units in both numerators and both denominators.

Examples

1. Solve the proportion for x: $\frac{3x-5}{2} = \frac{x-8}{3}$.

Answer:

$\frac{(3x-5)}{2} = \frac{(x-8)}{3}$	
$3(3x-5) = 2(x-8)$	Cross-multiply.

$$9x - 15 = 2x - 16$$
$$7x - 15 = -16$$
$$7x = -1$$
$$x = -\frac{1}{7}$$

Solve the equation for x.

2. A map is drawn such that 2.5 inches on the map equates to an actual distance of 40 miles. If the distance measured on the map between two cities is 17.25 inches, what is the actual distance between them in miles?

Answer:

$\frac{2.5}{40} = \frac{17.25}{x}$	Write a proportion where x equals the actual distance and each ratio is written as inches : miles.
$2.5x = 690$ $x = 276$ The two cities are **276 miles apart**.	Cross-multiply and divide to solve for x.

3. A factory knows that 4 out of 1000 parts made will be defective. If in a month there are 125,000 parts made, how many of these parts will be defective?

Answer:

$\frac{4}{1000} = \frac{x}{125,000}$	Write a proportion where x is the number of defective parts made and both ratios are written as defective : total.
$1000x = 500,000$ $x = 500$ There are **500 defective parts** for the month.	Cross-multiply and divide to solve for x.

PERCENTAGES

A PERCENT (or percentage) means per hundred and is expressed with a percent symbol (%). For example, 54% means 54 out of every 100. A percent can be converted to a decimal by removing the % symbol and moving the decimal point two places to the left, while a decimal can be converted to a percent by moving the decimal point two places to the right and attaching the % sign. A percent can be converted to a fraction by writing the percent as a fraction with 100 as the denominator and reducing. A fraction can be converted to a percent by performing the indicated division, multiplying the result by 100, and attaching the % sign.

The equation for finding percentages has three variables: the part, the whole, and the percent (which is expressed in the equation as a decimal). The equation, as shown below, can be rearranged to solve for any of these variables.

- part = whole × percent
- percent = $\frac{\text{part}}{\text{whole}}$
- whole = $\frac{\text{part}}{\text{percent}}$

This set of equations can be used to solve percent word problems. All that's needed is to identify the part, whole, and/or percent, and then to plug those values into the appropriate equation and solve.

Examples

1. Change the following values to the indicated form:

   (A) 18% to a fraction

   (B) $\frac{3}{5}$ to a percent

   (C) 1.125 to a percent

   (D) 84% to a decimal

   Answers:

   (A) The percent is written as a fraction over 100 and reduced: $\frac{18}{100} = \frac{9}{50}$.

   (B) Dividing 5 by 3 gives the value 0.6, which is then multiplied by 100: **60%**.

   (C) The decimal point is moved two places to the right: $1.125 \times 100 = \textbf{112.5\%}$.

   D. The decimal point is moved two places to the left: $84 \div 100 = \textbf{0.84}$.

2. In a school of 650 students, 54% of the students are boys. How many students are girls?

   Answer:

Percent of students who are girls = 100% – 54% = 46%	Identify the variables.
percent = 46% = 0.46	
whole = 650 students	
part = ?	
part = whole × percent = 0.46 × 650 = 299 **There are 299 girls.**	Plug the variables into the appropriate equation.

Percent Change

Percent change problems involve a change from an original amount. Often percent change problems appear as word problems that include discounts, growth, or markups. In order to solve percent change problems, it's necessary to identify the percent change (as a decimal), the amount of change, and the original amount. (Keep in mind that one of these will be the value being solved for.) These values can then be plugged into the equations below:

> Key terms associated with percent change problems include discount, sales tax, and markup.

- amount of change = original amount × percent change

- percent change = $\dfrac{\text{amount of change}}{\text{original amount}}$

- original amount = $\dfrac{\text{amount of change}}{\text{percent change}}$

Examples

1. An HDTV that originally cost $1,500 is on sale for 45% off. What is the sale price for the item?

   Answer:

original amount =$1,500 percent change = 45% = 0.45 amount of change = ?	Identify the variables.
amount of change = original amount × percent change = 1500 × 0.45 = 675	Plug the variables into the appropriate equation.
1500 − 675 = 825 **The final price is $825.**	To find the new price, subtract the amount of change from the original price.

2. A house was bought in 2000 for $100,000 and sold in 2015 for $120,000. What was the percent growth in the value of the house from 2000 to 2015?

   Answer:

original amount = $100,000 amount of change = 120,000 − 100,000 = 20,000 percent change = ?	Identify the variables.
percent change = $\dfrac{\text{amount of change}}{\text{original amount}}$ $= \dfrac{20,000}{100,000}$ $= 0.20$	Plug the variables into the appropriate equation.
0.20 × 100 = **20%**	To find the percent growth, multiply by 100.

EXPONENTS AND RADICALS

Exponents

An expression in the form b^n is in an exponential notation where b is the BASE and n is an EXPONENT. To perform the operation, multiply the base by itself the number of times indicated by the exponent. For example, 2^3 is equal to $2 \times 2 \times 2$ or 8.

Table 6.6. Operations with Exponents

RULE	EXAMPLE	EXPLANATION
$a^0 = 1$	$5^0 = 1$	Any base (except 0) to the 0 power is 1.
$a^{-n} = \dfrac{1}{a^n}$	$5^3 = \dfrac{1}{5^3}$	A negative exponent becomes positive when moved from numerator to denominator (or vice versa).
$a^m a^n = a^{m+n}$	$5^3 5^4 = 5^{3+4} = 5^7$	Add the exponents to multiply two powers with the same base.

RULE	EXAMPLE	EXPLANATION
$(a^m)^n = a^{mn}$	$(5^3)^4 = 5^{3(4)} = 5^{12}$	Multiply the exponents to raise a power to a power.
$\dfrac{a^m}{a^n} = a^{m-n}$	$\dfrac{5^4}{5^3} = 5^{4-3} = 5^1$	Subtract the exponents to divide two powers with the same base.
$(ab)^n = a^n b^n$	$(5 \times 6)^3 = 5^3 6^3$	Apply the exponent to each base to raise a product to a power.
$\left(\dfrac{a}{b}\right)^n = \dfrac{a^n}{b^n}$	$\left(\dfrac{5}{6}\right)^3 = \dfrac{5^3}{6^3}$	Apply the exponent to each base to raise a quotient to a power.
$\left(\dfrac{a}{b}\right)^{-n} = \left(\dfrac{b}{a}\right)^n$	$\left(\dfrac{5}{6}\right)^{-3} = \left(\dfrac{6}{5}\right)^3$	Invert the fraction and change the sign of the exponent to raise a fraction to a negative power.
$\dfrac{a^m}{b^n} = \dfrac{b^{-n}}{a^{-m}}$	$\dfrac{5^3}{6^4} = \dfrac{6^{-4}}{5^{-3}}$	Change the sign of the exponent when moving a number from the numerator to denominator (or vice versa).

Examples

1. Simplify: $\dfrac{(10^2)^3}{(10^2)^{-2}}$

   Answer:

$\dfrac{(10^2)^3}{(10^2)^{-2}}$	
$= \dfrac{10^6}{10^{-4}}$	Multiply the exponents raised to a power.
$= 10^{6-(-4)}$	Subtract the exponent in the denominator from the one in the numerator.
$= 10^{10}$ $= \mathbf{10{,}000{,}000{,}000}$	Simplify.

2. Simplify: $\dfrac{(x^{-2}y^2)^2}{x^3 y}$

   Answer:

$\dfrac{(x^{-2}y^2)^2}{x^3 y}$	
$= \dfrac{x^{-4}y^4}{x^3 y}$	Multiply the exponents raised to a power.
$= x^{-4-3}y^{4-1}$ $= x^{-7}y^3$	Subtract the exponent in the denominator from the one in the numerator.
$= \dfrac{y^3}{x^7}$	Move negative exponents to the denominator.

Radicals

RADICALS are expressed as $\sqrt[b]{a}$, where b is called the **INDEX** and a is the **RADICAND**. A radical is used to indicate the inverse operation of an exponent: finding the base which can be raised to b to yield a. For example, $\sqrt[3]{125}$ is equal to 5 because $5 \times 5 \times 5$ equals 125. The same operation can be expressed using a fraction exponent, so $\sqrt[b]{a} = \frac{1}{a^b}$. Note that when no value is indicated for b, it is assumed to be 2 (square root).

When b is even and a is positive, $\sqrt[b]{a}$ is defined to be the positive real value n such that $n^b = a$ (example: $\sqrt{16} = 4$ only, and not -4, even though $(-4)(-4) = 16$). If b is even and a is negative, $\sqrt[b]{a}$ will be a complex number (example: $\sqrt{-9} = 3i$). Finally if b is odd, $\sqrt[b]{a}$ will always be a real number regardless of the sign of a. If a is negative, $\sqrt[b]{a}$ will be negative since a number to an odd power is negative (example: $\sqrt[5]{-32} = -2$ since $(-2)^5 = -32$).

$\sqrt[n]{x}$ is referred to as the nth root of x.

- $n = 2$ is the square root
- $n = 3$ is the cube root
- $n = 4$ is the fourth root
- $n = 5$ is the fifth root

The following table of operations with radicals holds for all cases EXCEPT the case where b is even and a is negative (the complex case).

Table 6.7. Operations with Radicals

RULE	EXAMPLE	EXPLANATION
$\sqrt[b]{ac} = \sqrt[b]{a}\sqrt[b]{c}$	$\sqrt[3]{81} = \sqrt[3]{27}\sqrt[3]{3} = 3\sqrt[3]{3}$	The values under the radical sign can be separated into values that multiply to the original value.
$\sqrt[b]{\frac{a}{c}} = \frac{\sqrt[b]{a}}{\sqrt[b]{c}}$	$\sqrt{\frac{4}{81}} = \frac{\sqrt{4}}{\sqrt{81}} = \frac{2}{9}$	The b-root of the numerator and denominator can be calculated when there is a fraction under a radical sign.
$\sqrt[b]{a^c} = (\sqrt[b]{a})^c = a^{\frac{c}{b}}$	$\sqrt[3]{6^2} = (\sqrt[3]{6})^2 = 6^{\frac{2}{3}}$	The b-root can be written as a fractional exponent. If there is a power under the radical sign, it will be the numerator of the fraction.
$\frac{c}{\sqrt[b]{a}} \times \frac{\sqrt[b]{a}}{\sqrt[b]{a}} = \frac{c\sqrt[b]{a}}{a}$	$\frac{5}{\sqrt{2}}\frac{\sqrt{2}}{\sqrt{2}} = \frac{5\sqrt{2}}{2}$	To rationalize the denominator, multiply the numerator and denominator by the radical in the denominator until the radical has been canceled out.
$\frac{c}{b - \sqrt{a}} \times \frac{b + \sqrt{a}}{b + \sqrt{a}}$ $= \frac{c(b + \sqrt{a})}{b^2 - a}$	$\frac{4}{3 - \sqrt{2}}\frac{3 + \sqrt{2}}{3 + \sqrt{2}}$ $= \frac{4(3 + \sqrt{2})}{9 - 2} = \frac{12 + 4\sqrt{2}}{7}$	To rationalize the denominator, the numerator and denominator are multiplied by the conjugate of the denominator.

Examples

1. Simplify: $\sqrt{48}$

Answer:

$\sqrt{48}$	
$= \sqrt{16 \times 3}$	Determine the largest square number that is a factor of the radicand (48) and write the radicand as a product using that square number as a factor.

$$= \sqrt{16}\,\sqrt{3}$$
$$= \mathbf{4\sqrt{3}}$$

| | Apply the rules of radicals to simplify. |

2. Simplify: $\frac{6}{\sqrt{8}}$

Answer:

$\frac{6}{\sqrt{8}}$	
$= \frac{6}{\sqrt{4}\,\sqrt{2}}$ $= \frac{6}{2\sqrt{2}}$	Apply the rules of radicals to simplify.
$= \frac{6}{2\sqrt{2}}\left(\frac{\sqrt{2}}{\sqrt{2}}\right)$ $= \frac{\mathbf{3\sqrt{2}}}{\mathbf{2}}$	Multiply by $\frac{\sqrt{2}}{\sqrt{2}}$ to rationalize the denominator.

ALGEBRAIC EXPRESSIONS

The foundation of algebra is the VARIABLE, an unknown number represented by a symbol (usually a letter such as x or a). Variables can be preceded by a COEFFICIENT, which is a constant (i.e., a real number) in front of the variable, such as $4x$ or $-2a$. An ALGEBRAIC EXPRESSION is any sum, difference, product, or quotient of variables and numbers (for example $3x^2$, $2x + 7y - 1$, and $\frac{5}{x}$ are algebraic expressions). TERMS are any quantities that are added or subtracted (for example, the terms of the expression $x^2 - 3x + 5$ are x^2, $3x$, and 5). A POLYNOMIAL EXPRESSION is an algebraic expression where all the exponents on the variables are whole numbers. A polynomial with only two terms is known as a BINOMIAL, and one with three terms is a TRINOMIAL. A MONOMIAL has only one term.

EVALUATING EXPRESSIONS is another way of saying "find the numeric value of an expression if the variable is equal to a certain number." To evaluate the expression, simply plug the given value(s) for the variable(s) into the equation and simplify. Remember to use the order of operations when simplifying:

1.	Parentheses	4.	Division
2.	Exponents	5.	Addition
3.	Multiplication	6.	Subtraction

Example

If $m = 4$, find the value of the following expression:

$5(m - 2)^3 + 3m^2 - \frac{m}{4} - 1$

Answer:

$5(m - 2)^3 + 3m^2 - \frac{m}{4} - 1$	
$= 5(4 - 2)^3 + 3(4)^2 - \frac{4}{4} - 1$	Plug the value 4 in for m in the expression.
$= 5(2)^3 + 3(4)^2 - \frac{4}{4} - 1$	Calculate all the expressions inside the parentheses.

$= 5(8) + 3(16) - \frac{4}{4} - 1$	Simplify all exponents.
$= 40 + 48 - 1 - 1$	Perform multiplication and division from left to right.
$= 86$	Perform addition and subtraction from left to right.

OPERATIONS WITH EXPRESSIONS

Adding and Subtracting

Expressions can be added or subtracted by simply adding and subtracting LIKE TERMS, which are terms with the same variable part (the variables must be the same, with the same exponents on each variable). For example, in the expressions $2x + 3xy - 2z$ and $6y + 2xy$, the like terms are $3xy$ and $2xy$. Adding the two expressions yields the new expression $2x + 5xy - 2z + 6y$. Note that the other terms did not change; they cannot be combined because they have different variables.

Example

If $a = 12x + 7xy - 9y$ and $b = 8x - 9xz + 7z$, what is $a + b$?

Answer:

$a + b = (12x + 8x) + 7xy - 9y - 9xz + 7z =$ **$20x + 7xy - 9y - 9xz + 7z$**	The only like terms in both expressions are $12x$ and $8x$, so these two terms will be added, and all other terms will remain the same.

Distributing and Factoring

Distributing and factoring can be seen as two sides of the same coin. DISTRIBUTION multiplies each term in the first factor by each term in the second factor to get rid of parentheses. FACTORING reverses this process, taking a polynomial in standard form and writing it as a product of two or more factors.

Operations with polynomials can always be checked by evaluating equivalent expressions for the same value.

When distributing a monomial through a polynomial, the expression outside the parentheses is multiplied by each term inside the parentheses. Using the rules of exponents, coefficients are multiplied and exponents are added.

When simplifying two polynomials, each term in the first polynomial must multiply each term in the second polynomial. A binomial (two terms) multiplied by a binomial, will require 2 × 2 or 4 multiplications. For the binomial × binomial case, this process is sometimes called **FOIL**, which stands for first, outside, inside, and last. These terms refer to the placement of each term of the expression: multiply the first term in each expression, then the outside terms, then the inside terms, and finally the last terms. A binomial (two terms) multiplied by a trinomial (three terms), will require 2 × 3 or 6 products to simplify. The first

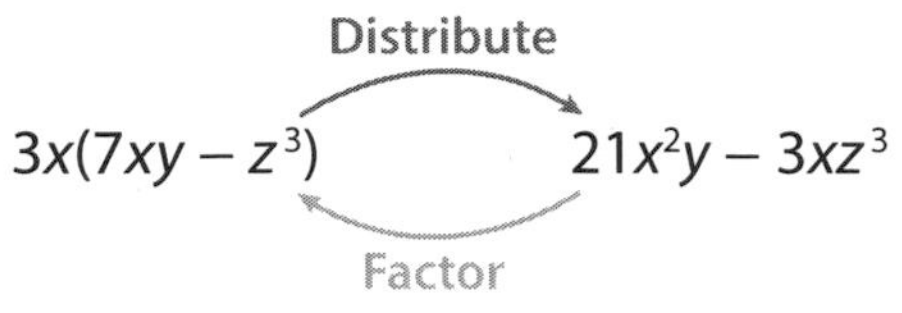

Distribute

$3x(7xy - z^3)$ $21x^2y - 3xz^3$

Factor

Figure 6.4. Distribution and Factoring

term in the first polynomial multiplies each of the three terms in the second polynomial, then the second term in the first polynomial multiplies each of the three terms in the second polynomial. A trinomial (three terms) by a trinomial will require 3 × 3 or 9 products, and so on.

Factoring is the reverse of distributing: the first step is always to remove ("undistribute") the GCF of all the terms, if there is a GCF (besides 1). The GCF is the product of any constants and/or variables that every term shares. (For example, the GCF of $12x^3$, $15x^2$ and $6xy^2$ is $3x$ because $3x$ evenly divides all three terms.) This shared factor can be taken out of each term and moved to the outside of the parentheses, leaving behind a polynomial where each term is the original term divided by the GCF. (The remaining terms for the terms in the example would be $4x^2$, $5x$, and $2y^2$.) It may be possible to factor the polynomial in the parentheses further, depending on the problem.

Example

1. Expand the following expression: $5x(x^2 - 2c + 10)$

   Answer:

$5x(x^2 - 2c + 10)$	
$(5x)(x^2) = 5x^3$ $(5x)(-2c) = -10xc$ $(5x)(10) = 50x$	Distribute and multiply the term outside the parentheses to all three terms inside the parentheses.
$= 5x^3 - 10xc + 50x$	

2. Expand the following expression: $(x^2 - 5)(2x - x^3)$

   Answer:

$(x^2 - 5)(2x - x^3)$	
$(x^2)(2x) = 2x^3$ $(x^2)(-x^3) = -x^5$ $(-5)(2x) = -10x$ $(-5)(-x^3) = 5x^3$	Apply FOIL: first, outside, inside, and last.
$= 2x^3 - x^5 - 10x + 5x^3$	Combine like terms and put them in order.
$= -x^5 + 7x^3 - 10x$	

3. Factor the expression $16z^2 + 48z$

   Answer:

	Both terms have a z, and 16 is a common factor of both 16 and 48. So the greatest common factor is $16z$. Factor out the GCF.
$16z^2 + 48z$ $= 16z(z + 3)$	

4. Factor the expression $6m^3 + 12m^3n - 9m^2$

$\longrightarrow$
CONTINUE

Answer:

$6m^3 + 12m^3n - 9m^2$
$= 3m^2(2m + 4mn - 3)$

All the terms share the factor m^2, and 3 is the greatest common factor of 6, 12, and 9. So, the GCF is $3m^2$.

LINEAR EQUATIONS

An **EQUATION** states that two expressions are equal to each other. Polynomial equations are categorized by the highest power of the variables they contain: the highest power of any exponent of a linear equation is 1, a quadratic equation has a variable raised to the second power, a cubic equation has a variable raised to the third power, and so on.

Solving Linear Equations

Solving an equation means finding the value or values of the variable that make the equation true. To solve a linear equation, it is necessary to manipulate the terms so that the variable being solved for appears alone on one side of the equal sign while everything else in the equation is on the other side.

The way to solve linear equations is to "undo" all the operations that connect numbers to the variable of interest. Follow these steps:

On multiple choice tests, it is often easier to plug the possible values into the equation and determine which solution makes the equation true than to solve the equation.

1. Eliminate fractions by multiplying each side by the least common multiple of any denominators.

2. Distribute to eliminate parentheses, braces, and brackets.

3. Combine like terms.

4. Use addition or subtraction to collect all terms containing the variable of interest to one side, and all terms not containing the variable to the other side.

5. Use multiplication or division to remove coefficients from the variable of interest.

Sometimes there are no numeric values in the equation or there are a mix of numerous variables and constants. The goal is to solve the equation for one of the variables in terms of the other variables. In this case, the answer will be an expression involving numbers and letters instead of a numeric value.

Examples

1. Solve for x: $\dfrac{100(x + 5)}{20} = 1$

Answer:

$\dfrac{100(x + 5)}{20} = 1$	
$(20)(\dfrac{100(x + 5)}{20}) = (1)(20)$ $100(x + 5) = 20$	Multiply both sides by 20 to cancel out the denominator.
$100x + 500 = 20$	Distribute 100 through the parentheses.

$100x = -480$	"Undo" the +500 by subtracting 500 on both sides of the equation to isolate the variable term.
$x = \dfrac{-480}{100}$	"Undo" the multiplication by 100 by dividing by 100 on both sides to solve for x.
$x = -4.8$	

2. Solve for x: $2(x + 2)^2 - 2x^2 + 10 = 42$

Answer:

$2(x + 2)^2 - 2x^2 + 10 = 42$	
$2(x + 2)(x + 2) - 2x^2 + 10 = 42$	Eliminate the exponents on the left side.
$2(x^2 + 4x + 4) - 2x^2 + 10 = 42$	Apply FOIL.
$2x^2 + 8x + 8 - 2x^2 + 10 = 42$	Distribute the 2.
$8x + 18 = 42$	Combine like terms on the left-hand side.
$8x = 24$	Isolate the variable. "Undo" +18 by subtracting 18 on both sides.
$x = 3$	"Undo" multiplication by 8 by dividing both sides by 8.

3. Solve the equation for D: $\dfrac{A(3B + 2D)}{2N} = 5M - 6$

Answer:

$\dfrac{A(3B + 2D)}{2N} = 5M - 6$	
$3AB + 2AD = 10MN - 12N$	Multiply both sides by $2N$ to clear the fraction, and distribute the A through the parentheses.
$2AD = 10MN - 12N - 3AB$	Isolate the term with the D in it by moving $3AB$ to the other side of the equation.
$D = \dfrac{(10MN - 12N - 3AB)}{2A}$	Divide both sides by $2A$ to get D alone on the right-hand side.

Graphs of Linear Equations

The most common way to write a linear equation is **SLOPE-INTERCEPT FORM**, $y = mx + b$. In this equation, m is the slope, which describes how steep the line is, and b is the y-intercept. Slope is often described as "rise over run" because it is calculated as the difference in y-values (rise) over the difference in x-values (run). The slope of the line is also the rate of change of the dependent variable y with respect to the independent variable x. The y-intercept is the point where the line crosses the y-axis, or where x equals zero.

To graph a linear equation, identify the y-intercept and place that point on the y-axis. If the slope is not written as a fraction,

 Use the phrase "Begin, Move" to remember that b is the y-intercept (where to begin) and m is the slope (how the line moves).

make it a fraction by writing it over 1 ($\frac{m}{1}$). Then use the slope to count up (or down, if negative) the "rise" part of the slope and over the "run" part of the slope to find a second point. These points can then be connected to draw the line.

To find the equation of a line, identify the y-intercept, if possible, on the graph and use two easily identifiable points to find the slope. If the y-intercept is not easily identified, identify the slope by choosing easily identifiable points; then choose one point on the graph, plug the point and the slope values into the equation, and solve for the missing value b.

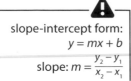

slope-intercept form:
$y = mx + b$

slope: $m = \frac{y_2 - y_1}{x_2 - x_1}$

- standard form: $Ax + By = C$
- $m = -\frac{A}{B}$
- x-intercept $= \frac{C}{A}$
- y-intercept $= \frac{C}{B}$

Another way to express a linear equation is standard form: $Ax + By = C$. In order to graph equations in this form, it is often easiest to convert them to point-slope form. Alternately, it is easy to find the x- or y-intercept from this form, and once these two points are known, a line can be drawn through them. To find the x-intercept, simply make $y = 0$ and solve for x. Similarly, to find the y-intercept, make $x = 0$ and solve for y.

Examples

1. What is the slope of the line whose equation is $6x - 2y - 8 = 0$?

Answer:

$6x - 2y - 8 = 0$	
$-2y = -6x + 8$ $y = \frac{-6x + 8}{-2}$ $y = 3x - 4$	Rearrange the equation into slope-intercept form by solving the equation for y.
$\boldsymbol{m = 3}$	The slope is 3, the value attached to x.

2. What is the equation of the following line?

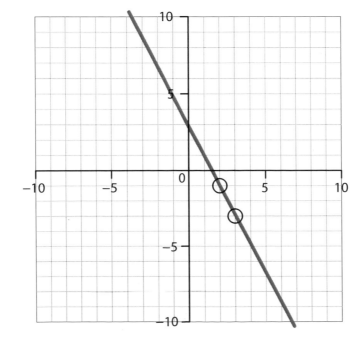

Answer:

$b = 3$	The *y*-intercept can be identified on the graph as $(0, 3)$.
$m = \frac{(-3) - (-1)}{3 - 2} = \frac{-2}{1} = -2$	To find the slope, choose any two points and plug the values into the slope equation. The two points chosen here are $(2, -1)$ and $(3, -3)$.
$y = -2x + 3$	Replace *m* with -2 and *b* with 3 in $y = mx + b$.

3. Write the equation of the line which passes through the points $(-2, 5)$ and $(-5, 3)$.

Answer:

$(-2, 5)$ and $(-5, 3)$	
$m = \frac{3 - 5}{(-5) - (-2)}$ $= \frac{-2}{-3}$ $= \frac{2}{3}$	Calculate the slope.
$5 = \frac{2}{3}(-2) + b$ $5 = \frac{-4}{3} + b$ $b = \frac{19}{3}$	To find *b*, plug into the equation $y = mx + b$ the slope for *m* and a set of points for *x* and *y*.
$y = \frac{2}{3}x + \frac{19}{3}$	Replace *m* and *b* to find the equation of the line.

4. What is the equation of the following graph?

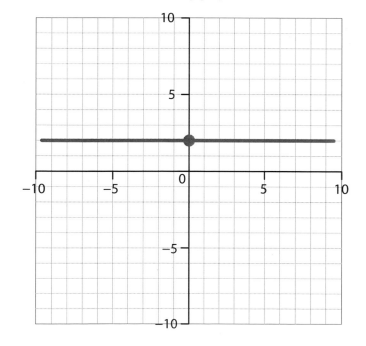

CONTINUE

Answer:

$y = 0x + 2$, or $y = 2$

The line has a rise of 0 and a run of 1, so the slope is $\frac{0}{1} = 0$. There is no x-intercept. The y-intercept is $(0, 2)$, meaning that the b-value in the slope-intercept form is 2.

PROPERTIES OF SHAPES

Basic Definitions

The basic figures from which many other geometric shapes are built are points, lines, and planes. A **POINT** is a location in a plane. It has no size or shape, but is represented by a dot. It is labeled using a capital letter.

A **LINE** is a one-dimensional collection of points that extends infinitely in both directions. At least two points are needed to define a line, and any points that lie on the same line are **COLINEAR**. Lines are represented by two points, such as A and B, and the line symbol: $(\overleftrightarrow{AB})$. Two lines on the same plane will intersect unless they are **PARALLEL**, meaning they have the same slope. Lines that intersect at a 90-degree angle are **PERPENDICULAR**.

A **LINE SEGMENT** has two endpoints and a finite length. The length of a segment, called the measure of the segment, is the distance from A to B. A line segment is a subset of a line, and is also denoted with two points, but with a segment symbol: $\overline{AB}$). The **MIDPOINT** of a line segment is the point at which the segment is divided into two equal parts. A line, segment, or plane that passes through the midpoint of a segment is called a **BISECTOR** of the segment, since it cuts the segment into two equal segments.

A **RAY** has one endpoint and extends indefinitely in one direction. It is defined by its endpoint, followed by any other point on the ray: $\overrightarrow{AB}$. It is important that the first letter represents the endpoint. A ray is sometimes called a half line.

Table 6.8. Basic Geometric Figures

TERM	DIMENSIONS	GRAPHIC	SYMBOL
point	zero	●	$\cdot A$
line segment	one	A ———— B	$\overline{AB}$
ray	one	A ——B——→	$\overrightarrow{AB}$
line	one	←————→	$\overleftrightarrow{AB}$
plane	two	▱	Plane M

A **PLANE** is a flat sheet that extends indefinitely in two directions (like an infinite sheet of paper). A plane is a two-dimensional (2D) figure. A plane can always be defined through any three noncollinear points in three-dimensional (3D) space. A plane is named using any three points that are in the plane (for example, plane **ABC**). Any points lying in the same plane are said to be COPLANAR. When two planes intersect, the intersection is a line.

Example

1) Which points and lines are not contained in plane *M* in the diagram below?

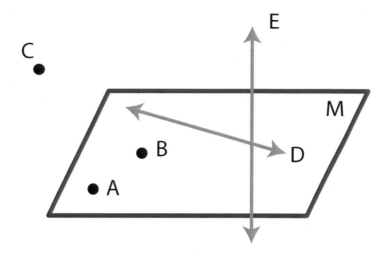

Answer:

Points *A* and *B* and line *D* are all on plane *M*. Point *C* is above the plane, and line *E* cuts through the plane and thus does not lie on plane *M*. The point at which line *E* intersects plane *M* is on plane *M* but the line as a whole is not.

Angles

ANGLES are formed when two rays share a common endpoint. They are named using three letters, with the vertex point in the middle (for example $\angle ABC$, where *B* is the vertex). They can also be labeled with a number or named by their vertex alone (if it is clear to do so). Angles are also classified based on their angle measure. A **right angle** has a measure of exactly 90°. **Acute angles** have measures that are less than 90°, and **obtuse angles** have measures that are greater than 90°.

Any two angles that add to make 90° are called COMPLEMENTARY ANGLES. A 30° angle would be complementary to a 60° angle. SUPPLEMENTARY ANGLES add up to 180°. A sup-plementary angle to a 60° angle would be a 120° angle; likewise, 60° is the SUPPLEMENT of 120°. Angles that are next to each other and share a common ray are called ADJACENT ANGLES. Angles that are adjacent and supplementary are called a LINEAR PAIR of angles. Their nonshared rays form a line (thus the *linear* pair). Note that angles that are supplementary do not need to be adjacent; their measures simply need to add to 180°.

 Angles can be measured in degrees or radians. Use the conversion factor 1 rad = 57.3 degrees to convert between them.

VERTICAL ANGLES are formed when two lines intersect. Four angles will be formed; the vertex of each angle is at the intersection point of the lines. The vertical angles across from each other will be equal in measure. The angles adjacent to each other will be linear pairs and therefore supplementary.

A ray, line, or segment that divides an angle into two equal angles is called an ANGLE BISECTOR.

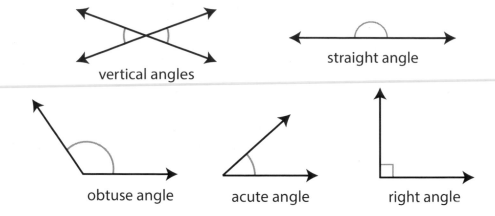

Figure 6.5. Types of Angles

Examples

1. If angles M and N are supplementary and $\angle M$ is 30° less than twice $\angle N$, what is the degree measurement of each angle?

Answer:

$\angle M + \angle N = 180°$ $\angle M = 2\angle N - 30°$	Set up a system of equations.
$\angle M + \angle N = 180°$ $(2\angle N - 30°) + \angle N = 180°$ $3\angle N - 30° = 180°$ $3\angle N = 210°$ $\angle N = 70°$	Use substitution to solve for $\angle N$.
$\angle M + \angle N = 180°$ $\angle M + 70° = 180°$ $\angle M = 110°$	Solve for $\angle M$ using the original equation.

2. How many linear pairs of angles are there in the following figure?

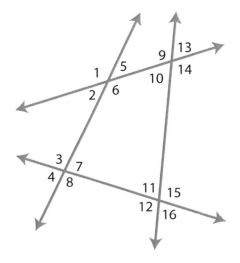

Circles

A CIRCLE is the set of all the points in a plane that are the same distance from a fixed point called the CENTER. The distance from the center to any point on the circle is the RADIUS of the circle. The distance around the circle (the perimeter) is called the CIRCUMFERENCE.

The ratio of a circle's circumference to its diameter is a constant value called pi (π), an irrational number which is commonly rounded to 3.14. The formula to find a circle's circumference is $C = 2\pi r$. The formula to find the enclosed area of a circle is $A = \pi r^2$.

Trying to square a circle means attempting to create a square that has the same area as a circle. Because the area of a circle depends on π, which is an irrational number, this task is impossible. The phrase is often used to describe trying to do something that can't be done.

Circles have a number of unique parts and properties:

- The DIAMETER is the largest measurement across a circle. It passes through the circle's center, extending from one side of the circle to the other. The measure of the diameter is twice the measure of the radius.

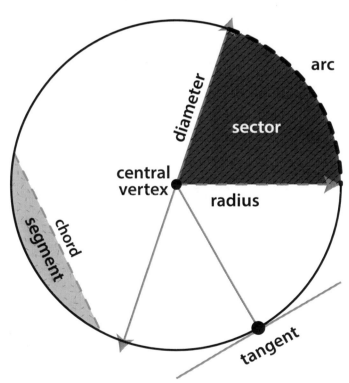

Figure 6.6. Parts of a Circle

- A line that cuts across a circle and touches it twice is called a SECANT line. The part of a secant line that lies within a circle is called a CHORD. Two chords within a circle are of equal length if they are are the same distance from the center.

- A line that touches a circle or any curve at one point is TANGENT to the circle or the curve. These lines are always exterior to the circle. A line tangent to a circle and a radius drawn to the point of tangency meet at a right angle (90°).

- An ARC is any portion of a circle between two points on the circle. The MEASURE of an arc is in degrees, whereas the LENGTH OF THE ARC will be in linear measurement (such as centimeters or inches). A MINOR ARC is the small arc between the two points (it measures less than 180°), whereas a MAJOR ARC is the large arc between the two points (it measures greater than 180°).

- An angle with its vertex at the center of a circle is called a CENTRAL ANGLE. For a central angle, the measure of the arc intercepted by the sides of the angle (in degrees) is the same as the measure of the angle.

- A SECTOR is the part of a circle *and* its interior that is inside the rays of a central angle (its shape is like a slice of pie).

	Area of Sector	Length of an Arc
Degrees	$A = \dfrac{\theta}{360°} \times \pi r^2$	$s = \dfrac{\theta}{360°} \times 2\pi r$
Radians	$A = \dfrac{1}{2}\pi^2\theta$	$s = r\theta$

- An INSCRIBED ANGLE has a vertex on the circle and is formed by two chords that share that vertex point. The angle measure of an inscribed angle is one-half the angle measure of the central angle with the same endpoints on the circle.

- A CIRCUMSCRIBED ANGLE has rays tangent to the circle. The angle lies outside of the circle.

- Any angle outside the circle, whether formed by two tangent lines, two secant lines, or a tangent line and a secant line, is equal to half the difference of the intercepted arcs.

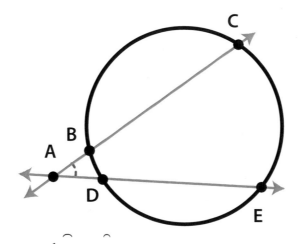

$$m\angle A = \tfrac{1}{2}(\overset{\frown}{CE} - \overset{\frown}{BD})$$

Figure 6.7. Angles Outside a Circle

- Angles are formed within a circle when two chords intersect in the circle. The measure of the smaller angle formed is half the sum of the two smaller arc measures (in degrees). Likewise, the larger angle is half the sum of the two larger arc measures.

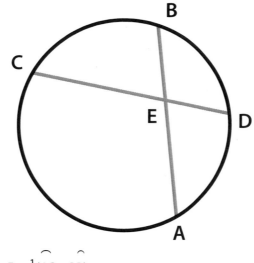

$$m\angle E = \tfrac{1}{2}(\overset{\frown}{AC} + \overset{\frown}{BD})$$

Figure 6.8. Intersecting Chords

- If a chord intersects a line tangent to the circle, the angle formed by this intersection measures one half the measurement of the intercepted arc (in degrees).

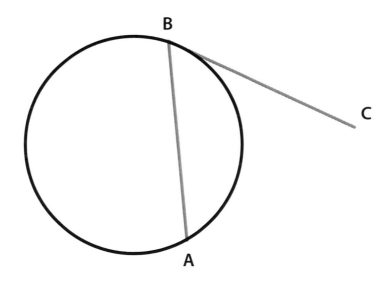

$$m\angle ABC = \tfrac{1}{2}m\,\overset{\frown}{AB}$$

Figure 6.9. Intersecting Chord and Tangent

CONTINUE

Examples

1. Find the area of the sector *NHS* of the circle below with center at *H*:

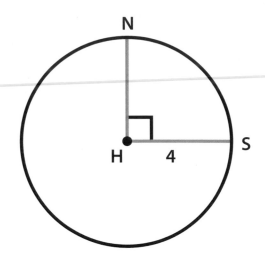

Answer:

$r = 4$ $\angle NHS = 90°$	Identify the important parts of the circle.
$A = \dfrac{\theta}{360°} \times \pi r^2$ $= \dfrac{90}{360} \times \pi(4)^2$	Plug these values into the formula for the area of a sector.
$= \dfrac{1}{4} \times 16\pi$ $\mathbf{= 4\pi}$	Plug these values into the formula for the area of a sector (continued).

2. In the circle below with center *O*, the minor arc *ACB* measures 5 feet. What is the measurement of *m∠AOB*?

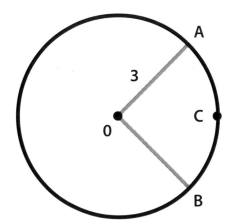

Answer:

$r = 3$ length of $\overset{\frown}{ACB} = 5$	Identify the important parts of the circle.

$$s = \frac{\theta}{360°} \times 2\pi r$$

$$5 = \frac{\theta}{360} \times 2\pi(3)$$

$$\frac{5}{6\pi} = \frac{\theta}{360}$$

$$\theta = 95.5°$$

$$m\angle AOB = 95.5°$$

Plug these values into the formula for the length of an arc and solve for θ.

Triangles

Much of geometry is concerned with triangles as they are commonly used shapes. A good understanding of triangles allows decomposition of other shapes (specifically polygons) into triangles for study.

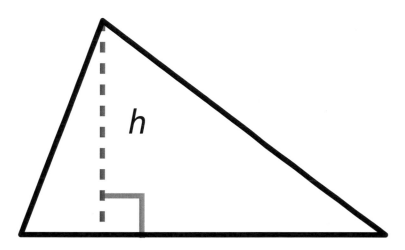

Figure 6.10. Finding the Base and Height of Triangles

Triangles have three sides, and the three interior angles always sum to 180°. The formula for the area of a triangle is $A = \frac{1}{2} bh$ or one-half the product of the base and height (or altitude) of the triangle.

Some important segments in a triangle include the angle bisector, the altitude, and the median. The **ANGLE BISECTOR** extends from the side opposite an angle to bisect that angle. The **ALTITUDE** is the shortest distance from a vertex of the triangle to the line containing the base side opposite that vertex. It is perpendicular to that line and can occur on the outside of the triangle. The **MEDIAN** extends from an angle to bisect the opposite side.

Angle Bisector
Divides angle in half

Altitude
Shortest distance to side

Median
Divides opposite side
in half

Figure 6.11. Important Segments in a Triangle

Triangles have two "centers." The CENTROID is where a triangle's three medians meet. The ORTHOCENTER is formed by the intersection of a triangle's three altitudes.

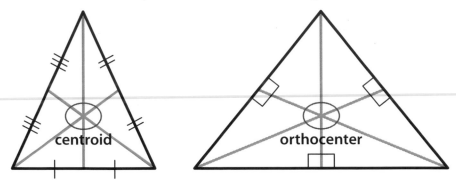

Figure 6.12. Centroid and Orthocenter of a Triangle

Triangles can be classified in two ways: by sides and by angles.

A SCALENE TRIANGLE has no equal sides or angles. An ISOSCELES TRIANGLE has two equal sides and two equal angles, often called BASE ANGLES. In an EQUILATERAL TRIANGLE, all three sides are equal as are all three angles. Moreover, because the sum of the angles of a triangle is always 180°, each angle of an equilateral triangle must be 60°.

Triangles Based on Sides

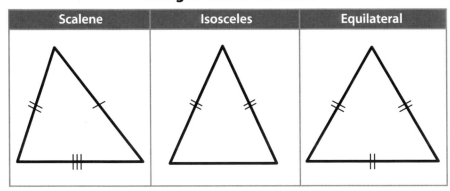

Triangles Based on Angles

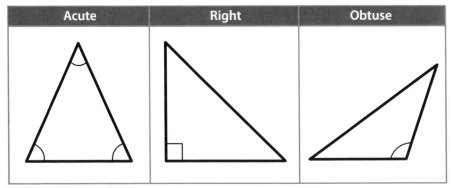

Figure 6.13. Types of Triangles

A RIGHT TRIANGLE has one right angle (90°) and two acute angles. An ACUTE TRIANGLE has three acute angles (all angles are less than 90°). An OBTUSE TRIANGLE has one obtuse angle (more than 90°) and two acute angles.

For any triangle, the side opposite the largest angle will have the longest length, while the side opposite the smallest angle will have the shortest length. The TRIANGLE INEQUALITY THEOREM states that the sum of any two sides of a triangle must be greater than the third side. If this inequality does not hold, then a triangle cannot be formed. A consequence of this theorem is the THIRD-SIDE RULE: if b and c are two sides of a triangle, then the measure of the third side a must be between the sum of the other two sides and the difference of the other two sides: $c - b < a < c + b$.

Trigonometric functions can be employed to find missing sides and angles of a triangle.

Solving for missing angles or sides of a triangle is a common type of triangle problem. Often a right triangle will come up on its own or within another triangle. The relationship among a right triangle's sides is known as the **PYTHAGOREAN THEOREM**: $a^2 + b^2 = c^2$, where c is the hypotenuse and is across from the 90° angle. Right triangles with angle measurements of 90° – 45° – 45° and 90° – 60° – 30° are known as "special" right triangles and have specific relationships between their sides and angles.

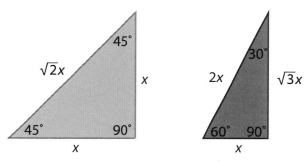

Figure 6.14. Special Right Triangles

Examples

1. Examine and classify each of the following triangles:

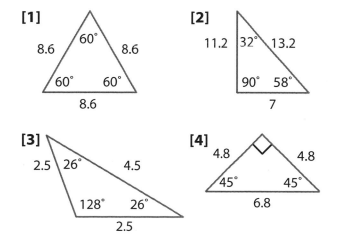

Answers:

Triangle 1 is an equilateral triangle (all 3 sides are equal, and all 3 angles are equal)

Triangle 2 is a scalene, right triangle (all 3 sides are different, and there is a 90° angle)

Triangle 3 is an isosceles triangle (there are 2 equal sides and, consequently, 2 equal angles)

Triangle 4 is a right, isosceles triangle (there are 2 equal sides and a 90° angle)

2. Given the diagram, if $XZ = 100$, $WZ = 80$, and $XU = 70$, then $WY = ?$

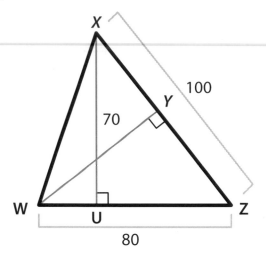

Answer:

$WZ = b_1 = 80$
$XU = h_1 = 70$
$XZ = b_2 = 100$
$WY = h_2 = ?$

$A = \frac{1}{2}bh$

$A_1 = \frac{1}{2}(80)(70) = 2800$

$A_2 = \frac{1}{2}(100)(h_2)$

The given values can be used to write two equation for the area of $\triangle WXZ$ with two sets of bases and heights.

$2800 = \frac{1}{2}(100)(h_2)$
$h_2 = 56$
$WY = 56$

Set the two equations equal to each other and solve for WY.

3. What are the minimum and maximum values of x to the nearest hundredth?

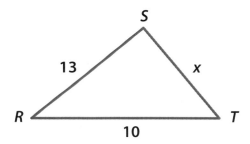

Answers:

The sum of two sides is 23 and their difference is 3. To connect the two other sides and enclose a space, x must be less than the sum and greater than the difference (that is, $3 < x < 23$). Therefore, **x's minimum value to the nearest hundredth is 3.01 and its maximum value is 22.99.**

Quadrilaterals

All closed, four-sided shapes are QUADRILATERALS. The sum of all internal angles in a quadrilateral is always 360°. (Think of drawing a diagonal to create two triangles. Since each triangle contains 180°, two triangles, and therefore the quadrilateral, must contain 360°.) The AREA OF ANY QUADRILATERAL is $A = bh$, where b is the base and h is the height (or altitude).

A PARALLELOGRAM is a quadrilateral with two pairs of parallel sides. A rectangle is a parallelogram with two pairs of equal sides and four right angles. A KITE also has two pairs of equal sides, but its equal sides are consecutive. Both a SQUARE and a RHOMBUS have four equal sides. A square has four right angles, while a rhombus has a pair of acute opposite angles and a pair of obtuse opposite angles. A TRAPEZOID has exactly one pair of parallel sides.

> ⚠ All squares are rectangles and all rectangles are parallelograms; however, not all parallelograms are rectangles and not all rectangles are squares.

Table 6.9. Properties of Parallelograms

TERM	SHAPE	PROPERTIES
Parallelogram		Opposite sides are parallel. Consecutive angles are supplementary. Opposite angles are equal. Opposite sides are equal. Diagonals bisect each other.
Rectangle		All parallelogram properties hold. Diagonals are congruent *and* bisect each other. All angles are right angles.
Square		All rectangle properties hold. All four sides are equal. Diagonals bisect angles. Diagonals intersect at right angles and bisect each other.
Kite		One pair of opposite angles is equal. Two pairs of consecutive sides are equal. Diagonals meet at right angles.
Rhombus		All four sides are equal. Diagonals bisect angles. Diagonals intersect at right angles and bisect each other.
Trapezoid		One pair of sides is parallel. Bases have different lengths. Isosceles trapezoids have a pair of equal sides (and base angles).

CONTINUE →

Examples

1. In parallelogram *ABCD*, the measure of angle *m* is is $m° = 260°$. What is the measure of $n°$?

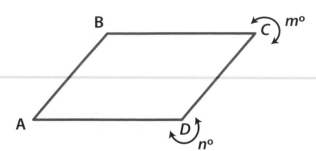

Answers:

$260° + m\angle C = 360°$ $m\angle C = 100°$	Find $\angle C$ using the fact that the sum of $\angle C$ and *m* is 360°.
$m\angle C + m\angle D = 180°$ $100° + m\angle D = 180°$ $m\angle D = 80°$	Solve for $\angle D$ using the fact that consecutive interior angles in a quadrilateral are supplementary.
$m\angle D + n = 360°$ $\mathbf{n = 280°}$	Solve for *n* by subtracting $m\angle D$ from 360°.

2. A rectangular section of a football field has dimensions of *x* and *y* and an area of 1000 square feet. Three additional lines drawn vertically divide the section into four smaller rectangular areas as seen in the diagram below. If all the lines shown need to be painted, calculate the total number of linear feet, in terms of *x*, to be painted.

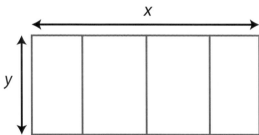

Answer:

$A = 1000 = xy$ $L = 2x + 5y$	Find equations for the area of the field and length of the lines to be painted (*L*) in terms of *x* and *y*.
$y = \frac{1000}{x}$ $L = 2x + 5y$ $L = 2x + 5(\frac{1000}{x})$ $\mathbf{L = 2x + \frac{5000}{x}}$	Substitute to find *L* in terms of *x*.

Polygons

Any closed shape made up of three or more line segments is a polygon. In addition to triangles and quadrilaterals, OCTAGONS and HEXAGONS are two common polygons.

The two polygons depicted below are REGULAR POLYGONS, meaning that they are equilateral (all sides having equal lengths) and equiangular (all angles having equal measurements). Angles inside a polygon are INTERIOR ANGLES, whereas those formed by one side of the polygon and a line extending outside the polygon are EXTERIOR ANGLES.

Breaking an irregular polygon down into triangles and quadrilaterals helps in finding its area.

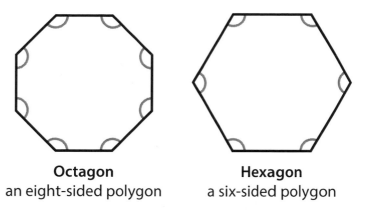

Octagon
an eight-sided polygon

Hexagon
a six-sided polygon

Figure 6.15. Common Polygons

The sum of all the exterior angles of a polygon is always 360°. Dividing 360° by the number of a polygon's sides finds the measure of the polygon's exterior angles.

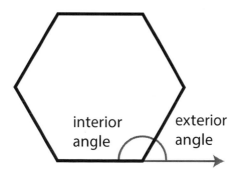

interior angle

exterior angle

Figure 6.16. Interior and Exterior Angles

To determine the sum of a polygon's interior angles, choose one vertex and draw diagonals from that vertex to each of the other vertices, decomposing the polygon into multiple triangles. For example, an octagon has six triangles within it, and therefore the sum of the interior angles is 6 × 180° = 1080°. In general, the formula for finding the sum of the angles in a polygon is *sum of angles* = $(n - 2) \times 180°$, where n is the number of sides of the polygon.

To find the measure of a single interior angle, simply divide the sum of the interior angles by the number of angles (which is the same as the number of sides). So, in the octagon example, each angle is $\frac{1080}{8} = 135°$.

In general, the formula to find the measure of a regular polygon's interior angles is: *interior angle* = $\frac{(n - 2)}{n} \times 180°$ where n is the number of sides of the polygon.

To find the area of a polygon, it is helpful to know the perimeter of the polygon (p), and the APOTHEM (a). The apothem is the shortest (perpendicular) distance from the polygon's center to one of the sides of the polygon. The formula for the area is: $area = \frac{ap}{2}$.

Finally, there is no universal way to find the perimeter of a polygon (when the side length is not given). Often, breaking the polygon down into triangles and adding the base of each triangle all the way around the polygon is the easiest way to calculate the perimeter.

Figure 6.17. Apothem in a Hexagon

Examples

1. The circle and hexagon below both share center point T. The hexagon is entirely inscribed in the circle. The circle's radius is 5. What is the area of the shaded area?

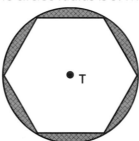

Answer:

$A_c = \pi r^2$ $= \pi(5)^2$ $= 25\pi$	The area of the shaded region will be the area of the circle minus the area of the hexagon. Use the radius to find the area of the circle.
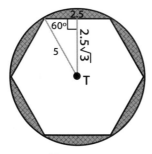 $a = 2.5\sqrt{3}$ $A_H = \frac{ap}{2}$ $= \frac{(2.5\sqrt{3})(30)}{2}$ $= 64.95$	To find the area of the hexagon, draw a right triangle from the vertex, and use special right triangles to find the hexagon's apothem. Then, use the apothem to calculate the area.
$= A_c - A_H$ $= 25\pi - 64.95$ $\approx \mathbf{13.59}$	Subtract the area of the hexagon from the circle to find the area of the shaded region.

2. What is the measure of an exterior angle and an interior angle of a regular 400-gon?

Answer:

The sum of the exterior angles is 360°. Dividing this sum by 400 gives $\frac{360°}{400}$ = **0.9°**. Since an interior angle is supplementary to an exterior angle, all the interior angles have measure 180 − 0.9 = **179.1°**. Alternately, using the formula for calculating the interior angle gives the same result:

interior angle = $\frac{400 - 2}{400} \times 180° = 179.1°$

THREE-DIMENSIONAL SHAPES

THREE-DIMENSIONAL SHAPES have depth in addition to width and length. VOLUME is expressed as the number of cubic units any shape can hold—that is, what it takes to fill it up. SURFACE AREA is the sum of the areas of the two-dimensional figures that are found on its surface. Some three-dimensional shapes also have a unique property called a slant height (ℓ), which is the distance from the base to the apex along a lateral face.

Table 6.10. Three-Dimensional Shapes and Formulas

TERM	SHAPE	FORMULA	
Prism		$V = Bh$ $SA = 2lw + 2wh + 2lh$ $d^2 = a^2 + b^2 + c^2$	B = area of base h = height l = length w = width d = longest diagonal
Cube		$V = s^3$ $SA = 6s^2$	s = cube edge
Sphere		$V = \frac{4}{3}\pi r^3$ $SA = 4\pi r^2$	r = radius
Cylinder		$V = Bh = \pi r^2 h$ $SA = 2\pi r^2 + 2\pi rh$	B = area of base h = height r = radius
Cone		$V = \frac{1}{3}\pi r^2 h$	r = radius h = height

Table 6.10. Three-Dimensional Shapes and Formulas (continued)

TERM	SHAPE	FORMULA	
Pyramid	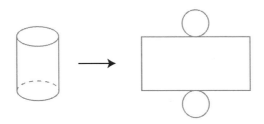	$V = \frac{1}{3}Bh$	B = area of base h = height

Finding the surface area of a three-dimensional solid can be made easier by using a **net**. This two-dimensional "flattened" version of a three-dimensional shape shows the component parts that comprise the surface of the solid.

Figure 6.18. Net of a Cylinder

Examples

1. A sphere has a radius z. If that radius is increased by t, by how much is the surface area increased? Write the answer in terms of z and t.

Answer:

$SA_1 = 4\pi z^2$	Write the equation for the area of the original sphere.
$SA_2 = 4\pi(z + t)^2$ $= 4\pi(z^2 + 2zt + t^2)$ $= 4\pi z^2 + 8\pi zt + 4\pi t^2$	Write the equation for the area of the new sphere.
$A_2 - A_1 = 4\pi z^2 + 8\pi zt + 4\pi t^2 - 4\pi z^2$ $\mathbf{= 4\pi t^2 + 8\pi zt}$	To find the difference between the two, subtract the original from the increased surface area.

2. A cube with volume 27 cubic meters is inscribed within a sphere such that all of the cube's vertices touch the sphere. What is the length of the sphere's radius?

Answer:

Since the cube's volume is 27, each side length is equal to $\sqrt[3]{27} = 3$. The long diagonal distance from one of the cube's vertices to its opposite vertex will provide the sphere's diameter:

$d = \sqrt{3^2 + 3^2 + 3^2} = \sqrt{27} = 5.2$

Half of this length is the radius, which is **2.6 meters**.

2

READING SKILLS

The Reading Skills test includes short reading passages followed by questions about those passages. The paper test will have 20 questions, and the computer adaptive test will have between 20 and 30 questions. The passages will cover simple, easy-to-understand topics, and no outside knowledge will be needed to answer the questions. The sections below will introduce the types of questions that are included on the test and explain how to answer them.

THE MAIN IDEA

The **MAIN IDEA** of a text describes the author's main topic and general concept; it also generalizes the author's point of view about a subject. It is contained within and throughout the text. The reader can easily find the main idea by considering how the main topic is addressed throughout a passage. In the reading test, the expectation is not only to identify the main idea but also to differentiate it from a text's theme and to summarize the main idea clearly and concisely.

The main idea is closely connected to topic sentences and how they are supported in a text. Questions may deal with finding topic sentences, summarizing a text's ideas, or locating supporting details. The sections and practice examples that follow detail the distinctions between these aspects of text.

Identifying the Main Idea

To identify the main idea, first identify the topic. The difference between these two things is simple: the **TOPIC** is the overall subject matter of a passage; the main idea is what the author wants to say about that topic. The main idea covers the author's direct perspective about a topic, as distinct from the **THEME**, which is a generally true idea that the reader might derive from a text. Most of the time, fiction has a theme, whereas nonfiction has a main idea. This is the case because in a nonfiction text, the author speaks more directly

 The author's perspective on the subject of the text and how he or she has framed the argument or story hints at the main idea. For example, if the author framed the story with a description, image, or short anecdote, this suggests a particular idea or point of view.

to the audience about a topic—his or her perspective is more visible. For example, the following passage conveys the topic as well as what the author wants to communicate about that topic.

The "shark mania" of recent years can be largely pinned on the sensationalistic media surrounding the animals: from the release of *Jaws* in 1975 to the week of ultra-hyped shark feeding frenzies and "worst shark attacks" countdowns known as Shark Week, popular culture both demonizes and fetishizes sharks until the public cannot get enough. Swimmers and beachgoers may look nervously for the telltale fin skimming the surface, but the reality is that shark bites are extremely rare and they are almost never unprovoked. Sharks attack people at very predictable times and for very predictable reasons. Rough surf, poor visibility, or a swimmer sending visual and physical signals that mimic a shark's normal prey are just a few examples.

Of course, some places are just more dangerous to swim. Shark attack "hot spots," such as the coasts of Florida, South Africa, and New Zealand try a variety of solutions to protect tourists and surfers. Some beaches employ "shark nets," meant to keep sharks away from the beach, though these are controversial because they frequently trap other forms of marine life as well. Other beaches use spotters in helicopters and boats to alert beach officials when there are sharks in the area. In addition, there is an array of products that claim to offer personal protection from sharks, ranging from wetsuits in different colors to devices that broadcast electrical signals in an attempt to confuse the sharks' sensory organs. At the end of the day, though, beaches like these remain dangerous, and swimmers must assume the risk every time they paddle out from shore.

The author of this passage has a clear topic: sharks and the relationship between humans and sharks. In order to identify the main idea of the passage, the reader must ask what the author wants to say about this topic, what the reader is meant to think or understand. The author makes sure to provide information about several different aspects of the relationship between sharks and humans, and points out that humans must respect sharks as dangerous marine animals, without sensationalizing the risk of attack. This conclusion results from looking at the various pieces of information the author includes as well as the similarities between them. The passage describes sensationalistic media, then talks about how officials and governments try to protect beaches, and ends with the observation that people must take personal responsibility. These details clarify what the author's main idea is. Summarizing that main idea by focusing on the connection between the different details helps the reader draw a conclusion.

⚠

Readers should identify the topic of a text and pay attention to how the details about it relate to one another. A passage may discuss, for example, topic similarities, characteristics, causes, and/ or effects.

Examples

The art of the twentieth and twenty-first centuries demonstrates several aspects of modern societal advancement. A primary example is the advent and ascendancy of technology: New technologies have developed new avenues for art making, and the globalization brought about by the Internet has both diversified the art world and brought it together simultaneously. Even as artists are able to engage in a global conversation about the categories and characteristics of art, creating a more uniform understanding, they can now express themselves in a diversity of ways for a diversity of audiences. The result has been a rapid change in how art is made and consumed.

1. This passage is primarily concerned with
   (A) the importance of art in the twenty-first century.
   (B) the use of art to communicate overarching ideals to diverse communities.
   (C) the importance of technology to art criticism.
   (D) the change in understanding and creation of art in the modern period.
   (E) artists' desires to diversify the media with which art is created.

   Answers:

   (A) is incorrect. The focus of the passage is what the art of the twentieth and twenty-first centuries demonstrates.

   (B) is incorrect. Although the passage mentions a diversity of audiences, it discusses the artists expressing themselves, not attempting to communicate overarching ideals.

   (C) is incorrect. The passage discusses how new technologies have "developed new avenues for art making," but nothing about criticism.

   (D) is correct. The art of the modern period reflects the new technologies and globalization possible through the Internet.

   (E) is incorrect. The passage mentions the diversity of ways artists express themselves, not the media specifically.

2. Which of the following best describes the main idea of the passage?
   (A) Modern advances in technology have diversified art making and connected artists to distant places and ideas.
   (B) Diversity in modern art is making it harder for art viewers to understand and talk about that art.
   (C) The use of technology to discuss art allows us to create standards for what art should be.
   (D) Art making before the invention of technology such as the Internet was disorganized and poorly understood.
   (E) Art making in the twenty-first century is dependent on the use of technology in order to meet current standards.

   Answers:

   (A) is correct. According to the text, technology and the Internet have "diversified the art world and brought it together simultaneously."

   (B) is incorrect. The passage explains that the global conversation about art has created a more uniform understanding.

   (C) is incorrect. The passage indicates that artists now engage in a global conversation about art, but this is one detail in the passage. The main idea of the passage concerns the advances in art in the twentieth and twenty-first centuries.

   (D) is incorrect. The invention of technology and the Internet have diversified art; however, that does not mean it was disorganized previously.

   (E) is incorrect. Technology is a means to an end; art is not dependent on it.

Topic and Summary Sentences

Identifying the main idea requires understanding the structure of a piece of writing. In a short passage of one or two paragraphs, the topic and summary sentences quickly relate what the paragraphs are about and what conclusions the author wants the reader to draw. These sentences function as bookends to a paragraph or passage, telling readers what to think and keeping the passage tied tightly together.

Generally, the TOPIC SENTENCE is the first, or very near the first, sentence in a paragraph. It is a general statement that introduces the topic, clearly and specifically directing the reader to access any previous experience with that topic.

A **summary** is a very brief restatement of the most important parts of an argument or text. Building a summary begins with the most important idea in a text. A longer summary also includes supporting details. The text of a summary should be much shorter than the original.

The SUMMARY SENTENCE, on the other hand, frequently—but not always!—comes at the end of a paragraph or passage, because it wraps up all the ideas presented. This sentence provides an understanding of what the author wants to say about the topic and what conclusions to draw about it. While a topic sentence acts as an introduction to a topic, allowing the reader to activate his or her own ideas and experiences, the summary statement asks the reader to accept the author's ideas about that topic. Because of this, a summary sentence helps the reader quickly identify a piece's main idea.

Examples

Altogether, Egypt is a land of tranquil monotony. The eye commonly travels either over a waste of waters, or over a green plain unbroken by elevations. The hills which inclose (*sic*) the Nile valley have level tops, and sides that are bare of trees, or shrubs, or flowers, or even mosses. The sky is generally cloudless. No fog or mist enwraps the distance in mystery; no rainstorm sweeps across the scene; no rainbow spans the empyrean; no shadows chase each other over the landscape. There is an entire absence of picturesque scenery. A single broad river, unbroken within the limits of Egypt even by a rapid, two flat strips of green plain at its side, two low lines of straight-topped hills beyond them, and a boundless open space where the river divides itself into half a dozen sluggish branches before reaching the sea, constitute Egypt, which is by nature a southern Holland—"weary, stale, flat and unprofitable."

—from *Ancient Egypt* by George Rawlinson

1. Which of the following best explains the general idea and focus indicated by the topic sentence?

   (A) Egypt is a boring place without much to do.

   (B) The land of Egypt is undisturbed; the reader will read on to find out what makes it so dull.

   (C) Egypt is a peaceful place; its people live with a sense of predictability.

   (D) The land of Egypt is quiet; the reader wants to know what is missing.

   (E) The reader is curious about how people survive in an area of worn-out uniformity.

   Answers:

   (A) is incorrect. The word *monotony* does suggest the idea of being bored; however, the focus is the land of Egypt, not what people have to do. In addition, tranquility is part of the general idea.

(B) is correct. This option indicates both the main idea and what the reader will focus on while reading.

(C) is incorrect. This option leaves out what the focus will be.

(D) is incorrect. This option leaves out the general idea of monotony.

(E) is incorrect. This option is inaccurate; the topic sentence does not suggest anything about survival.

2. Which of the following best states what the author wants the reader to understand after reading the summary sentence?

   (A) There is not much to get excited about while visiting Egypt.

   (B) Egypt is a poverty-stricken wasteland.

   (C) The land of Egypt is worn out from overuse.

   (D) The land of Egypt is quiet, but not worth visiting.

   (E) The land of Egypt lacks anything fresh or inspiring.

Answers:

(A) is incorrect. The summary describes the place, not a visit to the place.

(B) is incorrect. The word *unprofitable* suggests that the land of Egypt is unrewarding, not poverty stricken.

(C) is incorrect. The reason the land is stale and weary may not be due to overuse. This summary describes; it does not explain the reasons the land is worn.

(D) is incorrect. The first part of the sentence is correct, but the summary sentence does not indicate that Egypt is not worth visiting.

(E) is correct. The words *weary*, *stale*, and *unprofitable* suggest a lack of freshness or anything that stimulates enthusiasm.

SUPPORTING DETAILS

Between a topic sentence and a summary sentence, the rest of a paragraph is built with SUPPORTING DETAILS. Supporting details come in many forms; the purpose of the passage dictates the type of details that will support the main idea. A persuasive passage may use facts and data or detail specific reasons for the author's opinion. An informative passage will primarily use facts about the topic to support the main idea. Even a narrative passage will have supporting details—specific things the author says to develop the story and characters.

The most important aspect of supporting details is exactly what the term states: They support the main idea. Examining the various supporting details and how they work with one another will solidify how the author views a topic and what the main idea of the passage is. Supporting details are key to understanding a passage.

Identifying Supporting Details

How can the reader identify the most important pieces of information in a passage? Supporting details build an argument and contain the concepts upon which the main idea rests. While supporting details will help the reader determine the main idea, it is actually easier to find the most important supporting details by first understanding the main idea; the pieces that make up the main argument then become clear.

SIGNAL WORDS—transitions and conjunctions—explain to the reader how one sentence or idea is connected to another. These words and phrases can be anywhere in a sentence, and it is important to understand what each signal word means. Signal words can add information, provide counterarguments, create organization in a passage, or draw conclusions. Some common signal words include *in particular*, *in addition*, *besides*, *contrastingly*, *therefore*, and *because*.

Examples

The war is inevitable—and let it come! I repeat it, sir, let it come! It is in vain, sir, to extenuate the matter. Gentlemen may cry, "Peace! Peace!"—but there is no peace. The war is actually begun! The next gale that sweeps from the north will bring to our ears the clash of resounding arms! Our brethren are already in the field! Why stand we here idle? What is it that gentlemen wish? What would they have? Is life so dear, or peace so sweet, as to be purchased at the price of chains and slavery? Forbid it, Almighty God! I know not what course others may take; but as for me, give me liberty or give me death!

—from "Give Me Liberty or Give Me Death" speech by Patrick Henry

1. In the fourth sentence of the text, the word *but* signals

    (A) an example.

    (B) a consequence.

    (C) an exception.

    (D) a counterargument.

    (E) a reason

    Answers:

    (A) is incorrect. The author includes an example that the war has begun when he says "Our brethren are already in the field!" The word *but* does not signal this example.

    (B) is incorrect. The phrase "but there is no peace" is a fact, not a consequence.

    (C) is incorrect. In order to be an exception, the word *but* would have to be preceded by a general point or observation. In this case, *but* is preceded by a demand for peace.

    (D) is correct. The argument or claim that the country should be at peace precedes the word *but*. *But* counters the demand for peace with the argument that there is no peace; the war has begun.

    (E) is incorrect. *But* does not introduce a reason in this text; it introduces a contradictory point.

2. What argument does the author use to support his main point?

    (A) Life in slavery is not the goal of the country.

    (B) To die bravely is worthwhile.

    (C) Life without freedom is intolerable.

    (D) The cost of going to war is too great.

    (E) People cannot live in peace without going to war.

Evaluating Supporting Details

Besides using supporting details to help understand a main idea, the reader must evaluate them for relevance and consistency. An author selects details to help organize a passage and support its main idea. Sometimes, the author's bias results in details left out that don't directly support the main idea or that support an opposite idea. The reader has to be able to notice not only what the author says but also what the author leaves out.

To understand how a supporting detail relates to the main idea, the purpose of the passage should be discerned: what the author is trying to communicate and what the author wants from the reader. Every passage has a specific goal, and each paragraph in a passage is meant to support that goal. For each supporting detail, the position in the text, the signal words, and the specific content work together to alert the reader to the relationship between the supporting ideas and the main idea.

Close reading involves noticing the striking features of a text. For example, does a point made in the text appeal to the reader's sense of justice? Does a description seem rather exaggerated or overstated? Do certain words—such as *agonizing*—seem emotive? Are rhetorical questions being used to lead the reader to a certain conclusion?

Though the author generally includes details that support the text's main idea, the reader must decide how those details relate to one another as well as find any gaps in the support of the author's argument. This is particularly important in a persuasive piece of writing, when an author may allow bias to show through. Discovering the author's bias and how the supporting details reveal that bias is also key to understanding a text.

Examples

In England in the 'fifties came the Crimean War, with the deep stirring of national feeling which accompanied it, and the passion of gratitude and admiration which was poured forth on Miss Florence Nightingale for her work on behalf of our wounded soldiers. It was universally felt that there was work for women, even in war—the work of cleansing, setting in order, breaking down red tape, and soothing the vast sum of human suffering which every war is bound to cause. Miss Nightingale's work in war was work that never had been done until women came forward to do it, and her message to her countrywomen was educate yourselves, prepare, make ready; never imagine that your task can be done by instinct, without training and preparation. Painstaking study, she insisted, was just as necessary as a preparation for women's work as for men's work; and she bestowed the whole of the monetary gift offered her by the gratitude of the nation to form training-schools for nurses at St. Thomas's and King's College Hospitals.

—from *Women's Suffrage: A Short History of a Great Movement*
by Millicent Garrett Fawcett

1. Which of the following best states the bias of the passage?

   (A) Society underestimates the capacity of women.

   (B) Generally, women are not prepared to make substantial contributions to society.

   (C) If women want power, they need to prove themselves.

   (D) One strong woman cannot represent all women.

   (E) The strength of women is their ability to take care of others.

   Answers:

   (A) is correct. The author is suggesting that the work Florence Nightingale did had not been done before women came forward. Up till that point, what a woman could do had not been recognized.

   (B) is incorrect. This fact may have been true at the time this text was written, but only because educational opportunities were not available to women, and women were not encouraged to develop their abilities. Including this fact reveals the bias that women should be granted opportunities to train and to contribute.

   (C) is incorrect. This option does not apply; Florence Nightingale did more than prove herself.

   (D) is incorrect. The fact that Florence Nightingale donated the money awarded her to the training of women indicates that other women were preparing themselves to contribute.

   (E) is incorrect. This may or may not be true. It does not matter what kind of strength women have; the bias is that the strength of women wasn't really known.

2. Which of the following best summarizes what the author left out of the passage?

   (A) Women can fight in wars.

   (B) Other women should be recognized.

   (C) Women need to stop wasting time giving speeches at conventions and start proving themselves.

   (D) Without the contributions of women, society suffers.

   (E) Women are the ones who get the important work done.

   Answers:

   (A) is incorrect. "It was universally felt that there was work for women, even in war" suggests that women had much to offer and didn't need to be sheltered; however, "there was work" does not mean the author thought women should engage in combat.

   (B) is incorrect. Since the passage is specifically about Florence Nightingale, nothing in it suggests the author included information about what other women did.

   (C) is incorrect. Information about women's suffrage conventions is unrelated to the topic of the paragraph.

(D) is correct. The author emphasizes that "Miss Nightingale's work in war was work that never had been done until women came forward to do it."

(E) is incorrect. The author shows the importance of Miss Nightingale's work, but that does not suggest it was the only important work being done.

Facts and Opinions

Authors use both facts and opinions as supporting details. While it is usually a simple task to identify the two, authors may mix facts with opinions or state an opinion as if it were a fact. The difference between the two is simple: A FACT is a piece of information that can be verified as true or false, and it retains the quality of truthfulness or falsity no matter who verifies it. An OPINION reflects a belief held by the author and may or may not be something each reader agrees with.

To distinguish between fact and opinion, the reader should rely on what can be proven. Subjectivity is determined by asking if an observation varies according to the situation or the person observing.

Examples

I remember thinking how comfortable it was, this division of labor which made it unnecessary for me to study fogs, winds, tides, and navigation, in order to visit my friend who lived across an arm of the sea. It was good that men should be specialists, I mused. The peculiar knowledge of the pilot and captain sufficed for many thousands of people who knew no more of the sea and navigation than I knew. On the other hand, instead of having to devote my energy to the learning of a multitude of things, I concentrated it upon a few particular things, such as, for instance, the analysis of Poe's place in American literature—an essay of mine, by the way, in the current *Atlantic*. Coming aboard, as I passed through the cabin, I had noticed with greedy eyes a stout gentleman reading the *Atlantic*, which was open at my very essay. And there it was again, the division of labor, the special knowledge of the pilot and captain which permitted the stout gentleman to read my special knowledge on Poe while they carried him safely from Sausalito to San Francisco.

—from *The Sea-Wolf* by Jack London

1. Which of the following best summarizes an opinion stated by the narrator?

    (A) Poe has a place in American literature.

    (B) People have the time to read magazines like the *Atlantic* because there are other people to take care of other tasks.

    (C) The narrator has no knowledge of the sea and navigation.

    (D) Having specialized knowledge sets people apart and makes them superior.

    (E) Division of labor is a beneficial practice.

    Answers:

    (A) is incorrect. This is a fact. The *significance* of Poe's place in American literature is an opinion.

    (B) is incorrect. This is a fact. The reader is expected to agree with the point that if someone else had not been managing the boat, the people who wanted to get across the water would have had to do the work of getting themselves across.

    (C) is incorrect. This is a fact. The narrator admits to "this division of labor which made it unnecessary for me to study fogs, winds, tides, and navigation."

    (D) is incorrect. Although the narrator acknowledges that specialized knowledge exists, he does not indicate that he believes it creates superiority.

(E) is correct. The narrator provides several facts proving that he and the other passengers benefit from the specialized knowledge and labor of others.

2. Which of the following is an opinion expressed by the narrator that is NOT supported by facts within the passage?

   (A) People should live life focusing on and learning about only a few things.

   (B) Having general knowledge is good.

   (C) He has time to focus on writing about literature.

   (D) People depend on other people.

   (E) People can experience more freedom by depending on others.

   Answers:

   (A) is correct. When the narrator says "instead of having to devote my energy to the learning of a multitude of things, I concentrated it upon a few particular things," he conveys his view that he does not have to learn much. There are no facts to support the view that he has to learn only a few particular things in life.

   (B) is incorrect. The narrator does not express this opinion. He is speaking about specialized knowledge.

   (C) is incorrect. This is a fact that the narrator shares about his life.

   (D) is incorrect. The passage does offer facts to support this; both the narrator and the passenger reading depend on the pilot to navigate the boat safely.

   (E) is incorrect. This opinion is supported by the fact that the passenger has the freedom to sit back and read, and the narrator has the freedom to watch him read, while they both depend on the pilot.

TEXT STRUCTURE

The structure of a text determines how the reader understands the argument and how the various details interact to form the argument. There are many ways to arrange text, and various types of arrangements have distinct characteristics.

The organizing structure of a passage is defined by the order in which the author presents information and the transitions used to connect those pieces. Problem-and-solution and cause-and-effect structures use transitions that show causal relationships: *because, as a result, consequently, therefore.* These two types of structures may also use transitions that show contradiction. A problem-and-solution structure may provide alternative solutions; a cause-and-effect structure may explain alternative causes: *however, alternatively, although.*

> Authors often use repetition to reinforce an idea, including repeated words, phrases, or images.

Specific text structures include not only problem and solution and cause and effect, but also compare and contrast, descriptive, order of importance, and chronological. When analyzing a text, the reader should consider how text structure influences the author's meaning. Most important, the reader needs to be aware of how an author emphasizes an idea by the way he or she presents information. For instance, including a contrasting idea makes a central idea stand out, and including a series of concrete examples creates a force of facts to support an argument.

Examples

It was the green heart of the canyon, where the walls swerved back from the rigid plan and relieved their harshness of line by making a little sheltered nook and filling it to the brim with sweetness and roundness and softness. Here all things rested. Even the narrow stream ceased its turbulent down-rush long enough to form a quiet pool…. On one side, beginning at the very lip of the pool, was a tiny meadow, a cool, resilient surface of green that extended to the base of the frowning wall. Beyond the pool a gentle slope of earth ran up and up to meet the opposing wall. Fine grass covered the slope—grass that was spangled with flowers, with here and there patches of color, orange and purple and golden. Below, the canyon was shut in. There was no view. The walls leaned together abruptly and the canyon ended in a chaos of rocks, moss-covered and hidden by a green screen of vines and creepers and boughs of trees. Up the canyon rose far hills and peaks, the big foothills, pine-covered and remote. And far beyond, like clouds upon the border of the slay, towered minarets of white, where the Sierra's eternal snows flashed austerely the blazes of the sun.

—from "All Gold Canyon" by Jack London

1. The organizational structure of the passage is

   (A) order of importance.

   (B) cause and effect.

   (C) problem and solution.

   (D) descriptive.

   (E) chronological.

   Answers:

   (A) is incorrect. A series of reasons is not presented from most to least or least to most important. The passage describes a restful nook in the canyon.

   (B) is incorrect. The passage does not explain the origin of this nook or its effect on anything, although the reader understands from the details what makes the nook so restful.

   (C) is incorrect. The description of the nook presents no problem, although time in the nook could be seen as a solution for many problems.

   (D) is correct. The description of the nook begins with a general impression, moves from one side, to the area beyond the pool, to below the heart of the canyon, and finally to what is above the canyon.

   (E) is incorrect. The description does not include a sequence of events in time.

2. How does the text structure emphasize the central idea of the passage?

   (A) The logical reasons for needing to rest while hiking make the author's argument compelling.

   (B) By explaining the activities within the canyon, the author convinces the reader that the canyon is safe.

   (C) By describing the areas to the side, below, and above the canyon, the author is able to emphasize the softness at the heart of the canyon.

   (D) The concrete examples included in the passage demonstrate the author's view that beauty is found in nature.

   (E) The sensory details of the description make it easy for the reader to visualize and enjoy.

Answers:

(A) is incorrect. The passage does not indicate anything about a hike, although the valley is described as a restful place.

(B) is incorrect. The heart of the canyon is still, without activity; even the water stops rushing and forms a pool.

(C) is correct. The little restful nook is surrounded by the wall of the mountain, a "chaos of rocks," "boughs of trees," "far hills and peaks."

(D) is incorrect. The central idea of the passage is not finding beauty in nature but simply the restfulness of this nook.

(E) is incorrect. The passage does include sensory detail that's easy to visualize; however, this option does not indicate how the detail relates to the central idea.

DRAWING CONCLUSIONS

Reading text begins with making sense of the explicit meanings of information or a narrative. Understanding occurs as the reader draws conclusions and makes logical inferences. To draw a conclusion, the reader considers the details or facts. He or she then comes to a conclusion—the next logical point in the thought sequence. For example, in a Hemingway story, an old man sits alone in a café. A young waiter says that the café is closing, but the old man continues to drink. The waiter starts closing up, and the old man signals for a refill. Based on these details, the reader might conclude that the old man has not understood the young waiter's desire for him to leave.

When considering a character's motivations, the reader should ask what the character wants to achieve, what the character will get by accomplishing this, and what the character seems to value the most.

An inference is distinguished from a conclusion drawn. An **INFERENCE** is an assumption the reader makes based on details in the text as well as his or her own knowledge. It is more of an educated guess that extends the literal meaning. Inferences begin with the given details; however, the reader uses the facts to determine additional facts. What the reader already knows informs what is being suggested by the details of decisions or situations in the text. Returning to the example of the Hemingway story, the reader might infer that the old man is lonely, enjoys being in the café, and is reluctant to leave.

When reading fictional text, inferring character motivations is essential. The actions of the characters move the plot forward; a series of events is understood by making sense of why the characters did what they did. Hemingway includes contrasting details as the young waiter and an older waiter discuss the old man. The older waiter sympathizes with the old man; both men have no one at home and experience a sense of emptiness in life, which motivates them to seek the café.

Conclusions are drawn by thinking about how the author wants the reader to feel. A group of carefully selected facts can cause the reader to feel a certain way.

Another aspect of understanding text is connecting it to other texts. Readers may connect the Hemingway story about the old man in the café to other Hemingway stories about individuals struggling to deal with loss and loneliness in a dignified way. They can extend their initial connections to people they know or their personal experiences. When readers read a persuasive text, they often connect the arguments made to counterarguments and opposing evidence of which they are aware. They use these connections to infer meaning.

Examples

I believe it is difficult for those who publish their own memoirs to escape the imputation of vanity; nor is this the only disadvantage under which they labor: it is also their misfortune, that what is uncommon is rarely, if ever, believed, and what is obvious we are apt to turn from with disgust, and to charge the writer with impertinence. People generally think those memoirs only worthy to be read or remembered which abound in great or striking events, those, in short, which in a high degree excite either admiration or pity: all others they consign to contempt and oblivion. It is therefore, I confess, not a little hazardous in a private and obscure individual, and a stranger too, thus to solicit the indulgent attention of the public; especially when I own I offer here the history of neither a saint, a hero, nor a tyrant. I believe there are few events in my life, which have not happened to many: it is true the incidents of it are numerous; and, did I consider myself an European, I might say my sufferings were great: but when I compare my lot with that of most of my countrymen, I regard myself as a *particular favorite of Heaven*, and acknowledge the mercies of Providence in every occurrence of my life. If then the following narrative does not appear sufficiently interesting to engage general attention, let my motive be some excuse for its publication. I am not so foolishly vain as to expect from it either immortality or literary reputation. If it affords any satisfaction to my numerous friends, at whose request it has been written, or in the smallest degree promotes the interests of humanity, the ends for which it was undertaken will be fully attained, and every wish of my heart gratified. Let it therefore be remembered, that, in wishing to avoid censure, I do not aspire to praise.

—from *The Interesting Narrative of the Life of Olaudah Equiano,*
or Gustavus Vassa, The African by Olaudah Equiano

1. Which of the following best explains the primary motivation of the narrator?

(A) He wants his audience to know that he is not telling his story out of vanity.

(B) He is hoping people will praise his courage.

(C) He wants to give credit to God for protecting him.

(D) He is honoring the wishes of his friends.

(E) He is not seeking personal notoriety; he is hoping people will be influenced by his story and the human condition will improve.

Answers:

(A) is incorrect. That motive is how the passage begins, but it is not his primary motive.

(B) is incorrect. He says he does not aspire to praise, and he does not suggest that he was courageous.

(C) is incorrect. He does state that the "mercies of Providence" were always with him; however, that acknowledgement is not his primary motive.

(D) is incorrect. Although he says that he wrote it at the request of friends, the story is meant to improve humanity.

(E) is correct. In the passage "If it…in the smallest degree promotes the interests of humanity, the ends for which it was undertaken will be fully attained, and every wish of my heart gratified," the narrator's use of the word *humanity* could mean he wants to improve the human condition or he wants to increase human benevolence, or brotherly love.

2. Given the details of what the narrator says he is *not*, as well as what he claims his story is *not*, it can be inferred that his experience was

(A) a story that could lead to his success.

(B) an amazing story of survival and struggle that will be unfamiliar to many readers.

(C) an adventure that will thrill the audience.

(D) a narrow escape from suffering.

(E) an interesting story that is worthy of publication.

Answers:

(A) is incorrect. The narrator says that what is obvious in his story is what people "are apt to turn from with disgust, and to charge the writer with impertinence." The narrator is telling a story that his audience couldn't disagree with and might consider rude.

(B) is correct. By saying "what is uncommon is rarely, if ever, believed, and what is obvious we are apt to turn from with disgust," the narrator suggests that his experience wasn't common or ordinary and could cause disgust.

(C) is incorrect. The reader can infer that the experience was horrific; it will inspire disgust, not excitement.

(D) is incorrect. The narrator admits he suffered; he indicates that he narrowly escaped death. This is not an inference.

(E) is incorrect. By saying "If then the following narrative does not appear sufficiently interesting to engage general attention, let my motive be some excuse for its publication," the narrator makes clear that he does not think his narrative is interesting, but he believes his motive to help humanity makes it worthy of publication.

UNDERSTANDING THE AUTHOR

Many questions on the Reading Comprehension test will ask for an interpretation of an author's intentions and ideas. This requires an examination of the author's perspective and purpose as well as the way the author uses language to communicate these things.

In every passage, an author chooses words, structures, and content with specific purpose and intent. With this in mind, the reader can begin to comprehend why an author opts for particular words and structures and how these ultimately relate to the content.

The Author's Purpose

The author of a passage sets out with a specific goal in mind: to communicate a particular idea to an audience. The AUTHOR'S PURPOSE is determined by asking why the author wants the reader to understand the passage's main idea. There are four basic purposes to which an author can write: narrative, expository, technical, and persuasive. Within each of these general purposes, the author may direct the audience to take a clear action or respond in a certain way.

The purpose for which an author writes a passage is also connected to the structure of that text. In a NARRATIVE, the author seeks to tell a story, often to illustrate a theme or idea the reader needs to consider. In a narrative, the author uses characteristics of storytelling, such as chronological order, characters, and a defined setting, and these characteristics communicate the author's theme or main idea.

In an EXPOSITORY passage, on the other hand, the author simply seeks to explain an idea or topic to the reader. The main idea will probably be a factual statement or a direct assertion of a broadly held opinion. Expository writing can come in many forms, but one essential feature is a fair and balanced representation of a topic. The author may explore one detailed aspect or a broad range of characteristics, but he or she mainly seeks to prompt a decision from the reader.

Similarly, in TECHNICAL writing, the author's purpose is to explain specific processes, techniques, or equipment in order for the reader to use that process or equipment to obtain a desired result. Writing like this employs chronological or spatial structures, specialized vocabulary, and imperative or directive language.

In PERSUASIVE writing, though the reader is free to make decisions about the message and content, the author actively seeks to convince him or her to accept an opinion or belief. Much like expository writing, persuasive writing is presented in many organizational forms, but the author will use specific techniques, or RHETORICAL STRATEGIES, to build an argument. Readers can identify these strategies in order to clearly understand what an author wants them to believe, how the author's perspective and purpose may lead to bias, and whether the passage includes any logical fallacies.

Reading persuasive text requires an awareness of what the author believes about the topic.

Common rhetorical strategies include the appeals to ethos, logos, and pathos. An author uses these to build trust with the reader, explain the logical points of his or her argument, and convince the reader that his or her opinion is the best option.

An ETHOS—ETHICAL—APPEAL uses balanced, fair language and seeks to build a trusting relationship between the author and the reader. An author might explain his or her credentials, include the reader in an argument, or offer concessions to an opposing argument.

A LOGOS—LOGICAL—APPEAL builds on that trust by providing facts and support for the author's opinion, explaining the argument with clear connections and reasoning. At this point, the reader should beware of logical fallacies that connect unconnected ideas and build arguments on incorrect premises. With a logical appeal, an author strives to convince the reader to accept an opinion or belief by demonstrating that not only is it the most logical option but it also satisfies his or her emotional reaction to a topic.

Readers should consider how different audiences will react to a text. For example, how a slave owner's reactions to the narrative of Olaudah Equiano (on page 55) will differ from a slave trader's.

A PATHOS—EMOTIONAL—APPEAL does not depend on reasonable connections between ideas; rather, it seeks to remind the reader, through imagery, strong language, and personal connections, that the author's argument aligns with his or her best interests.

Many persuasive passages seek to use all three rhetorical strategies to best appeal to the reader.

Clues will help the reader determine many things about a passage, from the author's purpose to the passage's main idea, but understanding an author's purpose is essential to fully understanding the text.

Examples

Evident truth. Made so plain by our good Father in Heaven, that all *feel* and *understand* it, even down to brutes and creeping insects. The ant, who has toiled and dragged a crumb to his nest, will furiously defend the fruit of his labor, against whatever robber assails him. So plain, that the most dumb and stupid slave that ever toiled for a master, does constantly *know* that he is wronged. So plain that no one, high or low, ever does mistake it, except in a plainly *selfish* way; for although volume upon volume is written to prove slavery a very good thing, we never hear of the man who wishes to take the good of it, *by being a slave himself*.

Most governments have been based, practically, on the denial of the equal rights of men, as I have, in part, stated them; *ours* began, by *affirming* those rights. *They* said, some men are too *ignorant*, and *vicious*, to share in government. Possibly so, said we; and, by your system, you would always keep them ignorant and vicious. We proposed to give *all* a chance; and we expected the weak to grow stronger, the ignorant, wiser; and all better, and happier together.

We made the experiment; and the fruit is before us. Look at it. Think of it. Look at it, in its aggregate grandeur, of extent of country, and numbers of population, of ship, and steamboat.

—from Abraham Lincoln's speech fragment on slavery

1. The author's purpose is to
   (A) explain ideas.
   (B) narrate a story.
   (C) describe a situation.
   (D) persuade to accept an idea.
   (E) define a problem.

   Answers:

   (A) is incorrect. The injustice of slavery in America is made clear, but only to convince the audience that slavery cannot exist in America.

   (B) is incorrect. The author briefly mentions the narrative of America in terms of affirming the equal rights of all people, but he does not tell a story or relate the events that led to slavery.

   (C) is incorrect. The author does not describe the conditions of slaves or the many ways their human rights are denied.

   (D) is correct. The author provides logical reasons and evidence that slavery is wrong, that it violates the American belief in equal rights.

   (E) is incorrect. Although the author begins with a short definition of evident truth, he is simply laying the foundation for his persuasive argument that slavery violates the evident truth Americans believe.

2. To achieve his purpose, the author primarily uses
   (A) concrete analogies.
   (B) logical reasoning.
   (C) emotional appeals.
   (D) images.
   (E) figurative language.

Answers:

(A) is incorrect. The author mentions the ant's willingness to defend what is his but does not make an explicit and corresponding conclusion about the slave; instead, he says, "So plain, that the most dumb and stupid slave that ever toiled for a master, does constantly *know* that he is wronged." The implied parallel is between the ant's conviction about being wronged and the slave knowing he is wronged.

(B) is correct. The author uses logic when he points out that people who claim slavery is good never wish "to take the good of it, *by being a slave*." The author also points out that the principle of our country is to give everyone, including the "ignorant," opportunity; then he challenges his listeners to look at the fruit of this principle, saying, "Look at it, in its aggregate grandeur, of extent of country, and numbers of population, of ship, and steamboat."

(C) is incorrect. The author relies on logic and evidence, and makes no emotional appeals about the suffering of slaves.

(D) is incorrect. The author does offer evidence of his point with an image of the grandeur of America, but his primary appeal is logic.

(E) is incorrect. Initially, the author uses hyperbole when he says, "Evident truth. Made so plain by our good Father in Heaven, that all *feel* and *understand it*, even down to brutes and creeping insects." However, the author's primary appeal is logos.

The Audience

The structure, purpose, main idea, and language of a text all converge on one target: the intended audience. An author makes decisions about every aspect of a piece of writing based on that audience, and readers can evaluate the writing through the lens of that audience. By considering the probable reactions of an intended audience, readers can determine many things: whether or not they are part of that intended audience; the author's purpose for using specific techniques or devices; the biases of the author and how they appear in the writing; and how the author uses rhetorical strategies. While readers evaluate each of these things separately, identifying and considering the intended audience adds depth to the understanding of a text and helps highlight details with more clarity.

When reading a persuasive text, students should maintain awareness of what the author believes about the topic.

Several aspects identify the text's intended audience. First, when the main idea of the passage is known, the reader considers who most likely cares about that idea, benefits from it, or needs to know about it. Many authors begin with the main idea and then determine the audience in part based on these concerns.

Then the reader considers language. The author tailors language to appeal to the intended audience, so the reader can narrow down a broad understanding of that audience. The figurative language John Steinbeck uses in his novel *The Grapes of Wrath* reveals the suffering of the migrant Americans who traveled to California to find work during the Great Depression of the 1930s. Steinbeck spoke concretely to the Americans who were discriminating against the migrants. Instead of finding work in the "land of milk and honey," migrants faced unbearable poverty and injustice. The metaphor that gives the novel its title is "and in the eyes of the people there is the failure; and in the eyes of the hungry there is a

A logical argument includes a claim, a reason that supports the claim, and an assumption that the reader makes based on accepted beliefs. All parts of the argument need to make sense to the reader, so authors often consider the beliefs of their audience as they construct their arguments.

growing wrath. In the souls of the people the grapes of wrath are filling and growing heavy, growing heavy for the vintage." Steinbeck, used the image of ripening grapes, familiar to those surrounded by vineyards, to condemn this harsh treatment, provide an education of the human heart, and inspire compassion in his audience. Readers who weren't directly involved in the exodus of people from Oklahoma to the West, could have little difficulty grasping the meaning of Steinbeck's language in the description: "66 is the path of a people in flight, refugees from dust and shrinking land, from the thunder of tractors and invasion, from the twisting winds that howl up out of Texas, from floods that bring no richness to the land and steal what little richness is there."

Examples

In the following text, consideration should be made for how an English political leader of 1729 might have reacted.

It is a melancholy object to those, who walk through this great town, or travel in the country, when they see the streets, the roads and cabin-doors crowded with beggars of the female sex, followed by three, four, or six children, all in rags, and importuning every passenger for an alms. These mothers instead of being able to work for their honest livelihood, are forced to employ all their time in strolling to beg sustenance for their helpless infants who, as they grow up, either turn thieves for want of work, or leave their dear native country, to fight for the Pretender in Spain, or sell themselves to the Barbados.

I shall now therefore humbly propose my own thoughts, which I hope will not be liable to the least objection.

I have been assured by a very knowing American of my acquaintance in London, that a young healthy child well nursed, is, at a year old, a most delicious nourishing and wholesome food, whether stewed, roasted, baked, or boiled; and I make no doubt that it will equally serve in a fricassee.

I do therefore humbly offer it to public consideration, that of the hundred and twenty thousand children, already computed, twenty thousand may be reserved for breed, whereof only one fourth part to be males; which is more than we allow to sheep, black cattle, or swine, and my reason is, that these children are seldom the fruits of marriage, a circumstance not much regarded by our savages, therefore, one male will be sufficient to serve four females. That the remaining hundred thousand may, at a year old, be offered in sale to the persons of quality and fortune, through the kingdom, always advising the mother to let them suck plentifully in the last month, so as to render them plump, and fat for a good table. A child will make two dishes at an entertainment for friends, and when the family dines alone, the fore or hind quarter will make a reasonable dish, and seasoned with a little pepper or salt, will be very good boiled on the fourth day, especially in winter.

—from *A Modest Proposal for Preventing the Children of Poor People in Ireland From Being a Burden on Their Parents or Country, and for Making Them Beneficial to the Public* By Jonathan Swift

1. Which of the following best states the central idea of the passage?

    (A) Irish mothers are not able to support their children.

    (B) The Irish people lived like savages.

    (C) The people of England are quality people of fortune.

    (D) The poverty of the Irish forces their children to become criminals.

    (E) The kingdom of England has exploited the weaker country of Ireland to the point that the Irish people cannot support their families.

Answers:

(A) is incorrect. This is a fact alluded to in the passage, not a central idea.

(B) is incorrect. Although the author does refer to the Irish as savages, the reader recognizes that the author is being outrageously satirical.

(C) is incorrect. The author does say "That the remaining hundred thousand may, at a year old, be offered in sale to the persons of quality and fortune, through the kingdom," referring to the English. However, this is not the central idea; the opposite is, given that this is satire.

(D) is incorrect. The author does mention children growing up to be thieves, but this is not the central idea.

(E) is correct. The author is hoping to use satire to shame England.

2. The author's use of phrases like "humbly propose," "liable to the least objection," "wholesome food" suggests which of the following purposes?

   (A) to inform people about the attitudes of the English

   (B) to use satire to reveal the inhumane treatment of the Irish by the English

   (C) to persuade people to survive by any means

   (D) to express his admiration of the Irish people

   (E) to narrate the struggles of the English people

Answers:

(A) is incorrect. The author's subject is the poverty of the Irish, and his audience is the English who are responsible for the suffering of the Irish.

(B) is correct. The intended meaning of a satire sharply contradicts the literal meaning. Swift's proposal is not humble; it is meant to humble the arrogant. He expects the audience to be horrified. The children would make the worst imaginable food.

(C) is incorrect. The author is not serious. His intent is to shock his English audience.

(D) is incorrect. The author is expressing sympathy for the Irish.

(E) is incorrect. It is the Irish people who are struggling.

Tone and Mood

Two important aspects of the communication between author and audience occur subtly. The TONE of a passage describes the author's attitude toward the topic, distinct from the MOOD, which is the pervasive feeling or atmosphere in a passage that provokes specific emotions in the reader. The distinction between these two aspects lies once again in the audience: the mood influences the reader's emotional state in response to the piece, while the tone establishes a relationship between the audience and the author. Does the author intend to instruct the audience? Is the author more experienced than the audience, or does he or she wish to convey a friendly or equal relationship? In each of these cases, the author uses a different tone to reflect the desired level of communication.

 To determine the author's tone, students should examine what overall feeling they are experiencing.

Primarily DICTION, or word choice, determines mood and tone in a passage. Many readers make the mistake of thinking about the ideas an author puts forth and using those alone to determine particularly tone; a much better practice is to separate specific words from the text and look for patterns in connotation and emotion. By considering categories of words used by the author, the reader can discover both the overall emotional atmosphere of a text and the attitude of the author toward the subject.

> To decide the connotation of a word, the reader examines whether the word conveys a positive or negative association in the mind. Adjectives are often used to influence the feelings of the reader, such as in the phrase "an ambitious attempt to achieve."

Every word has not only a literal meaning but also a CONNOTATIVE MEANING, relying on the common emotions, associations, and experiences an audience might associate with that word. The following words are all synonyms: *dog, puppy, cur, mutt, canine, pet.* Two of these words—*dog* and *canine*—are neutral words, without strong associations or emotions. Two others—*pet* and *puppy*—have positive associations. The last two—*cur* and *mutt*—have negative associations. A passage that uses one pair of these words versus another pair activates the positive or negative reactions of the audience.

Examples

Day had broken cold and grey, exceedingly cold and grey, when the man turned aside from the main Yukon trail and climbed the high earth-bank, where a dim and little-travelled trail led eastward through the fat spruce timberland. It was a steep bank, and he paused for breath at the top, excusing the act to himself by looking at his watch. It was nine o'clock. There was no sun nor hint of sun, though there was not a cloud in the sky. It was a clear day, and yet there seemed an intangible *pall* over the face of things, a subtle gloom that made the day dark, and that was due to the absence of sun. This fact did not worry the man. He was used to the lack of sun. It had been days since he had seen the sun, and he knew that a few more days must pass before that cheerful orb, due south, would just peep above the sky-line and dip immediately from view.

—from "To Build a Fire" by Jack London

1. Which of the following best describes the mood of the passage?

    (A) exciting and adventurous

    (B) fierce and determined

    (C) bleak and forbidding

    (D) grim yet hopeful

    (E) intense yet filled with fear

Answers:

(A) is incorrect. The man is on some adventure as he turns off the main trail, but the context is one of gloom and darkness, not excitement.

(B) is incorrect. The cold, dark day is fierce, and the man may be determined; however, the overall mood of the entire passage is one of grim danger.

(C) is correct. The man is oblivious to the gloom and darkness of the day, which was "exceedingly cold and grey."

(D) is incorrect. The atmosphere is grim, and there is no indication the man is hopeful about anything. He is aware only of his breath and steps forward.

(E) is incorrect. The cold, grey scene of a lone man walking off the trail is intense, but "this fact did not worry the man."

2. The connotation of the words *intangible pall* is

   (A) a death-like covering.

   (B) a vague sense of familiarity.

   (C) an intimation of communal strength.

   (D) an understanding of the struggle ahead.

   (E) a refreshing sense of possibility.

Answers:

(A) is correct. Within the context of the sentence "It was a clear day, and yet there seemed an intangible *pall* over the face of things, a subtle gloom that made the day dark," the words *gloom* and *dark* are suggestive of death; the words *over the face* suggest a covering.

(B) is incorrect. The word *intangible* can mean a vague sense, but there is nothing especially familiar about a clear day that is dark, with no sunlight.

(C) is incorrect. The word *intangible* suggests intimation; however, from the beginning, the author shows the man alone, and reports, "the man turned aside from the main Yukon trail."

(D) is incorrect. A struggle may be indicated by the darkness and gloom, but the man has no understanding of this possibility. The text refers to the darkness, saying, "This fact did not worry the man. He was used to the lack of sun."

(E) is incorrect. The man is hiking this trail for some possibility, but he is not refreshed; he is pausing to catch his "breath at the top, excusing the act to himself by looking at his watch."

VOCABULARY IN CONTEXT

Vocabulary in context questions ask about the meaning of specific words in the passage. The questions will ask which answer choice is most similar in meaning to the specified word, or which answer choice could be substituted for that word in the passage.

When confronted with unfamiliar words, the passage itself can help clarify their meaning. Often, identifying the tone or main idea of the passage can help eliminate answer choices. For example, if the tone of the passage is generally positive, try eliminating the answer choices with a negative connotation. Or, if the passage is about a particular occupation, rule out words unrelated to that topic.

Passages may also provide specific CONTEXT CLUES that can help determine the meaning of a word.

One type of context clue is a DEFINITION, or DESCRIPTION, CLUE. Sometimes, authors use a difficult word, then include *that is* or *which is* to signal that they are providing a definition. An author also may provide a synonym or restate the idea in more familiar words:

> *Teachers often prefer teaching students with intrinsic motivation; these students have an internal desire to learn.*

The meaning of *intrinsic* is restated as an *internal desire*.

Similarly, authors may include an EXAMPLE CLUE, providing an example phrase that clarifies the meaning of the word:

Teachers may view extrinsic rewards as efficacious; however, an individual student may not be interested in what the teacher offers. For example, a student who is diabetic may not feel any incentive to work when offered a sweet treat.

Efficacious is explained with an example that demonstrates how an extrinsic reward may not be effective.

Another commonly used context clue is the CONTRAST, or ANTONYM, CLUE. In this case, authors indicate that the unfamiliar word is the opposite of a familiar word:

In contrast to intrinsic motivation, extrinsic motivation is contingent on teachers offering rewards that are appealing.

The phrase "in contrast" tells the reader that *extrinsic* is the opposite of *intrinsic*.

Examples

1. One challenge of teaching is finding ways to incentivize, or to motivate, learning.

   Which of the following is the meaning of *incentivize* as used in the sentence?

   (A) encourage

   (B) determine

   (C) challenge

   (D) improve

   (E) dissuade

   Answers:

   (A) is correct. The word *incentivize* is defined immediately with the synonym *motivate*, or *encourage*.

   (B) is incorrect. *Determine* is not a synonym for *motivate*. In addition, the phrase "to determine learning" does not make sense in the sentence.

   (C) is incorrect. *Challenge* is not a synonym for motivate.

   (D) is incorrect. *Improve* is closely related to motivation, but it is not the best synonym provided.

   (E) is incorrect. *Dissuade* is an antonym for motivate.

2. If an extrinsic reward is extremely desirable, a student may become so apprehensive he or she cannot focus. The student may experience such intense pressure to perform that the reward undermines its intent.

   Which of the following is the meaning of *apprehensive* as used in the sentence?

   (A) uncertain

   (B) distracted

   (C) anxious

   (D) forgetful

   (E) resentful

   Answers:

   (A) is incorrect. Nothing in the sentence suggests the student is uncertain.

   (B) is incorrect. *Distracted* is related to the clue "focus" but does not address the clue "pressure to perform."

(C) is correct. The reader can infer that the pressure to perform is making the student anxious.

(D) is incorrect. Nothing in the sentence suggests the student is forgetful.

(E) is incorrect. The clue describes the student as feeling pressured but does not suggest the student is resentful.

3

MECHANICAL COMPREHENSION

The Mechanical Comprehension section of the ASTB-E tests candidates' understanding of the basic principles of physics and how those principles are applied to real-world situations. Topics include Newton's laws of motion, work and energy, and simple machines. The ASTB-E includes approximately thirty mechanical comprehension questions to be answered in fifteen minutes.

FORCES

Newton's Laws

A fundamental concept of mechanics is INERTIA, which states that an object has a tendency to maintain its state of motion. An object at rest will stay at rest, and an object moving at constant velocity will continue to move at that velocity, unless something pushes or pulls on it. This push or pull is called a FORCE. The newton (N) is the SI unit for force (1 newton is 1 kg m/s²).

MASS is a fundamental property of matter and is a measure of the inertia of an object. The kilogram (kg) is the SI unit for mass. An object with a larger mass will resist a change in motion more than an object with a smaller mass will. For example, it is harder to throw an elephant than it is to throw a baseball (the elephant has much more mass than a baseball).

In 1687, Isaac Newton published three laws of motion that describe the behavior of force and mass. Newton's first law is also called the law of inertia. It states that an object will maintain its current state of motion unless acted on by an outside force.

Newton's second law is an equation:

$$F = ma$$

where F is the sum of the forces on an object (also called the net force), m is the mass of the object, and a is the acceleration. The law states that the net force on an object will lead

A **SYSTEM** is a collection of particles or objects that is isolated from its surroundings. All forces within a system are called internal forces, and forces outside the system are called external forces.

to an acceleration. Also, if an object has an acceleration, there must be a force that is causing it. Extending the previous example, if the same amount of force is applied to an elephant and a baseball, the baseball will have a much larger acceleration than the elephant (and so it is easier to throw).

An object in EQUILIBRIUM is either at rest or is moving at constant velocity; in other words, the object has no acceleration, or $a = 0$. Using Newton's second law, an object is in equilibrium if the net force on the object is 0, or $F = 0$ (this is called the equilibrium condition).

Newton's third law states that for every action (force), there will be an equal and opposite reaction (force). For instance, if a person is standing on the floor, there is a force of gravity pulling him toward the earth. However, he is not accelerating toward the earth; he is simply standing at rest on the floor (in equilibrium). So, the floor must provide a force that is equal in magnitude and in the opposite direction to the force of gravity.

Newton's second law, $F = ma$, can be used to remember all three laws.

If there is no outside force ($F = 0$), the object will not accelerate and thus will stay at rest or at a constant velocity (Newton's first law).

If an object is resting on the floor, it is not moving, and $a = 0$. To maintain this equilibrium, the weight of the object must be matched by the force pushing up from the floor (Newton's third law).

Another example is a person kicking a wall. While it may seem like kicking a wall would only damage the wall, the force applied to the wall from the person's foot is identical to the force applied to the person's foot from the wall.

Examples

1. When a car moving forward stops abruptly, which of the following describes what happens to the driver if she is wearing a seat belt?

    (A) The driver's body will continue to move forward due to inertia, and the seat belt will apply the required force to keep her in her seat.

    (B) The driver is inside the car, so she will stop with the car whether or not she is wearing a seat belt.

    (C) The driver will be pushed against the seat when the car stops; the seat belt has no effect.

    Answers:

    (A) is correct. The driver's body will continue moving forward due to inertia. A force is required to slow the driver down (Newton's first law).

    (B) is incorrect. Being inside the car does not matter; a force is required to slow the driver down.

    (C) is incorrect. The driver will be pushed against the seat only if the car is moving in reverse and comes to an abrupt stop.

2. Which example describes an object in equilibrium?

    (A) a parachutist after he jumps from an airplane

    (B) a person sitting still in a chair

    (C) a soccer ball when it is kicked

    Answers:

    (A) is incorrect. The parachutist will accelerate toward the earth.

    (B) is correct. The person is not accelerating.

    (C) is incorrect. During a kick, the soccer ball is accelerating.

Types of Forces

There are four **FUNDAMENTAL FORCES** that form the basis for all other forces. The **GRAVITATIONAL** force is the force that pulls mass together. It is an attractive force and is what holds stars and planets together as spheres and keeps them in orbit. It also keeps humans on the surface of the earth. The **WEAK** force is beyond the scope of this text, but it plays a role in nuclear reactions (like those in stars). The **ELECTROMAGNETIC** force is the force between electric charges. It is repulsive when the charges are the same sign (positive-positive or negative-negative) and is attractive when the charges are the opposite sign (positive-negative). This force holds the positive nuclei and negative electrons of atoms together. Finally, the **NUCLEAR** (or strong) force is so named because it holds together the nucleus in an atom. The nuclear force has a larger magnitude than the electromagnetic force that pushes protons (positive charges) away from each other in the nucleus.

Non-fundamental forces are defined as forces that can be derived from the four fundamental forces. These forces include tension, friction, the normal force, and the buoyant force. **TENSION** (F_T or T) is found in ropes pulling or holding up an object, and **FRICTION** (F_F) is created by two objects moving against each other. The **NORMAL FORCE** (F_N or N) occurs when an object is resting on another object. The normal force is always equal and opposite to the force pushing onto the surface. The **BUOYANT FORCE** (F_B) is the upward force experienced by floating objects. Finally, an **APPLIED FORCE** (F_A) is any force applied to an object by another object.

When working with forces, it is helpful to draw a **FREE-BODY DIAGRAM**, which shows all the forces acting on an object. Because forces are vectors, it is important to consider the direction of the force when drawing a diagram.

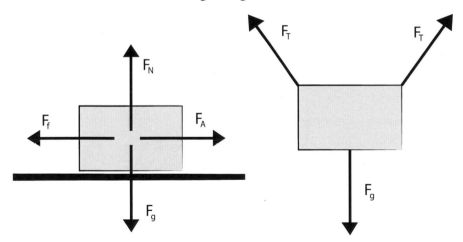

Figure 3.1. Free-Body Diagrams

Example

Which of the following forces causes oppositely charged ions to attract?

(A) nuclear

(B) electromagnetic

(C) tension

Answers:

(A) is incorrect. The nuclear force holds together the subatomic particles in an atom's nucleus.

(B) is correct. The electromagnetic force is the force between charged particles that causes them to attract or repel each other.

(C) is incorrect. Tension is a force that results from an object being pulled or hung from a rope or chain.

Weight

The gravitational force felt by an object on the surface of the earth is called the object's WEIGHT. The acceleration due to gravity on the surface of the earth is $g = 9.8$ m/s^2 and always points toward the center of the earth. Using Newton's second law, the weight W of an object of mass m is:

$$W = mg$$

Example

An object with a weight of 32 N on the moon is brought to Earth. If the acceleration due to gravity on the moon is 1.6 m/s^2, what is the weight of the object on Earth?

(A) 1.96 N

(B) 19.6 N

(C) 196 N

Answer:

(C) is correct.

$W = mg$ $32 = m(1.6)$ $m = 20$ kg	Use the formula for weight to find the object's mass using the acceleration due to gravity on the moon.
$W = mg$ $W = 20(9.8) = \mathbf{196\ N}$	Use the object's mass to find its weight on Earth using $g = 9.8$ m/s^2.

Tension

A common type of applied force is TENSION, the force applied by a rope or chain as it pulls on an object. In a free-body diagram, the vector for tension always points along the rope away from the object. Tension plays an important role in pulley systems, as shown in the figure on the right. The tension in the pulley's rope acts against the mass's weight, and the magnitude of the two forces determines whether the mass moves up or down.

Example

In Figure 3.2, if mass M is much greater than mass m, what direction do both masses move?

(A) Mass M will move down, and mass m will move up.

(B) Mass M will move up, and mass m will move down.

(C) Neither mass will move; the system is in equilibrium.

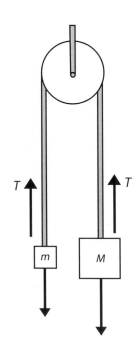

Figure 3.2. Pulley System

Friction

Microscopically, no surface is perfectly smooth. The irregular shape of the surfaces in contact will lead to interactions that resist movement. The resulting force is FRICTION. Friction opposes motion and describes the resistance of two surfaces in contact as they move across each other. On a free-body diagram, friction always points in the direction opposite the object's motion.

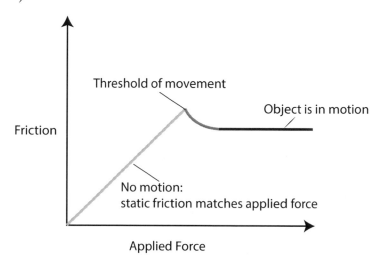

Figure 3.3. Static and Kinetic Friction

There are two types of friction: static and kinetic. STATIC FRICTION is applicable to an object that is not moving and is always equal to the force applied to the object. In other words, it is the amount of force that needs to be overcome for an object to move. For example, a small force applied to a large rock will not move the rock because static friction will match the applied force in the opposite direction. However, when enough force is applied, static friction can be overcome, and an object will begin moving. When this happens, the moving object experiences KINETIC friction.

The size of the friction force is dependent on an object's weight. Think of a couch being slid across a carpet. The couch becomes much harder to move if a person sits on the couch, and harder still if more people are added. This effect is written mathematically in terms of the normal force from the surface:

$$f_s \leq \mu_s N$$
$$f_k = \mu_k N$$

where f_s and f_k are the static and kinetic forces of friction, μ_s and μ_k are the static and kinetic coefficients of friction, and N is the normal force.

Examples

1. If a block is sliding down an inclined plane, in what direction will the friction vector point?

    (A) directly into (perpendicular to) the plane

    (B) down and parallel to the plane

    (C) up and parallel to the plane

    Answers:

    (A) is incorrect. This describes the direction of the component of the block's weight into the plane.

    (B) is incorrect. The force of friction will always oppose motion.

    (C) is correct. If the block is moving down the plane, the force of friction points up the plane.

2. In which of the following situations is an object experiencing static friction?

    (A) a rock sliding down a hill

    (B) a person in a moving car slamming on the brakes

    (C) a person leaning against a car

    Answers:

    (A) is incorrect. Kinetic friction will be in effect because the rock is moving.

    (B) is incorrect. Kinetic friction will be in effect because the car is moving.

    (C) is correct. The person is applying a force to the car, and static friction is keeping the car from moving.

Buoyant Force

When a boat or object is floating or under water or another liquid, the BUOYANT FORCE pushes vertically against the weight of the object. The magnitude of this force is calculated by considering the volume of the object that is submerged in the fluid. The object displaces a volume of liquid equal to its own volume, and the liquid pushes back by an amount that is exactly equal to the weight of the liquid that would exist in that volume. The buoyant force (always a vector pointing up), is given by:

Boats float by using the buoyant force. Ships that hold very large loads need a large buoyant force and so need to displace a large amount of water.

$$F_{buoyant} = m_{fluid} \, g = \rho V$$

where m_{fluid} is the mass of the fluid displaced, ρ is the density of the fluid, V is the volume of fluid that is displaced by the object, and g is the acceleration due to gravity.

Example

Which object will experience the largest buoyant force when fully submerged?

(A) a golf ball

(B) a baseball

(C) a basketball

Answer:

(C) ic correct. A basketball will have the largest volume and will displace the most water. This will lead to the largest buoyant force of the three.

Torque

TORQUE is the force required to rotate an object. The units for torque are N m (newton meters), and the equation is: $\tau = rF$, where r is the radius (the distance from the axis of rotation to the location of F), and F is the force. It is important to understand that r and F are vectors and that the equation is valid only in the case where r and F are perpendicular to each other.

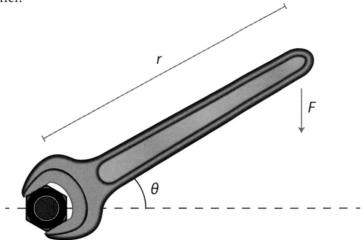

Figure 3.4. Torque

Remember that mass is a measure of inertia, where a larger mass is harder to accelerate with a force. MOMENT OF INERTIA is similarly used when discussing a rotating object to describe the object's inertia, or, its resistance to being rotated. A large amount of mass far away from the axis of rotation will have a larger moment of inertia than a smaller mass closer to the axis of rotation. For a single mass m at a distance r from a rotation axis, the moment of inertia is given by: $I = mr^2$.

For an object to be truly in equilibrium in terms of energy, it must not only be at rest or at constant velocity ($F = 0$); it must also not be rotating ($\tau = 0$). The object is then in ROTATIONAL EQUILIBRIUM.

Example

Which object has the highest moment of inertia? Assume all objects have the same mass.

(A) a solid disk with a radius of 5 cm

(B) a solid disk with a radius of 10 cm

(C) a hollow disk with a radius of 10 cm

Answers:

(A) is incorrect. An object's moment of inertia is largest when it has mass that is located far away from the axis of rotation. Compared to object C, the mass in this disk is closer to the axis of rotation.

(B) is incorrect. Compared to object C, most of the mass in this disk is closer to the axis of rotation.

(C) is correct. This object has identical mass to the other objects, but all the mass is located at a larger distance from the axis of rotation than the other objects.

WORK, ENERGY, AND POWER

Work

WORK is a scalar value that is defined as the application of a force over a distance. The SI unit for work is joule (J). The equation for work is:

$$W = Fd$$

where F is the force and d is the distance.

One example is a person lifting a book off the ground. As she lifts the book, the book has a weight, and her hand and arm are producing a force that is larger than that weight to make the book rise. In terms of work, the person's hand is doing work on the book to lift the book from the ground to its final position. If she drops the book, the force of gravity will push the book back to the ground. So, during a drop, gravity (the earth) is doing work on the book.

Another example is a person holding the book steady. Neither his hand nor gravity is doing work on the book because the book is not moving any distance. However, it is interesting to note that the person's hand and arm will get tired holding a book in the air. This is due to work that is done inside his body to keep his hand at its position while holding the book.

The sign of the work done is important. In the example of lifting a book, the person's hand is doing positive (+) work on the book. However, gravity is always pulling the book down, which means that during a lift, gravity is doing negative (–) work on the book. This can be expressed as such: If the force and the displacement are in the same direction, then the work is positive (+). If the force and the displacement are in opposite directions, then the work is negative (–). In the case of lifting a book, the net work done on the book is positive.

Example

Which situation requires the most work done on a car?

(A) pushing on the car, but it does not move

(B) towing the car up a steep hill for 100 meters

(C) pushing the car 5 meters across a parking lot

Answers:

(A) is incorrect. If the car does not move, then no work is done on the car.

(B) is correct. A steep hill requires a large force to counter the gravitational force. The large distance will also lead to a large amount of work done.

(C) is incorrect. Work will be done, but much less than in case B.

Energy

ENERGY is an abstract concept, but everything in nature has an energy associated with it. There are many types of energy, including mechanical, chemical, thermal, nuclear, electric, magnetic, and so on. The MECHANICAL ENERGY of an object is due to its motion (kinetic energy) and position (potential energy). Energy is a scalar and is given in the SI unit of joules (J).

There is an energy related to movement called the KINETIC ENERGY. Any object that has mass and is moving will have a kinetic energy. The equation for kinetic energy is:

$$KE = \frac{1}{2}mv^2$$

where m is the mass and v is the speed.

POTENTIAL ENERGY is understood as the potential for an object to gain kinetic energy. This can also be seen as energy stored in a system. There are several types of potential energy. ELECTRIC POTENTIAL ENERGY is derived from the interaction between positive and negative charges. Because opposite charges attract each other, and like charges repel, energy can be stored when opposite charges are moved apart or when like charges are pushed together. Similarly, compressing a spring stores ELASTIC POTENTIAL ENERGY. Energy is also stored in chemical bonds as CHEMICAL POTENTIAL ENERGY.

The energy stored in a book placed on a table is GRAVITATIONAL POTENTIAL ENERGY; it is derived from the pull of the earth's gravity on the book. The equation for gravitational potential energy is given by:

$$PE_g = mgh$$

where m is the mass, g is 9.8 m/s² (remember mg is an object's weight), and h is the height.

A simple way to understand gravitational potential energy is to consider an object's initial height. The speed of an object at a moment just before hitting the ground (and therefore the kinetic energy difference just before hitting the ground) after falling from a short stool to the ground may be compared to the speed of an object falling from the roof of a house to the ground. The jump from the roof will lead to a much higher kinetic energy, and so, the potential energy is higher on the roof.

Energy can be converted into other forms of energy, but it cannot be created or destroyed. This principle is called the CONSERVATION OF ENERGY. A swing provides a simple example of this principle. Throughout the swing's path, the total energy of the system remains the same. At the highest point of a swing's path, it has potential energy but no kinetic energy (because it has stopped moving momentarily as it changes direction). As the swing drops, that potential energy is converted to kinetic energy, and the swing's velocity increases. At the bottom of its path, all its potential energy has been converted into kinetic energy (meaning its potential energy is zero). This process repeats as the swing moves up and down. At any point in the swing's path, the kinetic and potential energies will sum to the same value.

Electrical power plants are energy converters. A hydroelectric plant converts gravitational energy (from water falling through the dam) into electrical energy. A nuclear power plant converts nuclear energy into electrical energy. Coal and gas power plants convert chemical energy into electrical energy. Solar panels convert light energy into electrical energy.

CONTINUE

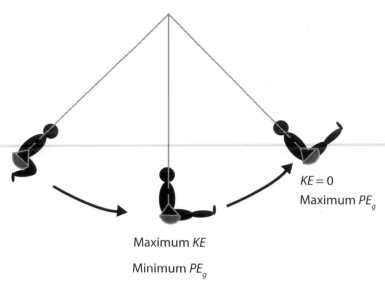

KE = 0

Maximum PE_g

Maximum KE

Minimum PE_g

Figure 3.5. Mechanical Energy in a Pendulum

In reality, there is air resistance against the swing, and there is friction between the swing's chain and the bar that holds the swing. Friction (and air resistance) convert mechanical energies into heat (thermal energy). This is why a swing will gradually slow down and reach lower heights with each back-and-forth motion. Energy loss through heat also occurs in electronics and motors.

Revisiting the concept of work, a change in position with the application of a force will necessarily lead to a velocity and therefore to kinetic energy. So, work is effectively an energy and can be related to kinetic energy with the following equation:

$$W = \Delta KE = \frac{1}{2}mv_2^2 - \frac{1}{2}mv_1^2$$

Examples

1. Imagine a roller coaster that does not have its own power and starts on a hill at a height of 100 meters. There is no air resistance or friction. It falls down to a height of 50 meters in the first dip and begins to move up the next hill that is 200 meters high. What will happen to the coaster on the next hill?

   (A) It will make it up to 150 m up the hill and move back down to the first dip.

   (B) It will make it up to 100 m up the hill and move back down to the first dip.

   (C) It will make it up to 75 m up the hill and move back down to the first dip.

   Answers:

   (A) is incorrect. It will not have enough energy to make it to 150 m.

   (B) is correct. Its maximum energy is from its starting point, the potential energy at 100 m, so it can never move higher than 100 m.

   (C) is incorrect. It has enough energy to make it past 75 m.

2. A pendulum with mass *m* is swinging back and forth. If it experiences both air resistance and friction, which of the following statements about the pendulum's speed is true?

   (A) The pendulum's maximum speed will always occur where the height of the mass off the ground is the lowest.

   (B) The pendulum's maximum speed will always occur where the height of the mass off the ground is the highest.

   (C) The mass will always travel at the same speed.

Power

As stated before, energy cannot be created or destroyed but can only change forms. A measure of this transfer of energy is called **POWER**, which is the rate of work done or energy conversion per time. The SI unit for power is a watt, W. Because work is defined as a force applied along a distance, power can also be written as a force multiplied by a speed. Power is a scalar with an equation that is given by:

$$P = \frac{W}{t} = Fv$$

where W is the work done (or energy converted) over an amount of time t, F is a force, and v is the speed.

Power is a commonly used measure of electrical devices. For example, light bulbs are labeled in terms of their wattage (40 W, 60 W, etc.). A 60 W light bulb will use 60 joules of electrical energy per second, and this energy will be converted into light energy (that is the light bulb's purpose), but also a great deal of that energy is converted into thermal energy (heat). The heat from light bulbs is wasted energy.

Electrical power from power companies is commonly charged in terms of kilowatt hours (kWh). From the equation for power above, the energy used during a time period can be calculated by multiplying the power by time. As an example, the energy used can be expressed as the amount kilowatts used multiplied by the number of hours. So, kilowatt hours is a unit of energy (1kWh = 3,600,000 J).

Examples

1. Which of the following is NOT a unit of energy?

   (A) joule

   (B) kilowatt hour

   (C) newton

   Answers:

   (A) is incorrect. A joule is the unit for energy.

   (B) is incorrect. Any form of watt multiplied by an amount of time is suitable for representing energy.

   (C) is correct. A newton is the unit for force.

2. A constant external force of 10 N is applied to an object to keep it moving at a constant speed of 10 m/s. Which of the following statements about the object is true?

   (A) No power is used to move the object.

   (B) The external force supplies power to keep the object moving at 10 m/s.

   (C) The object is not accelerating, so no power is used.

MOMENTUM AND COLLISIONS

The term *MOMENTUM* is a common one in the English language, but it has a specific meaning in mechanics: the mass of an object multiplied by its velocity. Any object that has mass and is also moving has momentum. Momentum is a vector and is given by the equation:

$$p = mv$$

where m is the mass and v is the velocity.

The concept of momentum can be used to describe a change in motion. For example, a baseball has a certain momentum when it is traveling through the air, but it has zero momentum once it has been caught. A change in velocity requires a force to cause an acceleration over a period of time, t. The change in momentum is called the IMPULSE and can be written as:

$$I = \Delta p = mv_2 - mv_1 = Ft$$

where p is the momentum; m and v are mass and speed, respectively; and F is the force over a time, t.

The relationship for impulse has interesting implications. If an object has a momentum change, then there was a force applied over a time t to cause that change. So, for an identical impulse value, a longer time requires less force to be used. Similarly, a shorter time requires more force. This is why a baseball catcher will wear a thick mitt and other padding to increase the interaction time that slows the ball. As a result, the catcher's hand feels a much smaller force than it would without the glove. Using the same reasoning, but in reverse, a baseball bat has no padding, which decreases the interaction time and relatively increases the force applied to the ball.

> ✓
> You are an astronaut in space and are holding a baseball in your hand. If you make the motion to throw the ball but never actually throw it, will you still move away as if you did?

Like energy, MOMENTUM IS CONSERVED. However, momentum is conserved only when there are no outside forces on the system. Conservation of momentum states that if an object in a system is given momentum, then all the other objects in the system will have a net momentum that will be opposite to the object. The total momentum of the system remains unchanged. For example, the sidebar on this page addresses an astronaut is at rest in space. If she throws an object to her right, her body will also move to the left in response.

Examples

1. Modern cars are designed to crumple during a collision. Using the concept of impulse, how does this protect the passengers?

   (A) By decreasing the interaction time, the crumple maximizes the force felt by the passengers.

   (B) By decreasing the interaction time, the crumple minimizes the force felt by the passengers.

   (C) By increasing the interaction time, the crumple minimizes the force felt by the passengers.

   Answers:

   (A) is incorrect. The crumple will increase the interaction time. A decrease in interaction time will increase the amount of force felt by the passengers.

   (B) is incorrect. The crumple will increase the interaction time. A decrease in interaction time will increase the amount of force felt by the passengers.

   (C) is correct. The crumple increases the time of interaction and so decreases the force felt by the passengers.

2. A man is sitting in a boat next to a dock and decides to jump from the boat to the dock. The boat is much lighter than the man. Using conservation of momentum, what will be the most likely result?

   (A) The man will most likely fall into the water.

   (B) The man will reach the dock.

   (C) The boat will slam into the dock.

   Answers:

   (A) is correct. The boat will move behind the man at high speed, while the man will move forward at low speed. He will most likely end up falling in the water.

   (B) is incorrect. The boat will move behind the man at high speed, while the man will move forward at low speed. He will most likely end up falling in the water.

   (C) is incorrect. If the man jumps toward the dock, the boat will move away from the dock.

SIMPLE MACHINES

A simple machine changes the magnitude or direction of an applied force, with the result leading to a **MECHANICAL ADVANTAGE** for the user. This advantage is the ratio of force that is output from the machine relative to the force input. The equation for mechanical advantage is given by:

$$MA = \frac{F_{output}}{F_{input}}$$

A **LEVER** is a simple machine based on the concept of torque. The axis of rotation and also where the lever rests is called the **FULCRUM**. Using the figure as a guide, $r_{input} F_{input} = r_{output} F_{output}$. Using the previous definition for mechanical advantages gives:

$$MA = \frac{r_{input}}{r_{output}}$$

There are three types of levers. A **FIRST-CLASS LEVER** has the fulcrum between the input and output forces, and the input force is in the opposite direction of the output force. A

SECOND-CLASS LEVER has the input and output forces on one common side of the fulcrum, and both are in the same direction. The output force is closer to the fulcrum than the input force is. Like the second-class lever, a THIRD-CLASS LEVER has the input and output forces on one common side of the fulcrum, and both are in the same direction. The input force is closer to the fulcrum than the output force is.

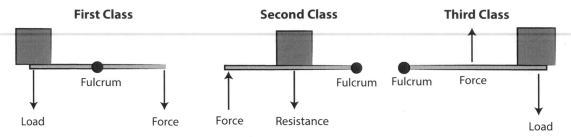

Figure 3.6. Types of Levers

An INCLINED PLANE is a simple machine (a ramp) that reduces the amount of force needed to raise a mass to a certain height. Earlier in this text it was shown that the weight of a mass on an inclined plane has a portion that pushes into the plane. Only a fraction of the weight is in the direction down the plane. This is the operating principle for this simple machine. In terms of work, the input work to move an object up an inclined plane of length L is $W_{in} = F_{input} \times L$. The output work is what is required to lift the object up to a height h, $W_{output} = F_{output} \times h$, where F_{output} is the object's weight. Combining these gives the mechanical advantage:

> The idea of simple machines was invented by Archimedes in the third century BCE.

$$MA = \frac{L}{h}$$

where L is the length of the inclined plane and h is the height.

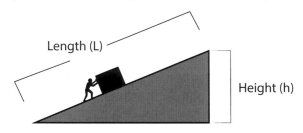

Figure 3.7. An Inclined Plane

A PULLEY is a simple machine that redirects force by supporting a rope that can move freely by rotating the pulley. A single pulley lifting a weight will have a mechanical advantage of 1. When a second pulley is added in a block-and-tackle configuration, the input force required to lift the weight is halved, and so the mechanical advantage is 2. Similarly, a three-pulley system will have a mechanical advantage of 3.

$$MA = \text{number of pulleys}$$

A WEDGE is a simple machine that converts an input force onto one surface into a force that is perpendicular to its other surfaces. A wedge is often used to separate material; common examples are an ax or knife. Using the same reasoning as used for an inclined plane

Figure 3.8. A Three-Pulley System

(a wedge is effectively two inclined planes on top of each other), the mechanical advantage is

$$MA = \frac{L}{W}$$

where L is the length of the inclined plane on the wedge, and W is the width (the length of the back edge).

A **WHEEL AND AXLE** is a simple machine that has a rotating structure with two different radii. The larger radius is the wheel, and the smaller radius is the axle. It is similar conceptually to a lever, where the different radii convert the torque on the wheel into a torque on the axle (or vice versa). The mechanical advantage is the same as for the lever:

$$MA = \frac{r_{input}}{r_{output}}$$

where r_{input} is the radius of the input, and r_{output} is the radius of the output.

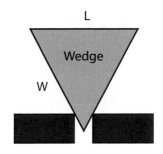

Figure 3.9. A Simple Wedge

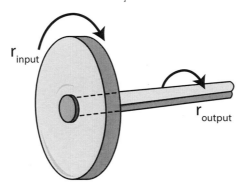

Figure 3.10. A Wheel and Axle

GEARS are simple machines that are circular and have notches or teeth along the outer edge. Several gears in contact form a gear train. Again, the force applied along a gear train is related to the torque, where a large-radius gear will apply a large torque to a smaller gear on the train. The number of teeth on a gear is directly related to the radius of the gear, allowing the mechanical advantage to be written as:

$$MA = \frac{\tau_{output}}{\tau_{input}} = \frac{N_{output}}{N_{input}}$$

where τ are the torques from each gear, and N is the number of teeth on each gear.

Another concept for a gear train is the **GEAR RATIO**, or speed ratio, which is a ratio of the angular velocity of the input gear to the angular velocity of the output gear. At the point of contact, the linear velocity must be the same, so $v = \omega_{input}\, r_{input} = \omega_{output}\, r_{output}$. So, the gear ratio is:

$$\frac{\omega_{input}}{\omega_{output}} = \frac{r_{output}}{r_{input}} = \frac{N_{output}}{N_{input}}$$

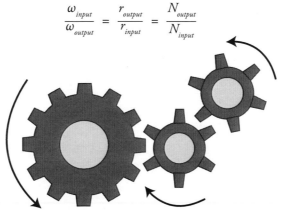

Figure 3.11. A Gear Train

A **SCREW** is a simple machine that converts rotational motion into linear motion. In general, a screw is a cylinder with an inclined plane wrapped around it. The wrapped inclined plane is called the thread, while the distance between the planes is called the pitch. The pitch is directed along the length of the screw. Again considering the work done, W_{input} = F_{input} $2\pi r$, where r is the radius of the screw; and W_{output} = F_{output} h, where h is the pitch. The mechanical advantage then becomes:

$$MA = \frac{2\pi r}{h}$$

where r is the radius of the screw, and h is the pitch.

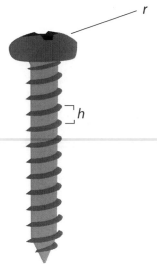

Figure 3.12. A Screw

Examples

1. Which is an example of a first-class lever?

   (A) wheelbarrow

   (B) scissors

   (C) tweezers

   Answers:

   (A) is incorrect. This is a second-class lever.

   (B) is correct. This is a first-class lever.

   (C) is incorrect. This is a third-class lever.

2. Which mechanical advantage is the best for the user?

   (A) 10

   (B) 5

   (C) 2

   Answer:

   (A) is correct. The highest mechanical advantage is the best for the user.

THE BASICS OF ELECTRICITY

Electric Charge

Electric **CHARGE** is a fundamental property of matter, like mass. When something is without charge, it is called **NEUTRAL**. Experimentally it was determined that there are two types of charges, named positive (+) and negative (–). As more was discovered about electric charge, it was shown that negative charge came from **ELECTRONS**, and positive charge came from **PROTONS**.

The unit of charge, e, is a fundamental constant (meaning it never changes) and has a value of e = 1.602 x 10^{-19} C, where C is coulombs. The charge of an electron is –e, and the charge of a proton is +e. Therefore, the total charge is always a multiple of e, and fractional values of e do not exist. For example, a charge of 14 e means there are 14 protons providing that charge.

As discussed in previous chapters, mass attracts other mass via the gravitational force. Similarly, an electric charge interacts with other electric charges through an electric force. Through experiments scientists determined that like charges repel (positive charges will repel positive charges and negative charges will repel negative charges), and unlike charges attract (positive charges will attract negative charges).

The magnitude of the electrical force, F, between charges is given in newtons, N, and is given by the equation:

$$F = \frac{kq_aq_b}{r^2}$$

where q_a and q_b are the charges, and r is the separation between them. k is a proportionality constant; $k = 9 \times 10^9$ Nm^2/C^2. It is important to consider direction when applying the force equation. For example, two electrons will each experience a force due to the other that pushes them apart. An electron and a proton will each experience a force due to the other that pulls them together.

Charges interact through this force through an **ELECTRIC FIELD** that is created by each individual charge. The electric field has direction and always moves away from positive charges and toward negative charges. The magnitude of the electric field (units N/C) at distance r from a charge q is given by:

$$E = \frac{kq}{r^2}$$

If another charge, q', is placed at r, the previous equation for the electric force is recovered:

$$F = q'E$$

Charges behave differently when placed in an electric field. A positive charge will be pushed along the direction of the electric field, while a negative charge will be pushed in the opposite direction of the electric field.

The words *force* and *field* are commonly used in our language. Think of your understanding of the words compared to how they are described here. It will help you remember!

Examples

1. Consider two scenarios: A) a proton and electron separated by 1 meter and B) two protons separated by 1 meter. What can be said about the electric force for each case?

   (A) The electric force will be the same strength, but for A) it will pull them together and for B) it will push them apart.

   (B) The electric force will be the same strength, but for A) it will push them apart and for B) it will pull them together.

   (C) The electric force will be stronger for case B) than case A).

   Answers:

   (A) is correct. The electric force equation will give the same value for both cases. Opposite charges attract and like charges repel.

   (B) is incorrect. The electric force equation will give the same value for both cases. Opposite charges attract and like charges repel.

   (C) is incorrect. The electric force equation will give the same value for both cases.

2. What comment about the electric field is true?

(A) The electric field can turn a proton turn into an electron.

(B) The electric field gets stronger the farther it is from a charge.

(C) The electric field always points from positive to negative charges.

Answers:

(A) is incorrect. An electric field cannot turn a proton into an electron.

(B) is incorrect. The electric field gets weaker the farther it is from a charge.

(C) is correct. The electric field does point from positive to negative charges.

Atomic Structure

Opposite charges attract, where the electric force will pull them together. However, this does not mean they will collide and stick together. Although the reasons are beyond the scope of this text, opposite charges will form systems called **ATOMS** when they are brought close together. In atoms, negatively charged electrons will orbit around a positively charged nucleus that contains protons and neutral particles called **NEUTRONS**.

⚠️ The neutron will radioactively decay into a positively charged proton and negatively charged electron (among other things).

Although it is possible for the number of protons in an atom to change (through nuclear reactions, like in the sun or a nuclear weapon), it is uncommon in daily experience. Outside of nuclear reactions, it is important to remember that electrons and protons are not created or destroyed.

The mass of a proton is 1.673×10^{-27} kg, and the mass of an electron is almost 2,000 times lighter, at 9.109×10^{-31} kg. Although their charges are equal and opposite, it is much harder to move the proton than the electron. Therefore, the much heavier nucleus may be considered rigid while the electrons move freely.

Electrons move around the nucleus in levels called shells. An atom's outermost shell is occupied by **VALENCE ELECTRONS**, which are farthest from the nucleus and therefore the most reactive of the atom's electrons. Atoms with a full valence shell are unreactive. Valence shells that are close to full will more easily accept electrons, and nearly empty valence shells will more easily lose electrons.

Valence shells determine a material's conductivity. The atoms in an **INSULATOR** have nearly full valence shells, meaning the electrons do not easily move. In a **CONDUCTOR**, the atoms have nearly empty valence shells, and electrons move freely. A **SEMICONDUCTOR'S** atoms are neither full nor empty, making them poor conductors and insulators. A semiconductor on its own will not conduct charge. However, other elements, or *dopants*, are added to change the material's electrical properties.

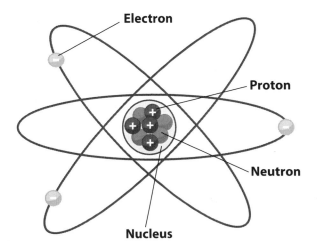

Figure 3.13. Atomic Structure

Examples

1. What configuration of particles can make an atom?

   (A) two neutrons

   (B) one proton and one electron

   (C) one neutron and one electron

   Answers:

   (A) is incorrect. Neutrons are neutral and will not attract and create an atom.

   (B) is correct. The proton and electron will attract and create an atomic system (in this case, a hydrogen atom).

   (C) is incorrect. The neutron has no charge, so it will not attract the electron to form an atom.

2. What best describes the properties of a semiconductor?

   (A) It is an insulator unless dopants are added.

   (B) It is a conductor unless dopants are added.

   (C) It has half the conducting properties of a conductor.

   Answers:

   (A) is correct. A semiconductor is an insulator whose conducting properties can be altered with dopants.

   (B) is incorrect. A semiconductor without dopants is an insulator.

   (C) is incorrect. Despite the name, a semiconductor does not have half the conducting properties of a conductor.

Current

CURRENT (I) is the amount of charge flow per time and is given by the equation:

$$I = \frac{\Delta q}{\Delta t}$$

where Δq is the amount of charge that moved past a location in Δt, the amount of time passed. Current is measured in amperes (amps), A.

Although current, by definition, does not need to be inside a material, for electronics, current flow is considered within a conductor (or semiconductor). As discussed previously, electrons are much lighter and therefore move much more easily than the heavy nuclei (nuclei are seen as basically rigid). Thus current flow is actually the flow of electrons. However, historically in electronics and circuits, current flow is positive in the direction of positive charge flow. This is called CONVENTIONAL CURRENT.

If a straight segment of conducting wire has an electric field applied along the wire, the electrons will move in the opposite direction of the field. If the nuclei are rigid and do not move, how is there positive charge flow? A simple analogy is bubbles in a liquid. The bubbles (air) are moving up through the liquid. The liquid moves down to fill the space left by the air. In electronics, the electrons act as the liquid, and the air (lack of electrons, also called HOLES) moves in the opposite direction. Therefore, conventional current flow is the direction of the flow of holes through a circuit.

Conceptually, a single electron or hole does not travel through the entire wire to create current. For example, a hole does not start at the battery and then move through the circuit back to the battery. Instead, the holes are colliding and moving at high speed in generally random directions in the wire. The electric field introduces a trend, or drift, in the hole movement that will make the holes move in the direction of the field, but rather slowly. Therefore, the electric field that is introducing the slow drift direction to the charge movement throughout the entire wire or circuit is what is measured as current flow.

Voltage from a battery, power supply, or across a circuit element is usually notated with + and – signs. Current always flows from + to – in the circuit.

There are two types of current sources, **DIRECT CURRENT** (**DC**) and **ALTERNATING CURRENT** (**AC**). Direct current is a constant current value, like that from a battery. For example, a battery will supply a constant 10mA to a circuit as long as the battery is good. In alternating current sources, the current value changes sign at a certain frequency.

As shown later in this chapter, alternating current is created by alternators, like those in a car and in power plants. Power outlets in our homes and businesses are AC sources (with typical frequencies of $f = 60$ Hz, $\omega = 377$ Hz). It is common to have electronic devices that convert AC sources to DC sources to power electronics, like laptops and smartphones.

Example

If charge is moving through a circuit at rate of 0.5 C every 2 seconds, what is the current in the circuit?

(A) 0.1 A

(B) 0.25 A

(C) 2.5 A

Answer:

(B) is correct. Use the formula for calculating current.

$$I = \frac{\Delta q}{\Delta t} = \frac{0.5}{2} = \textbf{0.25 A}$$

Resistance

RESISTIVITY is a measure of how easily an electron can move through a material. An insulator, where electrons are held close to the nuclei, will have a high resistivity. A conductor, where electrons can freely move throughout the entire material, has a low resistivity. The reciprocal of resistivity is called the conductivity; insulators have low conductivity and conductors have high conductivity. Resistivity is a material property and can vary by a huge amount.

Table 3.1. Resistivity of Common Materials

	MATERIAL	RESISTIVITY ($\Omega \times$ M)
Conductors	Copper	1.72×10^{-8}
	Gold	2.44×10^{-8}
Semiconductors	Silicon	2300
Insulators	Glass	$10^{10} - 10^{14}$
	Teflon	$>10^{13}$

RESISTANCE has units of ohms, Ω, and includes the material resistivity as well as the actual size of the device. For the case of a wire of length, L, cross-sectional area, A, and resistivity, ρ, the resistance is given by:

$$R = \frac{\rho L}{A}$$

Therefore, the resistance of a wire increases if the wire is made longer or if the wire is made thinner. Relatively, short and fat wires will have less resistance that long and thin wires.

Example

What is the best type of wire to use to get the highest resistance? Assume the material resistivity in the wire is identical.

(A) long, thin wire

(B) long, thick wire

(C) short, thin wire

Answers:

(A) is correct. From the equation $R = \frac{\rho L}{A}$, a larger length, L, means a higher resistance, R. A thinner wire (smaller A) will also have a higher resistance, R.

(B) is incorrect. The long wire will increase resistance, but a thick wire will have less resistance than a thin wire.

(C) is incorrect. The thin wire will increase resistance, but a short wire will decrease it.

Voltage

To understand voltage, it is helpful to revisit the concept of gravitational potential energy. Consider an individual standing on a box. She is not moving and therefore has zero kinetic energy. However, she has potential energy because if the box moves, she would fall to the floor. When the box moves, the person falls, and her potential energy becomes kinetic energy. As she falls, her kinetic energy increases and her potential energy decreases until she reaches the floor. There, her potential energy is zero because she cannot fall any further. (Her kinetic energy changes to other types of energy when she strikes the floor.)

 Kinetic energy is the energy associated with moving objects. Potential energy is the energy stored in an object.

Potential energy is defined by the relative position of the object. The woman on the box would have more potential energy if the box was tall because she would be farther from the floor; she'd have less potential energy if she was standing on a shorter box. In this analogy, potential (not potential energy) is defined only by the height of the box, not by the size of the person standing on the box.

In electronics, the electrical potential energy is conceptually the same. If two charges are separated by a distance, there is the potential for their energy to be turned into kinetic energy. For example, two opposite charges at a distance r that start at rest will be pulled together and have kinetic energy. Also, two similar charges (both positive or both negative) that start at rest at a distance r will move away and gain kinetic energy.

The ELECTRICAL POTENTIAL is defined as the electrical potential energy per unit charge. A higher electrical potential at a location means that a charge placed at that location has a higher potential energy. The potential difference is defined as the difference between the potentials at two separate locations. In electronics, the ELECTRIC POTENTIAL DIFFERENCE is called VOLTAGE and is given in volts, V.

It is important to remember that voltage is a relative measurement. If a measurement of voltage is relative to zero potential, for example, the reading may be 1,000 V at point A. If the same measurement is made at point B, the reading may be 1,001 V. The potential difference, or voltage, between points A and B is only 1 V. Therefore, a charged particle moving from A to B would have much less kinetic energy than a charged particle moving from A to zero potential (a difference of 1,000 V).

An important concept to consider is called the ELECTROMOTIVE FORCE, or **EMF**. EMF is also measured in volts. If the terminals of a AAA battery (1.5 V) are connected with a conducting copper wire, the electrons in the wire will move from the negative terminal to the positive terminal through the wire. (The electric field goes from the positive to the negative terminal through the wire, and the negatively charged electrons move opposite to the electric field.)

But why do the electrons flow through the wire and not directly through the battery itself? The field inside the battery will oppose the flow of electrons in the wire, so how does this work? The battery has a chemical process that moves the electrons in the opposite direction of the field (they move from the positive to negative terminals, not vice versa). This chemical process provides the EMF that drives the electrons through the wire (a simple circuit). EMF can be provided by photovoltaic cells (solar power), batteries (chemical processes), and generators (mechanical processes). As shown later in this chapter, the EMF in generators is created by a changing magnetic field.

Example

What is the source of the electromotive force in a battery?

(A) changing magnetic field

(B) mechanical movement

(C) chemical processes

Answers:

(A) is incorrect. Generators (not batteries) supply an electromotive force through a changing magnetic field.

(B) is incorrect. Generators (not batteries) supply an electromotive force by converting mechanical movement into electricity.

(C) is correct. A battery contains chemicals that produce an electromotive force through chemical reactions.

CIRCUITS

Circuit Basics

An electronic CIRCUIT is made up of conducting wires that connect circuit elements, such as resistors, capacitors, and inductors. To operate, an electric circuit requires a source of power. Some common circuit symbols are shown in Figure 3.14.

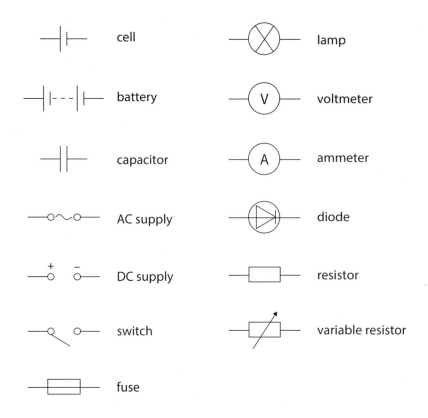

—┤├—	cell	—⊗—	lamp
—┤│- - -│├—	battery	—Ⓥ—	voltmeter
—┤├—	capacitor	—Ⓐ—	ammeter
—o∿o—	AC supply	—⊳|—	diode
—o o—	DC supply	—▭—	resistor
—o o—	switch	—▱↗—	variable resistor
—▭—	fuse		

Figure 3.14. Common Circuit Element Symbols

An important concept for circuits is **GROUND**. This is when the circuit is connected to the ground, or earth, which is ideally where charge of any amount can flow. Many buildings literally have a wire that goes into the earth outside as their ground. Ground is at zero potential.

There are many types of **VOLTAGE SOURCES**. The most common is the power outlet in our homes and businesses, and it provides V_{rms} = 120 V at 60Hz AC (the voltage goes from positive to negative to positive again at 60 times per second). Common DC sources include 9 V AA, AAA, C, and D batteries as well as batteries for our automobiles, smartphoncs, tablets, and laptops. These sources maintain a constant voltage. All voltage sources have an internal resistance, which is often assumed to be zero. However, this internal resistance can lead to actual voltage values that are less than expected. For example, a 1.5 V AAA battery may have a voltage measured at 1.3 V while connected to a device.

The electrical **LOAD** in a circuit consists of everything except for the power supply. The load is effectively the part of the circuit that uses power and performs a function. As shown later in this chapter, a complicated load circuit can often be reduced to a simpler, but equivalent, circuit. An example circuit with a power supply, an internal resistance, and a load resistance is shown in Figure 3.15.

A common circuit element is a **SWITCH**. It can either be an actual lever moved to connect or disconnect two wires, or it can be automated electronically. When the switch is open, the circuit is an open circuit, and current will not flow

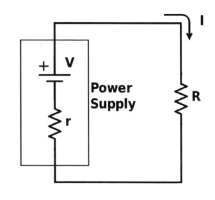

Figure 3.15. A Simple Circuit

through it. When the switch is closed, the circuit is a closed circuit, allowing current to flow.

A FUSE is a device that breaks the circuit (creates an open circuit) when too much current is flowing through it. At high currents, the heat caused by the power dissipated in the material will vaporize the material. Fuses can only be used once, and it is often easy to see when fuses have blown (the thin wire disappears). In homes, 10A and 20A to 40A fuses are common. A CIRCUIT BREAKER serves the same function as a fuse; however, it is a switch that is opened at high current and can be reused. It is common to have to manually reset the circuit breaker switch in homes.

Examples

1. Which circuit in the figure below shows a closed circuit with a power source and a load?

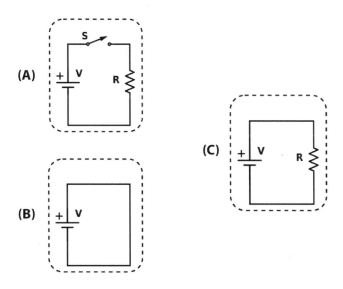

Answers:

(A) is incorrect. The circuit is not closed.

(B) is incorrect. There is no load on the power supply in this circuit.

(C) is correct. This circuit contains a power supply and a load.

2. Which electrical component would best turn a computer on and off?

(A) switch

(B) fuse

(C) circuit breaker

Answers:

(A) is correct. A switch would allow power to flow through the circuit when the computer is on, and it would not allow power to flow when it is off.

(B) is incorrect. A fuse is used to protect a circuit, and it breaks when too much current is applied.

(C) is incorrect. A circuit breaker is used to protect a circuit, and it flips a switch when too much current is applied.

Ohm's Law

OHM'S LAW is perhaps the most commonly used equation in electronics. When a voltage is applied across a resistive circuit element, the electrons in that material begin to move in the opposite direction of the electric field created. This creates a flow of charge and therefore a current flow. Remember that current is positive in the opposite direction of the flow of electrons.

The voltage from the power supply provides the energy to move the charges to create current, but the material limits the amount of current that can flow. This limitation is represented as the material's resistance. Through experimentation, current flow was found to be directly proportional to the voltage applied. This is understandable, as a stronger field should lead to more charge movement. Current flow was also found to be inversely proportional to the resistance of the material. Again, this is understandable, as less resistance from the material should allow more charge flow. Writing this mathematically gives Ohm's law:

When two values are directly proportional, they increase or decrease at the same time. When two values are indirectly proportional, one goes up when the other goes down (and vice versa).

$$V = IR$$

Where V is the voltage across the resistive element, I is the current through the element, and R is the element's resistance.

Example

What is the current flowing through a 100 kΩ resistor when a voltage of 2 V is applied across it?

(A) 20 μA

(B) 200 mA

(C) 20 A

Answer:

(A) is correct.

$V = IR$	Identify the appropriate equation.
$I = \frac{V}{R}$ $I = \frac{2V}{100\ k\Omega} = 0.00002\ A = \textbf{20 μA}$	Rewrite equation in terms of I, plug in values, and solve for the current.

Power

POWER is defined as the energy per unit of time (joules per second) and is measured in watts, W. Power is described by the equation:

$$P = \frac{\text{energy}}{\text{time}} = VI$$

where V is the voltage and I is the current through a circuit.

Power companies sell electric energy in units of kilowatt hours (kWh). 1 kWh = 3.6 × 10[6] J.

Using Ohm's law to replace V and I in the above equation, the equation for power can be written as:

$$P = VI = I^2R = \frac{V^2}{R}$$

where R is the resistance.

As charges move through a material, they collide with other charges and nuclei, which leads to heat. Therefore, the majority of electrical power used is converted into heat (except for an electrical motor, where electrical power is turned into mechanical power). This is why electronics get hot during use.

Example

What is the power dissipated in a 1 kΩ resistor when a voltage of 350 V is applied across it?

(A) 350 μW

(B) 0.35 W

(C) 122.5 W

Answer:

(C) is correct.

$P = \dfrac{V^2}{R}$	Identify the appropriate equation.
$P = \dfrac{(350V)^2}{1k\Omega} = \mathbf{122.5\,W}$	Plug in values and solve for power.

Series Circuits

When elements are in a SERIES CIRCUIT, the current flows through the elements along a single path. The current through elements in series will always be constant, and the total voltage for the resistors can be found by adding the voltage at each individual resistor.

The EQUIVALENT RESISTANCE of the circuit, which models a complicated circuit with many resistors as a single resistor, is found by adding the resistance of each resistor. This equivalent resistance can then be used to find the power for the circuit.

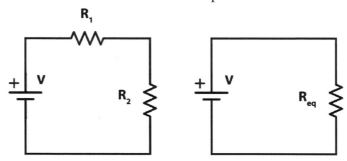

Figure 3.16. A Simple Series Circuit and Its Equivalent

Table 3.2. Series Circuits

Current	$I_1 = I_2 = I_3 = \ldots = I_n$
Voltage	$V_t = V_1 + V_2 + V_3 + \ldots + V_n$
Resistance	$R_{eq} = R_1 + R_2 + R_3 + \ldots + R_n$

Example

Find the equivalent resistance for the circuit in the figure below.

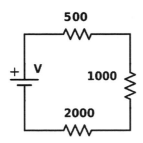

(A) 1.5 kΩ

(B) 2.5 kΩ

(C) 3.5 kΩ

Answer:

(C) is correct.

$R_{eq} = R_1 + R_2 + R_3$	Identify the appropriate equation.
$R_{eq} = 500 \ \Omega + 1 \ k\Omega + 2 \ k\Omega = 3{,}500 \ \Omega = \mathbf{3.5 \ k\Omega}$	Plug in values and solve for equivalent resistance.

Parallel Circuits

When elements are in a **PARALLEL CIRCUIT**, current may flow through multiple paths. For this type of circuit, the voltage across each element is constant, and the current for the circuit is found by adding the current passing through each resistor. Because electricity can flow through multiple paths (meaning it passes through each resistor) the equivalent resistance of the circuit will decrease as resistors are added.

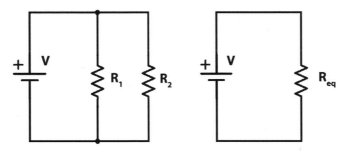

Figure 3.17. A Simple Parallel Circuit and Its Equivalent

Table 3.3. Parallel Circuits

Current	$I_t = I_1 + I_2 + I_3 + \dots + I_n$
Voltage	$V_1 = V_2 = V_3 = \dots = V_n$
Resistance	$\dfrac{1}{R_{eq}} = \dfrac{1}{R_1} + \dfrac{1}{R_2} + \dots + \dfrac{1}{R_N}$

Example

Find the equivalent resistance for the circuit in the figure below.

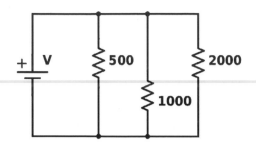

(A) 285.7 Ω

(B) 571.4 Ω

(C) 1.45 kΩ

Answer:

(A) is correct.

$\dfrac{1}{R_{eq}} = \dfrac{1}{R_1} + \dfrac{1}{R_2} + \dfrac{1}{R_3}$	Identify the appropriate equation.
$\dfrac{1}{R_{eq}} = \dfrac{1}{500\ \Omega} + \dfrac{1}{1\ k\Omega} + \dfrac{1}{2\ k\Omega} = 0.0035\ \dfrac{1}{\Omega}$ $R_{eq} = \textbf{285.7 } \Omega$	Plug in values to solve for equivalent resistance.

Complex Circuits

Series and parallel circuits can be combined to make more complex circuits. To determine the properties of these circuits, they must be broken down into individual series and parallel circuits that can be used to find the properties of each resistor or the overall circuit.

In the figure below, resistors R_2 and R_3 are in parallel, and both are wired in series with resistor R_1. To find the equivalent resistance of the circuit, find $R_{2,3}$ for R_2 and R_3 using the rules for parallel circuits. $R_{2,3}$ and R_1 are now in series, so the equivalent resistance of the entire circuit can be found using the rules for series circuits, as shown below.

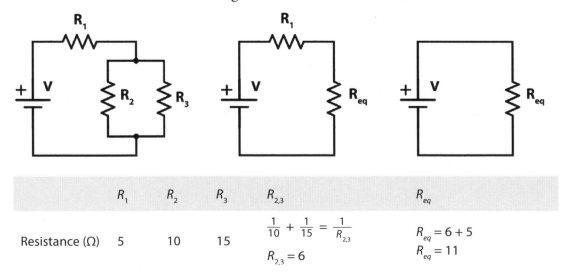

	R_1	R_2	R_3	$R_{2,3}$	R_{eq}
Resistance (Ω)	5	10	15	$\dfrac{1}{10} + \dfrac{1}{15} = \dfrac{1}{R_{2,3}}$ $R_{2,3} = 6$	$R_{eq} = 6 + 5$ $R_{eq} = 11$

Figure 3.18A. A Complex Circuit and Its Equivalent

In the next example below, resistor R_1 is in parallel with two resistors in series, R_2 and R_3. Again, the trick to finding the R_{eq} for this circuit is to work in steps. Using the equation for R_{eq} for series resistors, first reduce R_2 and R_3 to an equivalent resistance $R_{2,3}$. Now, R_1 and $R_{2,3}$ are in parallel, so use the rules for parallel circuits to find the equivalent resistance for the circuit.

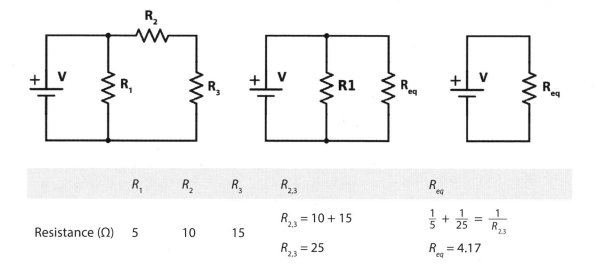

	R_1	R_2	R_3	$R_{2,3}$	R_{eq}
Resistance (Ω)	5	10	15	$R_{2,3} = 10 + 15$ $R_{2,3} = 25$	$\frac{1}{5} + \frac{1}{25} = \frac{1}{R_{2,3}}$ $R_{eq} = 4.17$

Figure 3.18B. A Complex Circuit and Its Equivalent

Example

Find the equivalent resistance for the circuit in the figure below.

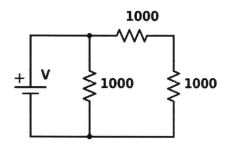

(A) 0.7 kΩ

(B) 1.5 kΩ

(C) 3.1 kΩ

Answer:

(B) is correct.

$\frac{1}{R_{eq}} = \frac{1}{R_1} + \frac{1}{R_2} + \frac{1}{R_3}$ $R_{eq} = R_1 + R_2$	Identify the appropriate equations.
$\frac{1}{R_{eq}} = \frac{1}{1\,k\Omega} + \frac{1}{1\,k\Omega} = 0.0021\frac{1}{\Omega}$ $R_{eq} = 500\ \Omega$	First, find the equivalent resistance of the parallel resistors.
$R'_{eq} = R + R_{eq} = 1\,k\Omega + 500\ \Omega = \mathbf{1.5\ k\Omega}$	Next, use that equivalent resistance in series with the last resistor to find the overall equivalent resistance.

Electrical Measurements

The previous sections discussed resistance, voltage, and current, all of which can be measured with a device called a **MULTIMETER**.

Electrical current is measured using a device called an **AMMETER**. An ammeter must be placed in series with the circuit element to accurately measure the current. An ammeter should have approximately zero internal resistance. Conceptually, the current going through the element also must be going through the ammeter.

Electric voltage is measured using a device called a **VOLTMETER**. A voltmeter must be placed in parallel to the circuit element to correctly measure the element's voltage. A voltmeter should have infinite resistance (an open circuit) so no current will flow through it. Because no current moves through the detector, a voltmeter can measure the voltage across the element without changing the circuit.

Resistance is measured using a device called an **OHMMETER**. An ohmmeter will either provide a voltage across an element and read the current that flows through it, or it will provide a current through an element and read the voltage across it. In either case, the resistance is calculated using Ohm's law.

Example

Which two diagrams in the figure below show the correct usage of an ammeter and a voltmeter to read the current through and voltage across the resistor shown?

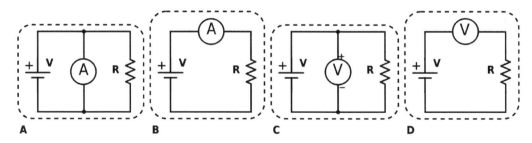

(A) A, C

(B) B, C

(C) A, D

Answers:

(A) is incorrect. An ammeter must be used in series, and a voltmeter must be used in parallel.

(B) is correct. An ammeter must be used in series, and a voltmeter must be used in parallel.

(C) is incorrect. An ammeter must be used in series, and a voltmeter must be used in parallel.

4

AVIATION INFORMATION

This Aviation section tests knowledge of topics related to aircraft operations, including the physics of flight, aircraft performance and structures, airfield and airspace operations, flight controls, and instrument comprehension, as well as a brief history of aviation.

THE PHYSICS OF FLIGHT

A successful aircraft flight is the result of an understanding of the scientific theories and principles involved in moving 300 to 400 tons of machinery through the skies at speeds ranging from 100 to 750 miles per hour (mph). Newton's laws of motion, Newton's law of universal gravitation, and Bernoulli's principle, along with weight, balance, the factors that constitute the flight envelope, and the axes of an aircraft all play a part in aeronautics.

Newton's Laws of Motion

Isaac Newton's three laws of motion detail the fundamental mechanics of motion. The first law focuses on inertia, the second law defines when an accelerated motion is applied to a force, and the third law explains the relationship of motion between any two objects.

NEWTON'S FIRST LAW OF MOTION, also called the LAW OF INERTIA, states that an object at rest will stay at rest, and an object in motion will remain in motion at a constant velocity unless acted upon by an unbalanced force. The unbalanced force may be any force, such as gravity or friction. For example, a ball sitting on the floor will remain still unless a force is exerted upon it—a kick from a foot, a push from a hand, or a strong wind moving it.

Inertia is the tendency of an object to resist changes in velocity whether the object is in motion or motionless.

There are four types of friction:

- SLIDING, or KINETIC, FRICTION results when the surface of one object slides along the surface of another object. This is commonly seen when pushing a solid object, such as a plate or book along a tabletop.

- **FLUID FRICTION** is the resistance on an object when it is moved through either air (gas) or water (liquid). This is witnessed when a fish moves through water, a bird flies through air, or an airplane creates drag.
- **ROLLING FRICTION** is similar to sliding friction except rolling friction occurs when an object rolls—instead of slides—across a surface. This is observed when a bowling ball rolls down an alley. The ball, once pushed, moves at a particular rate, or velocity, while also resisting that movement due to qualities of the surface on which it is rolling.
- **STATIC FRICTION** is what keeps an object at rest when that object is acted upon by an external force. A trash can initially remains in place due to static friction when an attempt is made to drag it across a floor.

As an example of the four frictions, if a car is traveling at 40 mph, the passengers and contents inside the car are also moving at a rate of 40 mph, until the driver applies the brakes to avoid a collision with a tree. If the passengers are not restrained by seat belts, the full effects of a collision pass from the vehicle to them as well as to the contents of the vehicle. The tires of the vehicle rolling along the road overcome rolling friction. The vehicle counteracts fluid friction from any oncoming wind. When the driver applies the brakes, the wheels may stop rolling but the car skids along the surface of the road, exemplifying sliding friction. At the moment of the car's impact with the tree, objects inside the vehicle overcome static friction as they scatter.

NEWTON'S SECOND LAW OF MOTION states that when a body is acted upon by a constant force, its resulting acceleration is inversely proportional to the mass of the body and directly proportional to the applied force.

The net force of an object is equal to the product of the mass of the object and the acceleration. The equation to determine the amount of force is $F = ma$. One unit of force (F) is defined as Newtons (N). Mass is weighed in kilograms (kg) and acceleration is measured in meters per second per second (m/s/s or m/s^2).

NEWTON'S THIRD LAW OF MOTION states that if two objects interact, the force exerted by the first object on the second object is equal in magnitude and opposite in direction to the force exerted by the second object on the first object.

For example, the force exerted by a tennis racket hitting a tennis ball is equal in magnitude and opposite the force exerted by the ball on the tennis racket. Likewise, during a launch of a rocket into space, the gases expelled under the rocket exert enough force to cause the rocket to lift off the launchpad in the opposite direction.

Example

Consider an object acted on by only two forces, as shown to the right. If the magnitudes of F_1 and F_2 are equal, which of the following statements is true?

(A) The velocity of the object must be zero.

(B) The velocity of the object must be constant.

(C) The velocity of the object must be increasing.

(D) The velocity of the object must be decreasing.

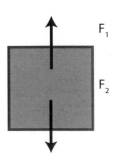

Answers:

(A) is incorrect. An object experiencing a net force of zero can be in motion.

(B) is correct. The velocity of an object experiencing a net force of zero will remain constant (meaning its acceleration is zero).

(C) is incorrect. The velocity of an object experiencing a net force of zero cannot change.

(D) is incorrect. The velocity of an object experiencing a net force of zero cannot change.

Newton's Law of Universal Gravitation

Isaac Newton's law of universal gravitation states that a particle attracts every other particle in the universe with a force that is directly proportional to the product of their masses and inversely proportional to the square of the distance between them. This law helps scientists understand the effects of gravity on aircraft during flight, because the gravitational force between two objects increases with mass and decreases with distance.

Equation: $F_g = G \dfrac{m_1 m_2}{d^2}$

F: unit of force (N) of gravity
G: gravitational constant value (e.g., 6.673×10^{-11} m³ kg⁻¹ s⁻²)
m₁: mass of object 1
m₂: mass of object 2
d: distance in meters between the centers of both objects

Example

Consider two objects a distance d apart. According to Newton's law of universal gravitation, what happens to the force between the two objects if the distance (d) is increased by a factor of 4?

(A) The force decreases by a factor of 4.

(B) The force increases by a factor of 4.

(C) The force increases by a factor of 2.

(D) The force decreases by a factor of 16.

Answer:

(D) is correct. In the equation for Newton's law of universal gravitation, increasing d by a factor of 4 decreases the value of F_g by a factor of d^2, or 16.

Bernoulli's Principle

Mathematician and physicist Daniel Bernoulli devised the following principle in relation to hydrodynamics: within a horizontal flow of fluid, points of faster fluid speed will experience less pressure than points of slower fluid speed.

This principle is imperative when analyzing the flow of hydraulic fluids through an aircraft. An accurate pressure flow of fluids is essential to the intricate operation of braking and flight control systems.

Bernoulli's principle also applies to airflow during the basic phases of flight: takeoff, in-flight, and landing. The curvature of an airplane wing causes air to pass faster over the top of the wing (creating a lower pressure area) than under the wing (a higher pressure area). During takeoff, this produces the lift an airplane requires. During flight and when landing, the aircraft must compensate for and utilize all four forces of flight: **WEIGHT** (the force of gravity pushing the aircraft down), **LIFT** (the force required to raise the aircraft), **THRUST** (the

Drag develops from friction and changes in air pressure, which cause an aircraft to slow down. Inputs to the flight controls affect weight, lift, thrust, and drag, resulting in the aircraft speeding up, slowing down, and/or gaining or losing altitude.

force applied in order to move the aircraft forward), and DRAG (the force that slows the aircraft down in preparation for landing).

Aircraft Weight and Balance

The calculation of an aircraft's weight and balance must be identified during preflight. It is important that the combination of passengers, baggage, usable and unusable fuel or fluids, and cargo are within established weight and balance limits. A predetermined *empty weight center of gravity (EWCG)* is provided by the aircraft's manufacturer along with a weight limit, which is specific to each aircraft.

The following are acronyms of other weight specifications:

- **MANUFACTURER'S EMPTY WEIGHT (MEW)** is the total weight of the aircraft as it was built. This includes systems and components required for the aircraft to operate. It does not include the weight of baggage, passengers, or either usable or unusable fuel or fluids.

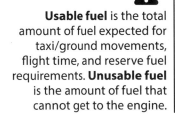

Usable fuel is the total amount of fuel expected for taxi/ground movements, flight time, and reserve fuel requirements. **Unusable fuel** is the amount of fuel that cannot get to the engine.

- **OPERATING EMPTY WEIGHT (OEW)** is the MEW plus the weight of the crew, fluids, unusable fuel, and the equipment required for flight. It does not include baggage, passengers, or usable fuel.

- **ALL-UP WEIGHT (AUW)**, or **AIRCRAFT GROSS WEIGHT (AGW)**, is the total aircraft weight at any given moment during a flight. The AUW decreases as fuel and fluids are consumed during the operation of the flight.

- **MAXIMUM LANDING WEIGHT (MLW)** is an aircraft's weight limit for landing. Exceeding this weight increases stress on the landing gear and may affect the distance required for a safe landing.

- **MAXIMUM ZERO FUEL WEIGHT (MZFW)** is the permissible weight of an aircraft with its contents and includes unusable fuel. The total MZFW excludes the weight of usable fuel on board and any consumable fluids.

- **MAXIMUM TAKEOFF WEIGHT (MTOW)** is an aircraft's weight limit for takeoff. Exceeding this limit increases the power required for takeoff, lengthens the runway distance needed for a successful lift off, and places excess stress on the aircraft structure.
- **MAXIMUM RAMP WEIGHT (MRW)** is the weight limit for an aircraft to taxi or be towed on the ground.

 Takeoff weight is determined by totaling the OEW, the cargo, the passengers, the baggage, and the taxi, flight, and reserve fuel requirements.

Example

Why is it important for an airplane not to exceed the MLW limit?

(A) All-up weight is calculated correctly.

(B) Most airplanes do not have to consider MLW.

(C) Undue stress may be placed on the landing gear system while landing.

(D) The airplane may not have enough fuel for the scheduled flight.

Answers:

(A) is incorrect. The all-up weight is the total weight of the airplane during all phases of flight, not just landing.

(B) is incorrect. Every pilot must consider MLW when assessing whether an aircraft's landing gear can support its weight and the runway is long enough for the aircraft's safe landing.

(C) is correct. By not exceeding the MLW, the pilot ensures that the landing gear will be able to support the weight of the aircraft and a longer than normal runway will not be required to land the plane.

(D) is incorrect. Although the MLW includes fuel on board, a pilot must ensure enough fuel is on board to reach his or her destination, or an alternate airfield if required.

The Flight Envelope

The **FLIGHT ENVELOPE** encompasses the limits of speed, altitude, and angle of attack required by any aircraft to maintain a stable flight. An incorrect combination of these factors may result in a stall, during which the aircraft experiences a decrease in lift and a reduction in airspeed.

The **ANGLE OF ATTACK (AOA)** is the angle between the direction of the airflow against the wing and the **CHORD**, an imaginary reference line that extends from the leading edge to the trailing edge of the wing.

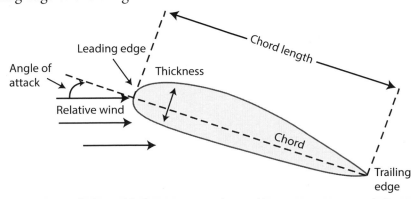

Figure 4.1. Identifying the AOA

An aircraft's airfoil section (wing) is designed for maximum lift and fuel efficiency. An aircraft wing is curved along its front, leading edge, which creates low pressure above and high pressure below as air passes by the wing. As air passes over the end of the wing, or over the end of a helicopter rotor blade, it changes direction, a deflection called DOWNWASH. This deflection of air downward helps produce lift. This is clearly visible when a helicopter hovers above water. The air deflected off the rotor blades accelerates downward, causing outward ripples in the water under the helicopter.

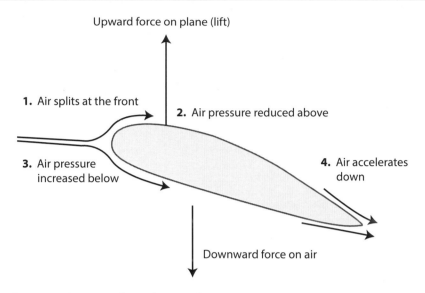

Figure 4.2. Downwash Producing Lift

The trailing edge of a wing has two control parts—ailerons and flaps—which extend outward and in opposite directions to aid the aircraft in rolling. The AILERONS are located from the midpoint of the trailing edge of the wing to the wing's tip. The FLAPS are located from the fuselage (main cabin body) to about the midpoint of the wing. Ailerons and flaps are in a closed position (flush against the wing's surface) during cruising altitude.

To land, the pilot first creates drag to slow the aircraft. SPOILERS are extended upward to help reduce airspeed. As the pilot approaches the runway, the wing flaps are progressively extended too. Once the aircraft is on the ground, raising the spoilers assists in slowing the airplane while the pilot also brakes. The following figure illustrates the positions of the flaps during takeoff, flight, and landing.

Drag is air resistance experienced during flight:

- **PARASITE DRAG** is just that—any "parasite" on the structure of the aircraft: low air pressure in the tires, skin friction, or anything that increases turbulence on the aircraft. *Skin friction* refers to any rough spot on the skin of the aircraft structure. This, along with rivet heads that may project above the skin, causes resistance to the air current flowing across the wing.

- **PROFILE DRAG** is produced mainly by the shape of the aircraft. A smaller, slimmer aircraft reduces profile drag.

- **INDUCED DRAG** is when, at the back of the wing, air flowing rapidly across the top meets air flowing more slowly underneath, creating a vortex. This type of drag depends on the performance of the aircraft. When lift, airspeed, and AOA increase, induced drag automatically increases too.

Best efficiency: for climbing,
cruising, and descent

Increased wing area: for
takeoff and initial climb

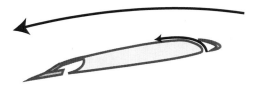

Maximum lift and high drag:
approach and landing

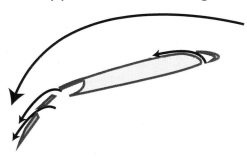

Maximum drag and reduced
lift: for braking on runway

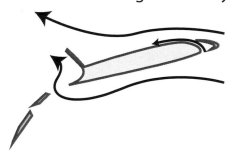

Figure 4.3. Wing Positions during Flight

Examples

1. What is an example of induced drag?

    (A) a decrease in airspeed

    (B) a decrease in AOA

    (C) a decrease in lift

    (D) an increase in AOA

Answers:

(A) is incorrect. A decrease in airspeed does not result in a form of induced drag.

(B) is incorrect. A decrease in the AOA also does not result in a form of induced drag.

(C) is incorrect. A decrease in lift does not result in induced drag either.

(D) is correct. An increase in AOA, lift, or airspeed will result in induced drag on an airplane.

2. When an airplane increases its lift, which statement is true about the air pressure flowing above and below its wings?

(A) Air pressure is equal above and below the wings since the wings split the air evenly.

(B) Air pressure is higher above the wings and lower below the wings.

(C) Air pressure is lower above the wings and higher below the wings.

(D) Air pressure causes the trailing edges of the wings to extend outward.

Answers:

(A) is incorrect. Air pressure is not equal above and below the wings.

(B) is incorrect. Air pressure is not higher above the wings, which would defeat the purpose of lift.

(C) is correct. Air pressure is lower above the wings and higher below the wings, producing lift.

(D) is incorrect. A pilot's input at the controls causes the wings to extend outward.

The Axes of an Aircraft

Aircraft fly on a combination of three axes: longitudinal, lateral, and vertical. The LONGI-TUDINAL AXIS (roll) runs lengthwise from the nose (front) of the aircraft to the tail (rear) of the aircraft; the LATERAL AXIS (pitch) runs wingtip to wingtip; and the VERTICAL AXIS (yaw) runs perpendicular to the wings at the center of the aircraft.

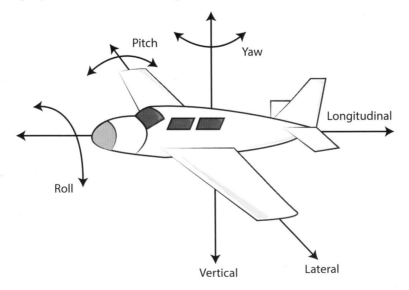

Figure 4.4. Aircraft Axes

Controlling the axes of the aircraft is necessary to keep the aircraft in TRIM, its desired position. ROLL along the aircraft's longitudinal axis is controlled by an adjustment of the ailerons, located at the trailing edges of the wings. PITCH—the lateral angle of ascent or descent—is controlled by the elevators, located in the rear portion of the horizontal tail assembly. YAW is controlled by the rudder, located in the rear portion of the vertical tail assembly; movement of the rudder causes the nose of the aircraft to move from side to side.

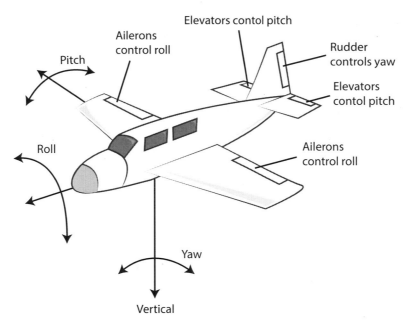

Figure 4.5. Controls for Roll, Pitch, and Yaw

Example

Which components increase the pitch of an airplane?

(A) the ailerons and elevators along the longitudinal axis

(B) the ailerons and rudder along the vertical axis

(C) the elevators along the lateral axis

(D) the elevators along the longitudinal axis

Answers:

(A) is incorrect. The ailerons control roll along the longitudinal axis.

(B) is incorrect. Neither component nor the vertical axis affects the pitch of an airplane.

(C) is correct. The elevators may increase or decrease the pitch of an airplane along the lateral axis.

(D) is incorrect. The elevators affect the lateral axis, not the longitudinal axis.

The Atmosphere

Atmospheric pressure is an extreme concern for a pilot when flying. Air weighs approximately 14.7 pounds per square inch (psi), and flight controls are calibrated for a standard atmosphere. Humidity and low air density levels reduce an aircraft's capability for power, thrust, and lift. When the intake engines receive less air, the propellers are less efficient, and thin air applies less force on the wings, resulting in less than maximum lift.

Altitude, pressure, temperature, and humidity all affect the performance of an aircraft. The **PRESSURE ALTIMETER** in the cockpit is automatically calibrated for 29.92 inches of mercury (Hg). A pilot resets the pressure altitude indicator after departing an airfield to ensure the correct pressure altitude of the aircraft is displayed for the destination airfield (if it is different from the departure airfield). If this is not done, the aircraft may be at a lower altitude than what the altimeter displays.

All aircraft perform more efficiently in colder temperatures because the air is denser than when the air is warm. However, if the temperature drops too low, de-icing of the wings may be required during preflight procedures, extending the time required to complete preflight checks.

Example

How does air density affect the performance of an airplane?

(A) Low air density and humidity increase engine performance.

(B) High air density decreases engine performance.

(C) High air density increases engine performance.

(D) Low temperatures and low air density increase engine performance.

Answers:

(A) is incorrect. Low air density and humidity decrease engine performance.

(B) is incorrect. High air density does not decrease engine performance.

(C) is correct. High air density increases engine performance.

(D) is incorrect. Low temperatures and low air density levels decrease engine performance.

FIXED-WING AIRCRAFT STRUCTURE

The Fuselage

The **FUSELAGE** of an aircraft is the main section that holds the crew, passengers, and cargo. The wings, tail, engines, and landing gear attach to the fuselage, so this structure must be extremely strong to withstand stresses while minimizing weight. The fuselage also functions in the stabilization of an aircraft during flight.

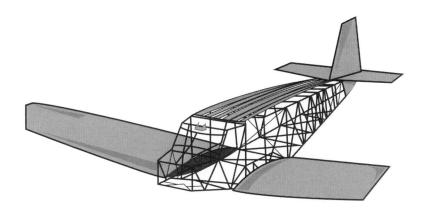

Figure 4.6. Truss Structure

The two main types of aircraft structures are truss and monocoque. A **TRUSS STRUCTURE** consists of welded steel-tubing longerons separated by diagonal members to endure the loads placed upon the aircraft.

A **MONOCOQUE STRUCTURE** consists of a thin sheet-aluminum alloy curved to fit the shell of the fuselage. This metal skin is designed to withstand the stress of loads and minimize the total weight of the aircraft.

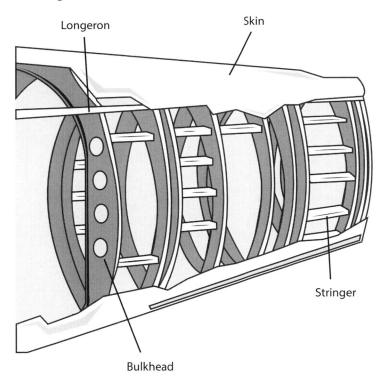

Figure 4.7. Monocoque Structure

Example

What considerations do aircraft manufacturers address when selecting materials for a fuselage?

(A) a large enough area to hold the fuel tanks under the fuselage

(B) a non-bending material to withstand stress while flying

(C) a strong plastic framing that does not break easily

(D) the weight and strength of a material

Answers:

(A) is incorrect. Fuel tanks are typically placed inside the wings.

(B) is incorrect. The material must be able to curve around the frame of a fuselage.

(C) is incorrect. Plastic is not used.

(D) is correct. Both weight and strength are considered when selecting materials for fuselages.

The Wings

Several designs of wings are in use in aircraft. Wings may be attached to the bottom of the fuselage (what's called a **LOW WING**), to the middle of the fuselage (a **MID WING**), or on top of the fuselage (a **HIGH WING**). If no external braces are required, the wing is of a **CANTILEVER** design. Some smaller fixed-wing aircraft are made with a **SEMI-CANTILEVER** design, meaning external braces are attached to the wings. An aircraft with two levels of wings (one above the other) is called a **BIPLANE**.

Wings also may be **DIHEDRAL** or **ANHEDRAL** to assist with stabilization. Note the angle of the wings in Figure 4.8.

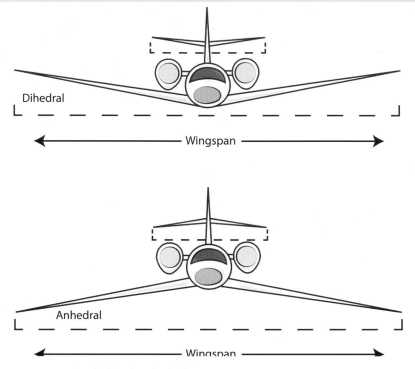

Figure 4.8. Dihedral and Anhedral Wings

The wings of an aircraft enable lift; the characteristics of the airfoil determine the lift capabilities.

The **CHORD**, touched on earlier, is the imaginary line in an airfoil; it establishes a baseline for the amount of camber and width required of the wing along its wingspan (the distance from one wingtip to the other wingtip). When the measurements of the chord line and the camber line differ greatly, the curvature of the wing will provide more lift.

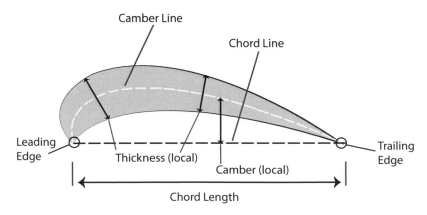

Figure 4.9. Wing Chord Length

THICKNESS is a percentage of the wing chord; it typically ranges from 6.5 to 13.5 percent.

The CAMBER LINE is the amount of curvature of the wing. This additional imaginary line runs halfway between the upper and lower surfaces of the wing.

There are four types of wing planforms:

- The RECTANGULAR is the simplest type, highly inefficient, and typically used for light general aviation.
- The ELLIPTICAL is the most efficient style, with the lowest possible induced drag.
- The TAPERED is a cross between a rectangular and an elliptical, providing better lift distribution and moderate efficiency. Aircraft with these wings have a wide range of speeds.
- The SWEPT is tapered back to reduce drag. This category includes slightly swept, moderately swept, and sharply swept types. The disadvantages of the swept wing planform include its tendency to twist under stress. The delta wing, found on supersonic aircraft, is a highly swept triangular type that is very strong and has the ability to hold a large volume of fuel. Unlike the more standard swept wings, though, the delta has a high incidence of induced drag.

Example

Complete the following sentence with the term that establishes the size of the wing and the amount of camber an aircraft requires: *The amount of lift generated is dependent on the difference between the camber line and the _____.*

(A) anhedral

(B) wingspan

(C) chord line

(D) dihedral

Answers:

(A) is incorrect. Anhedral is a type of wing.

(B) is incorrect. Though the total surface area of a wing indeed influences lift, that area is not considered in relation to the camber line.

(C) is correct. When the measurements of the chord line and the camber line differ greatly, the curvature of the wing will provide more lift.

(D) is incorrect. The dihedral is another type of wing.

The Powerplant

An aircraft's POWERPLANT encompasses the engines and propellers as well as the induction, exhaust, electrical, cooling, lubrication, and fuel systems.

In accordance with Newton's third law of motion, an aircraft must generate enough thrust to create enough lift to overcome the drag produced during flight. Thrust is accomplished by converting an exploding gas-air mixture into mechanical energy in an ENGINE. In modern turbofan engines, this mechanical energy turns the fan to produce thrust, much the same as a propeller on a smaller aircraft. The fan or propeller has an airfoil shape which produces "lift" in the forward direction, referred to as thrust. Typically, aircraft with a cruising speed not exceeding 250 mph use a *reciprocating engine*. Larger, more powerful aircraft use a *gas turbine engine*. Aircraft traveling at high altitudes (above 30,000 feet) use a *turbo-supercharged reciprocating engine*. Aircraft operating at Mach 1 or higher use a *turbojet engine*; the afterburner on this engine enhances the power to reach such high speeds.

Thrust Horsepower equation:

$$thp = \frac{thrust \times aircraft\ speed\ (in\ mph)}{375\ pph}$$

thp: thrust horsepower
Aircraft speed: in miles per hour (mph)
pph: pounds per hour

All engines must also meet certain requirements for fuel efficiency. During takeoff, engines operate at maximum performance. The level of power is cut back during the climb and then reduced to a fuel-efficient level when the aircraft levels off at cruising speed.

There are a few types of **PROPELLERS**. The *fixed pitch propeller* is set by the manufacturer. The *variable pitch propeller* allows the pilot to adjust the blade pitch during flight. A *pusher propeller* is installed on the rear of an aircraft and faces to the rear; the thrust created from its rotation pushes instead of pulls the aircraft, contrary to the fixed and variable pitch propellers. The pitch of any style of propeller affects the way it cuts through the air, producing air mass.

Example

If an engine produces 3500 pounds of thrust and travels at 500 mph, what is the thp?

(A) 3500 thp

(B) 3550.75 thp

(C) 4000 thp

(D) 4666.67 thp

Answers:

(A) is incorrect. Thrust is not the answer.

(B) is incorrect.

(C) is incorrect. Do not just add the thrust and the airspeed.

(D) is correct. Multiply the thrust by the aircraft speed and then divide that amount by 375.

The Landing Gear

The landing gear must support the weight of an aircraft during takeoff, landing, and ground maneuvering. The styles of landing gear include the following: tail wheel, tandem, and tricycle landing gear.

When an aircraft's main landing gear is positioned forward of its center of gravity, the use of a **TAIL WHEEL** system is required. This type of landing gear consists of a third wheel assembly, which is beneficial for landing on non-paved runways. Improvements to the assembly allow for steering the tail wheel through the rudder.

TANDEM landing gear has both main and tail portions mounted along the longitudinal axis of the aircraft. This style supports the use of very flexible wings.

TRICYCLE landing gear includes a main gear and a nose gear, which together support increased braking ability, higher landing speeds, and better visibility for ground operations. The nose gear is steered through either mechanical linkage or, in larger aircraft, hydraulic power. Having multiple wheels on each main gear improves safety if one tire fails.

Example

Match the type of landing gear (letters A through C) with its design and purpose (numbers 1 through 4). A through C may be attributed to more than one design and purpose.

(A) tail wheel

(B) tandem

(C) tricycle

1. This functional style is helpful when landing on non-paved runways.

2. The main and tail portions of this style are positioned along the longitudinal axis.

3. This style includes nose gear.

4. This style is required when the main landing gear is positioned forward of the aircraft's center of gravity.

Answers:

1. **(A)** Tail wheel gear is preferred when landing on non-paved runways.

2. **(B)** Tandem landing gear is positioned along the longitudinal axis of an aircraft.

3. **(C)** Tricycle landing gear includes nose and main portions.

4. **(C)** The nose gear helps support the aircraft's weight since the center of gravity is forward of the main landing gear.

The Tail Assembly

The rear portion of an aircraft is the tail assembly (also known as the *empennage*). It provides stability to the aircraft and consists of a rudder, a vertical stabilizer, a horizontal stabilizer, the trim tabs, and two elevators.

The **RUDDER** and the **VERTICAL STABILIZER** are part of the *vertical tail structure*. The rudder is at the rear of the vertical tail structure and is used to keep the aircraft in coordinated flight. The vertical stabilizer, further forward, prevents the aircraft from yawing back and forth.

The **HORIZONTAL STABILIZER** and the **ELEVATORS** are part of the *horizontal tail structure*. The horizontal stabilizer is at the front of the horizontal tail structure; it prevents the aircraft from pitching up and down. The elevators are hinged to the horizontal stabilizer; they direct the up and down motion of the aircraft's nose.

TRIM TABS are on the trailing edges of the wings toward the fuselage, the rudder, and the elevators. Adjusting angles of the trim tabs acts as a secondary flight control system, helping to offset an undesirable attitude of the aircraft and relieving pressure on the controls. Moving trim tabs on the elevators shifts the elevators in the opposite direction: aiming the trim tabs down moves the elevators up, and aiming the trim tabs up moves the elevators down, relieving pressure on the controls. (Trim tabs located on the wings assist with

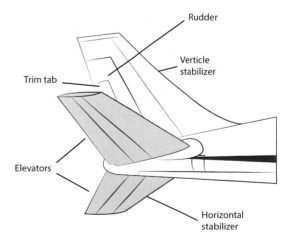

Figure 4.10. Tail Assembly

stabilizing the aircraft if a wing dips left or right unnecessarily, maintaining the aircraft's center of gravity.)

Trim tabs

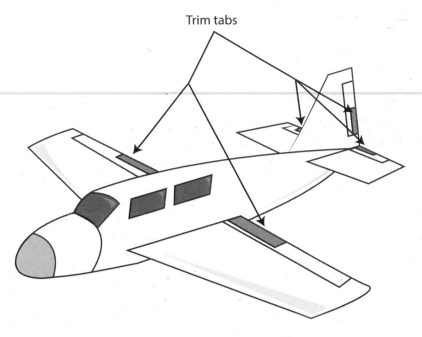

Figure 4.11. Aircraft Trim Tabs

Example

What component is designed to relieve pressure on the controls?

(A) the empennage

(B) the horizontal stabilizer

(C) the rudder

(D) the trim tabs

Answers:

(A) is incorrect. The empennage, or tail assembly, includes the rudder, the vertical stabilizer, the horizontal stabilizer, and two elevators. The empennage controls the stability of the aircraft.

(B) is incorrect. The horizontal stabilizer helps to control the pitch of an aircraft.

(C) is incorrect. The rudder is used to turn an aircraft left or right.

(D) is correct. The trim tabs relieve pressure on the controls.

The Flight Controls

Flight control instrumentation devices in the cockpit allow the pilot to manage the performance, attitude, and movement of an aircraft. Every aircraft has both a primary and a secondary flight control system.

The **PRIMARY FLIGHT CONTROL SYSTEM** manages the *ailerons*, *elevators*, and *rudder*. These devices are designed for the safe maneuvering of the aircraft and the elimination of over-controlling measures introduced by the pilot. An input to this system changes the airflow and pressure distribution needed to ensure a smooth flight. As mentioned earlier, all aircraft fly along three axes: longitudinal, vertical, and lateral. A smooth adjustment correcting aircraft movement directly affects roll, pitch, and yaw of the aircraft. The ailerons keep roll in check along the longitudinal axis. The elevators stabilize pitch along the lateral axis. The rudder controls yaw movement along the vertical axis.

The SECONDARY FLIGHT CONTROL SYSTEM manages the *wing flaps, leading edge devices, spoilers*, and *trim tabs*. This system assists the pilot in optimizing aircraft performance during flight. An input to this system increases lift and adjusts drag. During takeoff and landing, a pilot maximizes the airflow needed for lift by adjusting the wing flaps. Devices such as moveable slats are added to the leading edges of the flaps to increase the available AOA and avoid a stall. The trailing edges of the flaps extend from the wings to increase drag and thus slow the aircraft when landing. Spoilers are also used to reduce lift, increase drag, and control speed when descending. Additionally, they assist the aircraft to roll (bank) to the right or left. The trim system, as mentioned earlier, improves the overall attitude of an aircraft by relieving pressure on the controls.

Also inside the cockpit are the throttle, joystick or control wheel, and pedals, which coordinate the movement of the aircraft. The THROTTLE increases and decreases power. The JOYSTICK or CONTROL WHEEL directs the aircraft left, right, nose up, and nose down. The PEDALS shift the rudder, which moves the aircraft left or right.

Example

Which component(s) help optimize the performance of an aircraft as part of the secondary flight control system?

(A) the elevators

(B) leading edge devices

(C) the spoilers

(D) both B and C

Answers:

(A) is incorrect. The elevators are part of the primary flight control system.

(B) is incorrect. Leading edge devices are indeed part of the secondary flight control system, but so are the spoilers, so the best answer is D.

(C) is incorrect. The spoilers are indeed part of the secondary flight control system, but so are leading edge devices, so the best answer is D.

(D) is correct. Leading edge devices and the spoilers are part of the secondary flight control system, and they optimize the performance of that system.

THE FOUR FUNDAMENTAL FLIGHT MANEUVERS

The four fundamentals of flight are STRAIGHT-AND-LEVEL FLIGHT, TURNS, CLIMBS, and DESCENTS.

Straight-and-Level Flight

The key to smooth flight is the handling of the flight controls by the pilot. The controls should be held with a light touch, not gripped strongly. Straight-and-level flight is achieved when the aircraft is in cruising mode and the four forces of flight—weight, lift, thrust, and drag—are in balance. Straight-and-level flight still requires a monitoring of the controls, but it does not necessarily require moving the controls when the aircraft is not set to autopilot. Avoiding rash inputs on the flight controls maintains a smooth flight.

When an aircraft banks, it tends to change attitude while in the turn. After the turn is complete, the altitude indicator (among the flight instruments discussed later) will confirm the aircraft's heading. The pilot must ensure the natural reference point of the horizon and the perpendicular positions of the wings to return to level flight.

Example

Which of the following is NOT considered necessary to achieve straight-and-level flight?

(A) monitoring the controls

(B) setting the aircraft in cruising mode

(C) moving the flight controls

(D) using a light touch

Answers:

(A) is incorrect. Monitoring the controls assures a successful straight-and-level flight.

(B) is incorrect. A straight-and-level flight is achieved when the aircraft is in cruising mode.

(C) is correct. Moving the controls is not always necessary to maintain a straight-and-level flight.

(D) is incorrect. A light touch is essential to a straight-and-level flight.

Turns

When an aircraft is turned, its ailerons should be banked toward the direction of the turn. The degree of the bank angle determines how much input and adjustment a pilot must make to restore the airplane or helicopter to level flight. The lift force acts at the same angle as the angle of bank to tilt the aircraft away from the vertical. To return to level flight, the vertical lift component must equal the weight of the aircraft. When a pilot pulls back on the stick (or cyclic in helicopters), the total lift is greater than the total aircraft weight, counterbalancing the vertical lift component with the weight to maintain altitude. The horizontal lift component becomes unbalanced and causes the aircraft to accelerate inward to perform the turn.

To perform a turn, the following actions are required.

- The pilot first moves the stick (or cyclic): to the left for left turns or to the right for right turns.
- Enough power or pitching up is also added to counteract the loss of lift.
- The controls are neutralized to stop any increase in the bank angle and to maintain the desired bank angle.
- After the turn is accomplished, the ailerons are leveled to resume flight.

During a turn maneuver, a pilot must maintain visual reference with the horizon and keep alert to the aircraft limits of airspeed and attitude displayed on the flight instruments.

Typically, altitude and airspeed decrease in a turn. The elevators are used to hold altitude, and the throttle is used to increase speed. As airspeed and altitude decrease, a stall and loss of lift on the wings may result. In this case, the pilot must lower the AOA by one of several means to apply power.

There are three types of turns: shallow, medium, and steep turns. A SHALLOW TURN consists of a bank of up to 20 degrees; after such a turn, the stability of an aircraft naturally returns it to level flight without pilot interference. The bank of a MEDIUM TURN is between 20 and 45 degrees; the pilot during this turn must input aileron pressure to return the aircraft to level flight. A STEEP TURN includes any bank greater than 45 degrees; after a steep turn the pilot must input opposite pressure on the controls to return the aircraft to level flight.

Example

What action must a pilot perform when flying out of a steep turn that is not usually required during a shallow or medium turn?

(A) apply drag by lowering the aileron on the rising wing

(B) decrease airspeed

(C) exceed aircraft limits to finish the turn as soon as possible

(D) input opposite pressure on the controls

Answers:

(A) is incorrect. Additional drag during turns should not be applied. Airspeed and altitude decrease naturally due to the airflow around the wings.

(B) is incorrect. Aircraft airspeed decreases naturally. An additional loss of airspeed may result in a stall.

(C) is incorrect. An aircraft's limitations should never be exceeded.

(D) is correct. An input of opposite pressure on the controls will return the aircraft to level flight.

Climbs

A CLIMB is when an aircraft flight path changes from a lower to a higher level in altitude. During this maneuver, a pilot must increase lift to overcome the aircraft's weight. Climbing without increasing thrust results in a decrease in airspeed. The corrective action is to input additional thrust without exceeding the aircraft's maximum power settings.

A NORMAL CLIMB—sometimes referred to as a CRUISE CLIMB—is performed within the aircraft manufacturer's standards; the aircraft increases airspeed, but it may not be operating at its optimum performance. A BEST RATE OF CLIMB (V_y) involves gaining the most altitude in a given amount of time using the most power available to reach cruising altitude. This climb is steeper than a normal climb and results in the greatest altitude gain over a set amount of time. It is used when an aircraft must take off or gain altitude quickly. A BEST ANGLE OF CLIMB (V_x) involves gaining the most altitude over a given distance. This climb is also used during takeoff but especially at airports where there are obstructions in the flight path. Navigating obstacles typically requires this climbing technique.

Example

Which statement is correct regarding the best rate of climb?

(A) The least amount of power should be applied.

(B) Obstructions in the flight path require a best rate of climb.

(C) The most altitude in a given amount of time can be obtained.

(D) The best rate of climb accomplishes the best climb angle over a given distance.

Answers:

(A) is incorrect. The best rate of climb requires the most amount of available power.

(B) is incorrect. Obstructions in the flight path require a best angle of climb.

(C) is correct. The best rate of climb results in the most altitude gain over a given amount of time.

(D) is incorrect. The best rate of climb is not the best angle of climb.

Descents

The opposite of a climb in aviation is a DESCENT. When lift is decreased, induced drag is minimized, and the aircraft has a tendency to gain airspeed and thrust. Engine power levels must be reduced to maintain airspeed and avoid an excess speed situation.

A PARTIAL POWER DESCENT is the preferred way to decrease altitude. During this type of descent the aircraft should drop at a rate of 500 feet per minute (fpm). A DESCENT AT MINIMUM SAFE AIRSPEED (MSA) is a nose-high controlled descent used to clear obstacles on short approach to a short runway. The aircraft's angle during this descent is steeper than during a partial power descent. An EMERGENCY DESCENT occurs when the aircraft rapidly loses altitude. Emergency procedures dictate the power settings and control positions for all emergency descents.

A fixed-wing aircraft is by design able to GLIDE for a short distance, including during a descent with little or no engine power; gravity naturally takes over. The best glide speed allows for traveling the greatest distance while still airborne.

Example

What is the standard rate of descent for a partial power descent?

(A) 100 fpm

(B) 200 fpm

(C) 500 fpm

(D) 1,000 fpm

Answers:

(A) is incorrect. This is not the preferred rate of descent.

(B) is incorrect. This is not the preferred rate of descent.

(C) is correct. This is indeed the preferred rate of descent for a partial power descent.

(D) is incorrect. This is not the preferred rate of descent.

ROTARY-WING AIRCRAFT

Disclaimer: For the purposes of this section we will be discussing a helicopter with an underslung rotor system and skid-type landing gear. Popular versions of this type of aircraft include the Bell 206B3 (US Army TH-67) and the Bell 205 (US Army UH-1).

Rotary-Wing Aircraft Structure

The major components of a rotary-wing aircraft allow the aircraft to hover and fly directionally. Some of the most vital of these will be detailed in this section.

The MAST (also known as the SHAFT) is a long cylindrical component that extends vertically from the main rotor transmission up to the MAIN ROTOR HUB. The mast is responsible for the rotational drive force that turns the main rotor hub, where all components of the main rotor head are attached. These include the blade grips, the rotor blades, the pitch horn (or yoke), the stabilizer bar and weight (or flybar), and the teeter hinge (or trunnion).

The BLADE GRIPS connect the rotor blades to the rotor system. The primary responsibility of the blade grips is to allow the rotor blades to feather. *Feathering* is a term used to describe the change of the blades' angle relative to their rotation plane (also known as *angle of attack*).

ROTOR BLADES are most often made of metal, but as rotorcraft and composite technologies evolve, more rotor blades are being made of composites such as fiberglass or carbon fiber. The rotor blades give a rotary-wing aircraft lift. Shaped much like airplane wings, the airfoils of rotor blades, when spun along a rotational axis, ultimately create lift for the aircraft.

The PITCH HORN (or YOKE) extends perpendicular to the main rotor blades. It connects directly to the blade grips and stabilizer bar and receives control inputs from the pitch links. Its job is to collect control input from the pilot and translate that input into force, moving the blade grips. This force feathers the blades, or changes their angle of attack.

The twisting movement of helicopter blade grips is due to a component installed inside them. Wire is wrapped several hundred times around two opposing spindles and then completely covered in a flexible polymer that forms a blade grip. As blade grips twist on their ball bearings, these internal wire tension-torsion (TT) straps work like large rubber bands to prevent centrifugal force from allowing the blades to be pulled from the rotor head. Without these straps the rotational forces exerted on the rotor blades would be so great they would fly off in opposite directions.

The STABILIZER BAR AND WEIGHT (or FLYBAR) help to maintain a constant plane of rotation for the rotor blades. The stabilizer bar is connected to the swashplate (described more fully later in this section) via a series of mechanical linkages, which combine with the stabilizer bar to dampen any over-control by the pilot as well as help the aircraft weather extreme wind gusts, thereby reducing pilot workload.

The TEETER HINGE (also known as the TRUNNION) connects the mast to the main rotor hub. The teeter hinge allows the rotor hub and blades to flap up or down depending on control input and aerodynamic forces. As one blade rises, the teeter hinge enables the opposite blade to fall in its plane of rotation, much like the up and down of a teeter-totter.

Below the mast and the main rotor hub's components is the main rotor transmission. Mounted to this transmission is the SWASHPLATE, without which directional control of a rotary-wing aircraft would not be possible. Although there are a number of helicopter rotor designs, from the single main rotor to the tandem rotor (like the CH-47 Chinook) to the coaxial rotor (like the Kamov KA-50), all these aircraft have a swashplate. The two primary components of the swashplate—the inner, or non-rotating, swashplate and the outer, or rotating, swashplate—form concentric rings, which rest on a type of bearing. This bearing allows the swashplate to tilt along a horizontal plane as well as move up and down. The mast runs through the center of the swashplate, and as the mast turns, driving the main rotor system, a SCISSORS LINK connected to the mast in turn drives the outer, rotating swashplate. The inner, non-rotating swashplate lifts and tilts, controlling the directional movement of the outer, rotating swashplate, which changes the pitch of the rotor blades.

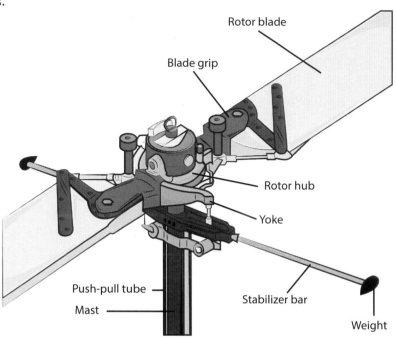

Figure 4.12. Main Rotor System Assembly

PITCH LINKS, or PUSH-PULL TUBES, connect to both the rotating swashplate and the stabilizer bar, or directly to the pitch horn. Pitch links are the mechanical linkage that translates pilot input to control the blade's pitch.

The TAIL BOOM is the structural component of the helicopter that supports the tail rotor and in some cases the directional fins.

> ✔ The tail boom of most light rotary-wing aircraft has almost no internal support structure. On the Bell 206B3 Jet Ranger there is structural reinforcement where the tail boom couples with the fuselage and where the tail rotor gearbox couples with the tail boom, but the rest of the tail boom is hollow.

In a helicopter design known as a NOTAR (no tail rotor), a DUCTED FAN is used in place of a traditional tail rotor to cancel out torque effect or the counter-rotating force applied to the airframe as a main rotor system turns. This ducted fan is usually connected to the engine, and as the fan rotates, it creates thrust similar to that of a rotating propeller. As this thrust is forced through a duct in the tail boom it is vented out the back of the aircraft at a 90-degree angle and is controlled by a louver that allows either more or less air to pass out of the thrust opening. It is this vectored thrust that gives a NOTAR rotary-wing aircraft directional control in the hover and cancels out torque effect.

COWLINGS are removable pieces of an aircraft's outer skin that protect important areas of the aircraft from aerodynamic and environmental forces. They also allow for inspection or maintenance of those areas.

SKIDS, a type of landing gear, allow a rotary-wing aircraft to land safely without damaging its undercarriage. Skids are often made of tubular steel and run parallel to the airframe.

Example

Which rotary-wing aircraft component allows the rotor hub and blades to flap?

(A) the teeter hinge

(B) the rotor hub

(C) the swashplate

(D) the skids

Answers:

(A) is correct. The teeter hinge allows the blades to flap up and down.

(B) is incorrect. The rotor hub is the center attachment point for the rotor head components.

(C) is incorrect. The swashplate is the component that allows for directional movement of the aircraft.

(D) is incorrect. The skids are used as landing gear on a rotary-wing aircraft.

The Physics of Rotary-Wing Aircraft

Hovering flight is the balance of the four aerodynamic forces—weight, lift, thrust, and drag—at a given period of time. In a rotary-wing aircraft during a hover, these forces are in opposition straight up and straight down. In order for the aircraft to hover, it has to overcome its weight via the generation of lift. If lift is greater than the aircraft's weight, then the helicopter rises from the ground.

A rotary-wing aircraft creates lift via the rotational movement of its airfoils. As its rotor blades turn, the slow-moving high-pressure air below the blades pushes up against the faster-moving low-pressure air above the blades. This upward force is known as the **M**AGNUS EFFECT.

Once the aircraft is airborne, it must produce enough lift and thrust to counteract the weight and drag of the aircraft and keep the aircraft in the air. As long as the helicopter maintains a balance between these forces, it will remain in a stabilized hover, suspended in a column of air created by the rotational movement of the rotor blades. This column of air passing through the rotor blades is known as **I**NDUCED FLOW, or downwash.

> ✓
> The Magnus effect was first described (though not named) by Isaac Newton in 1672. In fact, in 1742 a British mathematician named Benjamin Robins arguably described the Magnus effect, though only as it relates to the trajectory of a spinning musket ball. However, the force itself would not actually be *called* the Magnus effect until 1852, when German physicist Gustav Magnus officially "discovered" it.

While the aircraft is in a stabilized hover, it is attempting to counteract another aerodynamic principle of vertical flight: translating tendency. **T**RANSLATING TENDENCY is the tendency of a rotary-wing aircraft to drift laterally due to tail rotor thrust. The tail rotor of a rotary-wing aircraft is used to counteract torque and to provide directional control of the aircraft. As the main rotor blades turn, the airframe wants to rotate opposite to that movement. The tail rotor creates the horizontal thrust necessary to counteract that rotational pull of the airframe, which results in the helicopter drifting laterally—its translating tendency.

GYROSCOPIC PRECESSION is another aerodynamic factor exhibited in rotary-wing aircraft. When a force is applied to a rotating rotor, the force will be felt 90 degrees later in the plane of rotation, just as it would in a gyroscope. For example, if force is applied at the six o'clock position of a counterclockwise spinning component, the force is felt or viewed at the three o'clock position.

As a rotary-wing aircraft moves forward, the next aerodynamic factor it will encounter is known as TRANSVERSE FLOW EFFECT. When the helicopter begins to accelerate, the induced flow created by the lifting action of the rotor blades drops to nearly zero in the front half of the rotor system and increases in the rear half of the rotor system. This drop in induced flow causes the angle of attack in the front half of the rotor system to increase, causing the blades to flap up. In contrast, as the induced flow increases in the rear half of the rotor system, the angle of attack decreases, causing the blades to flap down. Due to gyroscopic precession, the displacement of the flapping blades is not felt until 90 degrees later in the plane of rotation, which causes the rotary-wing aircraft to roll laterally.

TRANSLATIONAL LIFT is another factor that rotary-wing aircraft have to contend with. While a rotary-wing aircraft hovers, the induced flow created is nearly vertical. As this vertical column of air hits the ground, it extends outward in all directions and often is pulled back vertically to be recirculated through the aircraft's rotor system. This movement of air creates vortices at the ends of the rotor blades. It is these vortices that hinder the effectiveness of the rotor system, requiring more power for the aircraft to stay aloft.

To achieve an *effective translational lift (ETL)*, the efficiency of the main rotor system must be increased. When an aircraft moves either forward or laterally, it begins to outrun its rotor vortices and thereby creates greater efficiency in the rotor system. The efficiency is not directionally equal, though, since the rotor system does not outrun different vortices at the same time. As the forward half of the rotor system becomes more efficient, the blades flap up, creating more lift and causing the nose of the aircraft to pitch up and, due to gyroscopic precession, to roll laterally. Both transverse flow effect and translational lift can be countered by using the cyclic pitch control (detailed in the upcoming controls section), which can tip the aircraft's plane of rotation.

Lifting forces in the main rotor are not equal at all times either. DISSYMMETRY OF LIFT is an unequal lifting of forces created by the advancing and retreating blades. As a rotary-wing aircraft moves forward through the air, *relative wind* is created, which is the motion of air across an airfoil. As a counterclockwise rotating blade moves an aircraft forward, it encounters fast-moving air along the right-hand side of that aircraft. As it encounters this fast-moving air, more lift is created. Conversely, the leading edge of the airfoil on the left-hand side of the aircraft—the retreating blade—does not run into fast-moving air; therefore lift decreases. Due to this difference in lift between the advancing and retreating halves of the rotor system, the aircraft is inclined to roll toward the left.

One of the things that make a rotary-wing aircraft unique is its ability to autorotate. AUTOROTATION is a situation in which the rotor blades are driven by relative wind rather than by the aircraft's powerplant. For example, in the event of an engine failure a pilot can adjust his or her flight controls to allow the induced flow of air through the rotor system to reverse the aircraft's direction. As gravity pulls the aircraft back to the ground, this induced flow can travel vertically through the rotor system and continue to drive the blades in their plane of rotation. As long as the rotor system is turning, the pilot can maintain full directional control of the aircraft and steer it to a suitable landing area. The rotor system stores inertia, giving the pilot an opportunity to cushion the helicopter upon landing. This is a skilled maneuver and if not performed well can cause the rotor system to lose all rotational movement and, in turn, the last remaining vestiges of lift.

Example

Which direction will a rotary-wing aircraft roll due to the transverse flow effect?

(A) upside down

(B) vertically

(C) backward

(D) laterally

Answers:

(A) is incorrect. The aircraft will not roll upside down.

(B) is incorrect. The aircraft will not roll vertically.

(C) is incorrect. The aircraft will not roll backward.

(D) is correct. The aircraft will roll laterally due to the transverse flow effect.

Rotary-Wing Aircraft Controls

There are four primary controls of the rotary-wing aircraft. The CYCLIC CONTROL SYSTEM, mounted on the flight deck floor and centered between the pilot's legs, is utilized to adjust the aircraft's pitch and roll axes. A causal effect of the spinning motion of rotor blades is vertical thrust. As the blades spin, a column of air is created that the pilot can manipulate via the use of the helicopter's flight controls. When the cyclic control is pushed forward, the column of air supporting the rotary-wing aircraft is directed aft, creating a forward lift vector that moves the helicopter forward. This cyclic movement is able to change the direction of the lift vector up to 360 degrees around the aircraft, allowing a pilot to hover in one location.

The COLLECTIVE CONTROL, located to the left of the pilot's seat, is used to "collectively" change the pitch of the rotor blades. When the pilot raises the collective, the pitch angle of the blades increases simultaneously. As the pitch angle increases, so does the angle of attack of the blades; this in turn creates more lift. To perform a level climb the pilot simply pulls the collective up; to descend, he or she pushes it down.

Yaw control of the aircraft is adjusted by the use of the TAIL ROTOR PEDALS, or the DIRECTIONAL CONTROLS. Much like the collective control over the main rotor system, the tail rotor pedals change the pitch of the tail rotor blades, causing a larger or smaller horizontal lifting vector.

Many modern rotary-wing aircraft also have a self-governing THROTTLE CONTROL, meaning once the throttle is switched to a flight setting, engine performance is managed by a computer. Smaller as well as some older aircraft have a manual throttle control, which requires the pilot to increase and reduce the throttle to maintain optimal flying parameters. The throttle can be located in a variety of places within the aircraft, but the majority of throttle controls are found on the collective control in the form of an attached twisting grip, very similar to a collar. By twisting this grip, the throttle can be either increased or decreased.

Example

Which primary rotary-wing flight control increases the pitch angle of the blades simultaneously?

(A) the cyclic

(B) the directional controls

(C) the ducted fan

(D) the collective

Answers:

(A) is incorrect. The cyclic controls the pitch and roll axes of the aircraft.

(B) is incorrect. The directional controls manage the aircraft's yaw.

(C) is incorrect. The ducted fan is a component of the NOTAR aircraft design.

(D) is correct. The collective control changes the pitch of the blades simultaneously.

FLIGHT INSTRUMENTS

A pilot uses outside visual reference cues against the horizon to maneuver a helicopter. When weather degrades to less than the minimum visual flight rules (VFR), flight instruments must be relied upon for guiding the helicopter along the flight path, providing altitude, heading, and airspeed. The altimeter, the airspeed indicator, and the vertical speed indicator are common pitot-static instruments. A pitot tube and static ports extend outside the aircraft's structure to collect the outside air and static pressure. The air passes through a pitot line to the instruments calibrated to measure the aircraft's altitude and speed.

Altimeter

An altimeter displays the altitude of a helicopter. It computes this by measuring the atmospheric pressure at the aircraft's current altitude and comparing this to a preset value. Air pressure decreases 1 inch of mercury for each 1,000 feet of altitude.

There are three types of altimeters: the three-pointer, the counter drum, and the encoding.

Figure 4.13. Three-Pointer Altimeter

Of the three "hands" on a **THREE-POINTER ALTIMETER**, the longest, thinnest hand displays altitude in tens of thousands of feet; the shortest hand displays thousands of feet; and the medium-length hand displays hundreds of feet. The box on the right side of the altimeter displays the set ground atmospheric pressure. This setting may be adjusted using the knob at the bottom left of the instrument.

Figure 4.14. Counter Drum Altimeter

The **COUNTER DRUM ALTIMETER** digitally displays the altitude without needing manual figuring. Just as the three-pointer altimeter does, it also displays the set ground atmospheric pressure.

The **ENCODING ALTIMETER** converts the altitude into a digital code, which is then relayed to ground control radar via a transponder.

Several types of altitudes may be displayed on an altimeter:

- **INDICATED ALTITUDE** is the altitude actually displayed on the altimeter.
- **TRUE ALTITUDE** is the height of the aircraft above mean sea level (MSL).
- **ABSOLUTE ALTITUDE** is the height of the aircraft above ground level (AGL).
- **PRESSURE ALTITUDE** is a pre-calibrated altitude with a standard atmosphere level setting of 29.92 inches of Hg. (This altitude is often used in flight planning calculations.)
- **DENSITY ALTITUDE** is pressure altitude modified for a nonstandard temperature.

Figure 4.15. Encoding Altimeter

Example

Air pressure decreases 1 inch of mercury for each _____ feet of altitude.

(A) 100

(B) 500

(C) 1,000

(D) 1,500

Answers:

(A) is incorrect. Changes in air pressure are not measured at 1 inch of mercury for each 100 feet of altitude.

(B) is incorrect. Changes in air pressure are not measured at 1 inch of mercury for each 500 feet of altitude.

(C) is correct. Air pressure indeed decreases 1 inch of mercury for each 1,000 feet of altitude.

(D) is incorrect. Changes in air pressure are not measured at 1 inch of mercury for each 1,500 feet of altitude.

Vertical Speed Indicator

A vertical speed indicator (VSI) displays the vertical speed of an aircraft, in 500-foot increments, measured in thousands of feet per minute, and indicates if the aircraft is climbing, descending, or in level flight, and it shows the rate of climb or descent. The instrument uses a diaphragm to compare the static pressure outside the aircraft to the static pressure surrounding the diaphragm inside the instrument. The difference in the pressures

Figure 4.16. Vertical Speed Indicator

identifies a climb or a descent. When the aircraft is on the ground, the pilot may reset the indicator to zero with a *zeroing screw*.

The VSI does not display in real time; there is typically a six- to nine-second delay, or *lag*, in the reading. *Trend information* (a sudden climb or descent) shows initially, then the feet per minute rate is displayed.

Example

An increase in the static pressure, as measured around the diaphragm inside the VSI, indicates an aircraft is in which of the following maneuvers?

(A) a bank

(B) a climb

(C) a descent

(D) a straight-and-level flight

Answers:

(A) is incorrect. A level bank would not cause a difference between the static pressure of the aircraft and the static pressure surrounding the diaphragm of the flight instrument.

(B) is correct. An increase in static pressure surrounding the diaphragm indicates the aircraft is in a climb.

(C) is incorrect. A descent would cause a decrease in the static pressure surrounding the diaphragm versus the static pressure of the aircraft.

(D) is incorrect. Straight-and-level flight does not cause a decrease in the static pressure surrounding the diaphragm versus the static pressure of the aircraft.

Airspeed Indicator

The airspeed indicator is a differential pressure gauge that determines how fast the aircraft is moving by contrasting the ambient (inside) air pressure with the ram (outside) air pressure using the aircraft's pitot tube and static ports. A diaphragm in the indicator expands and contracts, causing the linkage to the indicator pointer to move. Airspeed is measured in knots, and each level of airspeed is color-coded:

- The **WHITE ARC** displays the flap operating speed. The lower limit of the white arc (V_{SO}) is the stalling speed with the flaps down. The upper limit (V_{FE}), where the white and green arcs meet, indicates the maximum speed at which the flaps can be extended.

- The **GREEN ARC** displays the aircraft's normal operating range, from the lowest limit (V_{S1}) to the highest limit(V_{NO}), also known as the *maximum structural cruising speed*.

Figure 4.17. Airspeed Indicator

- The **RED RADIAL LINE** represents the never-exceed speed (V_{NE}).

There are different types of airspeed: INDICATED AIRSPEED is what is displayed on the indicator instrument; CALIBRATED AIRSPEED is the indicated airspeed corrected for position error; EQUIVALENT AIRSPEED is the calibrated airspeed corrected for non-standard pressure; and TRUE AIRSPEED is the equivalent airspeed corrected for non-standard density.

Example

Which type of airspeed is displayed on the airspeed indicator?

(A) calibrated airspeed

(B) equivalent airspeed

(C) indicated airspeed

(D) pressure airspeed

Answers:

(A) is incorrect. Calibrated is the airspeed on the indicator corrected for position error.

(B) is incorrect. Equivalent airspeed is the calibrated airspeed measurement corrected for non-standard pressure.

(C) is correct. Indicated airspeed is indeed what is displayed on the airspeed indicator instrument.

(D) is incorrect. This is not a type of airspeed.

Turn and Slip Indicator

The turn and slip indicator combines a turn indicator pointer and a slip indicator ball (inclinometer) in the same housing to measure the yaw rotation of the aircraft. This instrument indicates if the pilot is making a coordinated left or right standard turn. The turn and slip indicator operates on a gyro in a vertical plane aligned with the longitudinal axis, and displays the bank of the aircraft along its vertical axis as well as the rate at which the aircraft turns. A 360-degree turn completed in 2 minutes, at 3 degrees per second, would be considered a standard turn.

The indicator also displays the direction of the turn the aircraft takes.

- In a SLIPPING TURN, there is more bank than needed and gravity is greater than the centrifugal force reaction on the slip indicator ball, thus the ball moves toward the inside of the turn.

- In a SKIDDING TURN, the centrifugal force reaction is greater than gravity on the slip indicator ball, and the ball moves toward the outside of the turn.

- In a COORDINATED TURN, centrifugal force and gravity react equally on the slip indicator ball, and the ball remains in the lowest part of the glass.

Example

What is the purpose of the turn and slip indicator?

(A) to display the aircraft's angle of descent

(B) to display the degree of a turn

(C) to indicate whether an increase of altitude is needed

(D) to indicate if the pilot is making a coordinated left or right standard turn

Attitude Indicator

The attitude indicator provides real-time and direct attitude information during changes in an aircraft's pitch (along the lateral axis) and when banking (along the longitudinal axis). It displays the relationship of the aircraft's orientation to an artificial horizon. Modern aircraft may have additional features included in the attitude indicator to assist with flight navigation.

The indicator's BANK SCALE represents the sky in blue and the ground/horizon in brown or black. The numbers are in degrees of attitude. The top hashes are degrees of bank, displayed in 30-degree increments. The POINTER at the 12 o'clock position of the indicator (an upside down triangle) is used to check the aircraft's position; it turns toward the direction the aircraft banks.

Figure 4.18 displays a straight-and-level flight in progress. If the aircraft is performing, for example, a *level left bank*, the indicator would show the miniature aircraft tilting to the left with the center of the aircraft wings remaining at the horizontal bar. A *climbing*

Figure 4.18. Attitude Indicator

right bank would be displayed with the aircraft's wings above the horizontal bar and the artificial horizon dipping to the left and rising on the right (thus the right wing would be closer to the ground). In a *level climb* or *dive* the wings would be displayed parallel along the horizontal bar, and the aircraft would be moving toward the blue portion of the indicator for a climb or the brown or black portion for a dive.

Example

The lateral axis of an aircraft controls what?

(A) a bank

(B) a level left bank

(C) pitch

(D) a shallow turn

Answers:

(A) is incorrect. The longitudinal axis controls banking.

(B) is incorrect. The longitudinal axis controls all banks.

(C) is correct. The lateral axis controls the pitch of the aircraft.

(D) is incorrect. The longitudinal axis controls turns.

Magnetic Compass

The magnetic compass is a navigational instrument that displays the cardinal headings (north, south, east, and west) in 30-degree increments. Long vertical hash marks identify 10-degree increments, and short vertical hashes identify 5-degree increments. Due to nearby electromagnetic interference from metal structures and electrical components in an aircraft, COMPASS MAGNETIC DEVIATION exists. This deviation is allowable up to 10 degrees.

When the compass card is not level, the magnets dip downward toward Earth. This process, called MAGNETIC DIP, happens when the aircraft is in a bank toward the west or east or when it is accelerating or decelerating while on a west or east heading. Also, when on a west or east heading, any increase in airspeed during a turn causes the compass to reflect a false turn toward the north. A decrease in airspeed during the turn causes the compass to reflect a false turn toward the south.

Compass deviations are caused by electromagnetic influences on the magnets in the compass.

Also, it is common for the direction on magnetic compasses to lag when an aircraft makes a turn. For example, when turning left from a north heading, the compass turns right to 30 degrees and will reset itself once 270 degrees is reached. When turning from a south heading, the compass leads at the same rate of location at degrees latitude. If the aircraft was at 40 degrees latitude, the pilot would have to roll back approximately 40 degrees past the south reading.

A number of other variations and errors can occur with a compass. A compass dial aligns itself with the north and south MAGNETIC POLES, not with geographic true north and south. Pilots fly with the aid of sectional charts that use the geographic poles instead. The difference between true north or south and magnetic north or south is called MAGNETIC VARIATION.

To identify the variation (in degrees) between magnetic and geographic north, say, a pilot must convert true north (from the sectional charts) to magnetic north (from the aircraft's magnetic compass). If the magnetic variation is east of true north, the degree of variation is subtracted from the map's true heading. If the magnetic variation is west of true north, that degree of variation is added to the map's true heading. The line where the true north and magnetic north variation is zero degrees is called an AGONIC LINE. Lines where the variation is greater or less than zero degrees are called ISOGONIC LINES.

East is least, west is best. Subtract the degree of variation if the variation is east of true north; add the degree of variation if the variation is west of true north.

Compass deviations may be corrected by using an airfield's compass rose. These indications are recorded on a compass compensation card placed near the compass in the cockpit.

> ### Example
> If the variation between the magnetic north pole and the true north pole is greater than +12 degrees west, how does a pilot adjust for the compass heading?
>
> **(A)** by adding 6 degrees to the compass heading displayed
>
> **(B)** by adding 12 degrees to the compass heading displayed
>
> **(C)** No adjustment is needed; the magnetic compass automatically adjusts for the degree of variation.
>
> **(D)** by subtracting 6 degrees to the compass heading displayed

Heading Indicator

The heading indicator is similar to a magnetic compass but functions with a gyroscope and is not subject to the magnetic deviations inherent in magnetic compasses. Direction in this indicator is defined by the aircraft's horizontal plane. When this plane does not match Earth's horizon, a gimbal error exists, called a DRIFT. This drift needs to be corrected every ten to fifteen minutes by confirming the heading using the magnetic compass.

Figure 4.19. Heading Indicator

Example

Using Figure 4.19, what is the closest degree heading of this aircraft?

(A) 25 degrees

(B) 80 degrees

(C) 250 degrees

(D) 260 degrees

Answers:

(A) is incorrect. Add a zero after the numeral increment. The heading is closer to 260 degrees.

(B) is incorrect. Read the compass needle at the nose of the miniature aircraft on the dial for its heading, not at the tail of the aircraft.

(C) is incorrect. The compass needle is closer to 260 than 250.

(D) is correct. The aircraft is on a 260-degree heading.

Vertical Card Compass

A vertical card compass is a dry compass, not a float-type compass. As seen in Figure 4.20, it is etched out in 30-degree increments with 3 representing 30, 6 representing 60, etc., and there is no overshoot with delayed readings. The heading is read from the 12 o'clock position and the nose of the miniature aircraft on the instrument.

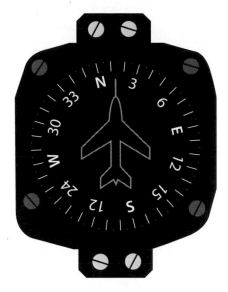

Figure 4.20. Vertical Card Compass

Example

Using Figure 4.20, what is the degree heading of this aircraft?

(A) 10 degrees

(B) 20 degrees

(C) 100 degrees

(D) 190 degrees

Answers:

(A) is correct. Add a zero after the numeral increment. The heading is 10 degrees.

(B) is incorrect. The heading is closer to 10 degrees than 20 degrees.

(C) is incorrect. A 100-degree heading would be an easterly heading.

(D) is incorrect. Do not read the compass from the tail of the miniature aircraft.

AIRPORTS AND FLIGHT PROTOCOLS

Runway Design and Function

The Federal Aviation Administration (FAA) oversees airport designs and improvements for federal airports, and has established a twenty-year structural design life expectancy for runway pavements. Runway materials must hold up to the stresses placed on them from the weight and impact of aircraft, and foreign object damage (FOD). Runways must also avoid causing undue wear on aircraft tires and provide water runoff and protection from harsh weather conditions.

Currently runways must be 9 to 12 inches deep at regional airfields capable of servicing smaller aircraft. Hub airports frequented by jumbo jets require a 15- to 18-inch depth of pavement. Of the different runway designs, a **FLEXIBLE PAVEMENT** consists of hot-mix asphalt installed on a base course and subbase, if required. This type of pavement resists cracking (versus rigid pavements). A FULL-DEPTH ASPHALT PAVEMENT contains asphaltic cement as its main material. A RIGID PAVEMENT may use rubberized Portland cement as a subbase. All pavement styles consist of layers: a base course (stabilized), a subbase, and a subgrade, and it is important that loose, gritty material does not exist between the layers.

Runway lengths are dependent on several factors, including the type of aircraft expected to use the runway, the expected maximum takeoff weight (MTOW), the elevation of the airfield, and the maximum local air temperature.

The movement area of an airfield includes the aprons and areas for takeoff, landing, and taxiing. Runway markings are designed to guide an aircraft through a safe landing and takeoff. Runways are defined by their markings, and there are three types.

VISUAL RUNWAY MARKINGS are visible so a pilot can view them as the aircraft approaches the runway. These runways are commonly small airstrips.

A NONPRECISION INSTRUMENT RUNWAY is generally found in small- to medium-size airports and displays a centerline, a threshold mark, and designators, as well as a visual cue called an *aiming point*—a wide strip located on both sides of the runway and approximately 1,000 feet from the landing threshold. This signifies the runway contains navigation facilities for an instrument approach with only horizontal guidance.

A PRECISION INSTRUMENT RUNWAY, found in larger airports, displays all the same markings of a nonprecision instrument runway as well as a touchdown zone and side stripes. This type of runway also contains an *instrument landing system (ILS)* or *precision approach radar (PAR)*. An ILS approach receives radio responses that provide both vertical and horizontal guidance (if a pilot is too low or too high, or too far left or right, as the aircraft approaches). Additionally, a runway number identifies the approach direction as read from a magnetic azimuth and left, center, and right designations identify parallel runways.

Along with physical design, features such as approach lighting and instrumentation requirements limit the type of aircraft a runway may service. RUNWAY END IDENTIFICATION LIGHTS (REILs) are synchronized illuminated lights placed on each side of the runway threshold to help a pilot identify the approach end of a runway. Additionally, the lights at the end of the runway are red, and outward from the runway end they are green, to indicate the threshold. RUNWAY EDGE LIGHTS identify the edges of the runway. These are of variable intensity and white in color, although instrument runways have yellow edge lighting along the last 2,000 feet, or half the length of runway, whichever is less.

An APPROACH LIGHT SYSTEM (ALS) assists a pilot in transitioning from instrument flight to visual flight for landing. Some airports have the flashing lights blink sequentially to guide a pilot to the end of the runway under instrument landings. A VISUAL APPROACH SLOPE INDICATOR (VASI) will assist with descents during visual landings. Each indicator has a white light on the upper portion and a red light on the lower portion to identify to the pilot his or her position along the glide path to the runway.

Example

Which answer lists different types of marked runways?

(A) approach, instrument, and visual

(B) FOD, REIL, and VASI

(C) precision instrument, non-precision instrument, and visual

(D) REIL and visual

Answers:

(A) is incorrect. Approach is not a type of marked runway.

(B) is incorrect. FOD is not a marked runway and REIL and VASI are lighting systems.

(C) is correct. These are the three types of marked runways.

(D) is incorrect. Visual is a type of marked runway; however, REIL is not.

Airspace

Controlled airspace is the area controlled and maintained by the FAA-regulated air traffic control (ATC) service. This service controls the movement of all aviation assets within its designated area.

Airspace is divided into six classes by the FAA. (Note that aircraft must have operable equipment and meet certain certification to operate in certain classes. Student and recreational pilots must also be certified to conduct flight operations in certain classes of airspace. Pilots are required to contact the ATC controller to obtain clearance, when necessary, prior to inadvertently entering any controlled airspace.)

- **CLASS A**—Airspace from 18,000 feet MSL to pressure altitude of 60,000 feet, 12 nautical miles (NM) off the coast of the United States, and international airspace beyond 12 NM that is within the navigational signal of ATC radar. All aircraft must operate under instrument flight rules (IFR) at this level.

- **CLASS B**—Airspace from ground level to 10,000 feet MSL surrounding the busiest airports capable of IFR operations and commercial passenger traffic. ATC clearance is required to enter and leave this airspace. Aircraft and pilots must be certified to operate in this airspace.

- **CLASS C**—Airspace from ground level to 4,000 feet above the airport elevation surrounding airports with an operational control tower and serviced by radar approach control, IFR operations, and commercial passenger traffic. Airspace extends from 5 NM radius (surface to 4,000 feet above airport elevation) to 10 NM radius from 1,200 to 4,000 feet. No pilot certification is required to operate in this airspace; however, clearance is required to enter and exit this airspace. A two-way radio and an operable radar beacon transponder with automatic altitude reporting equipment are required.

- **CLASS D**—Airspace from ground level to 2,500 feet above the airport elevation surrounding airports with an operational control tower. Notices to Airmen (NOTAM) identify any specific requirements for pilots to operate in this controlled airspace. A two-way radio is required to operate in this airspace.

- **Class E**—Any controlled airspace not included in class A through class D. Special VFR operations are permitted with prior clearance obtained by the controlling facility. Class E airspace is distinguished on sectional charts in blue or magenta, and white on low altitude en route charts. No specific pilot or equipment requirement exists.
- **Class G**—Uncontrolled airspace with visibility requirements of 1 mile during the day and 3 miles at night. This airspace is valid for altitudes 1,200 feet AGL to 10,000 feet MSL. Above 10,000 feet, 5 miles of visibility is required day or night. Class G airspace is identified on sectional maps by a faded, thick blue line.

For any airspace, required flight visibility is 3 statute miles, except in Class A and Class E. There are established elevations where aircraft must remain clear of clouds in the controlled airspace. These restrictions are typically 1,000 feet above the clouds, 500 feet below the clouds, and anywhere from 1,000 feet to 1 statute mile when horizontal with the clouds. Obstacles and urban development may preclude the ability to abide by these set restrictions, but a pilot must display good judgment in this case.

Requirements to establish radio communications with a pilot are different among the classes of airspace.
- **Classes A and B**—The ATC controller must verbally grant clearance. Acknowledgment of the aircraft call sign is not considered an established communication.
- **Classes C and D**—If the ATC controller acknowledges with the aircraft call sign, communication is considered established. This is true even if the ATC controller responds with the aircraft call sign and instructs the pilot to "standby."

Example

Which of the following statements is true about controlled airspace?

(A) An operable two-way radio is all that is required for communications in any airspace.

(B) ATC controllers must verbally grant clearance for entry and exit of Class B through Class D airspaces.

(C) Controllers of Class A through Class D airspaces may establish communications by acknowledging the pilot with the aircraft call sign.

(D) Flight visibility required for Class B airspace is 5 NM.

Answers:

(A) is incorrect. Class D is the only airspace that requires only an operable two-way radio.

(B) is correct. Clearance is required to enter and exit the airspace.

(C) is incorrect. Airspace Classes A and B require the ATC controller to grant clearance—not merely by acknowledging with the aircraft call sign.

(D) is incorrect. Flight visibility for Class B is 3 statute miles.

Right-of-Way

All aircraft have an inherent duty to steer clear of other aircraft and hot-air balloons. Steering clear means that an aircraft may not pass over, under, or ahead of another aircraft unless it is well clear. The following six rules establish the right-of-way for certain situations:

1. An aircraft in distress always has the right-of-way over all other air traffic.

2. When two aircraft of the same category approach each other (except head-on) at generally the same altitude, the aircraft on the right has the right-of-way.

3. When approaching aircraft are of different categories, refer to the following list, presented in order of right-of-way:

   - Hot-air balloons
   - Gliders
   - Airships
   - Powered parachutes
   - Powered hang gliders and ultra-light aircraft
   - Airplanes
   - Rotorcraft

   An exception to this list is an aircraft towing or refueling another aircraft, which has the right-of-way over all other engine-driven aircraft.

4. When two aircraft approach head-on, the pilot of each aircraft should change course to the right.

5. An overtaking aircraft has the right-of-way, and the pilot of the aircraft being overtaken must shift course to the right to stay clear.

6. When landing, an aircraft on final approach or beginning to land has the right-of-way, as long as it does not force an already landed aircraft off the runway. When two aircraft are landing at the same time, the aircraft at a lower altitude has the right-of-way but cannot cut in front of the other aircraft to become the lower level aircraft.

Example

Which right-of-way statement is true?

(A) An aircraft being towed must yield to a rotorcraft when the two aircraft approach each other.

(B) Aircraft in distress have the right-of-way despite their category.

(C) A landing aircraft on short final approach may force a landed aircraft to move off the runway.

(D) Rotorcraft has the right-of-way over a glider when both are approaching at the same time.

Answers:

(A) is incorrect. An aircraft in tow has the right-of-way over the rotorcraft (an engine-driven aircraft).

(B) is correct. Any aircraft in distress always has the right-of-way.

(C) is incorrect. An aircraft on short final approach may not force an already landed aircraft off the runway.

(D) is incorrect. A glider has the right-of-way over a rotorcraft when they approach at the same time.

AVIATION HISTORY

Since 1900, the year of the first flight of a Zeppelin, aircraft technology and capabilities have evolved beyond expectations. The following timeline includes some of the milestones in aviation history.

July 2, 1900: The Zeppelin makes its first flight.

October 22, 1900: The Wright brothers make their first glider flight.

December 17, 1903: The Wright brothers complete the first powered, manned, heavier-than-air controlled flight (it lasted twelve seconds).

February 22, 1920: The first transcontinental mail service is established, from San Francisco to New York.

May 3, 1923: The first nonstop coast-to-coast airplane flight travels from New York to San Diego.

May 21, 1927: Charles A. Lindbergh accomplishes the first nonstop solo flight across the Atlantic Ocean.

June 29, 1927: The first trans-Pacific flight travels from California to Hawaii.

June 1, 1937: Amelia Earhart is lost en route to Howland Island from New Guinea.

June 28, 1939: Pan American Airways flies the first trans-Atlantic passenger service.

October 14, 1947: Captain Charles E. Yeager exceeds the sound barrier in a rocket.

May 5, 1961: Alan Shepard pilots the first US manned space flight.

February 20, 1962: John Glenn becomes the first American to orbit Earth.

December 27, 1968: Apollo 8 is the first human flight to orbit the moon.

September 3, 1971: The Concorde makes its first transatlantic crossing.

1978: The US Airline Deregulation Act ends government regulation of airline routes and rates.

October 24, 2003: The Concorde supersonic jet makes its last flight.

NAUTICAL INFORMATION

PARTS OF A SHIP

Ship directions are terms used to describe various parts of a vessel. The **BOW** of any ship is the forward-most part. Moving **FORE**, or forward, takes one toward the bow of the ship, and moving **AFT** takes one toward the **STERN**, or back, of the ship. Between the bow and the stern in this fore-and-aft direction is the **MIDSHIPS** section, with **AMIDSHIPS** being the actual center point of the ship. The imaginary lengthwise line down the center of the vessel is called the **CENTERLINE**. When on the ship and facing toward the bow, the **PORT** side is to the left and the **STARBOARD** side is to the right.

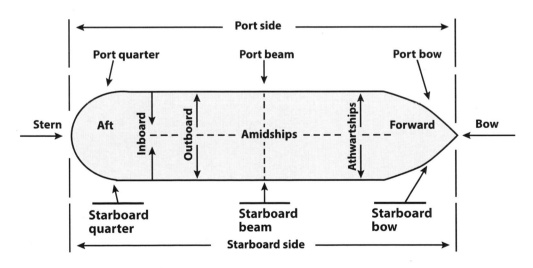

Figure 5.1. Onboard Orientation

The ship's body, called the **HULL**, is watertight to give it strength and buoyancy (the ability to float). The **KEEL** is the bottom-most structure of the ship. It runs along the centerline for the entire length of the hull from bow to stern, forming the backbone of the hull. **FRAMES** are sections that run longitudinally (fore and aft) or transversely (side to side) throughout the vessel, much like a skeletal structure.

Shell plating forms the skin of the hull. The DECKS are horizontal portions of the structure supported by beams. Just as tall buildings have multiple floors, most ships have more than one deck. The main deck is the uppermost deck that spans completely from bow to stern. The shell plating begins at the keel and continues up to the main deck, meeting at the gunwale.

The vertical wall-like structures that further divide a vessel's interior into various compartments are BULKHEADS, vital to both the strength of the ship and in preventing the spread of damage (fire, smoke, or flooding). HATCHES, either on a deck or in the shell plating, are openings that allow access for loading of supplies and should be securely closed when not in use. Many types of ships have cargo holds to store supplies.

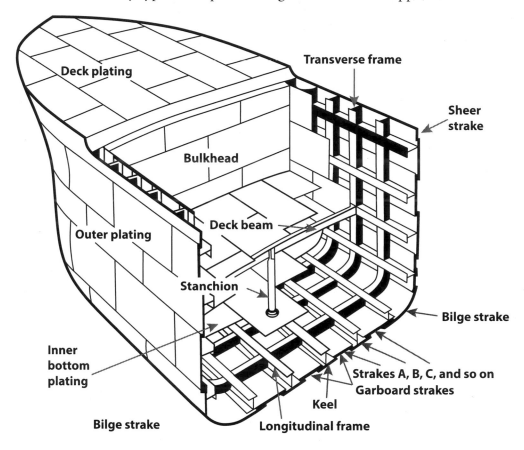

Figure 5.2. Construction of the Hull

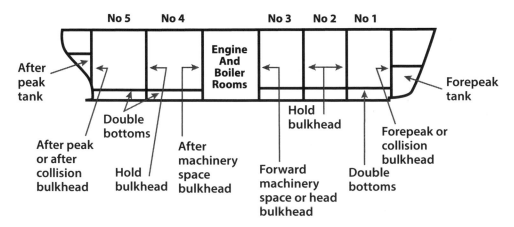

Figure 5.3. Bulkheads, Decks, and Holds

The FORECASTLE is the forward-most compartment on a ship. The SUPERSTRUCTURE is above the main deck or uppermost complete deck, while the BRIDGE, being the key point from which the ship navigates, is part of the superstructure. In the bridge is the HELM, the apparatus used to control the direction of the ship. The helm is connected by various methods (hydraulic, for example) to the RUDDER or rudders. Attached to the hull near the stern of the ship, the rudder controls the ship's direction from underwater.

Antennas and sensors are mounted on one or more tower-like MASTS. Sections splitting off from the masts are called yardarms; flags are often flown from these masts. Heading aft to the stern is the FANTAIL, the aftermost (farthest aft) space or deck of the ship, with the TRANSOM being the aftermost wall or shell plating of the ship's hull.

 A term commonly associated with the helm is the **Conn**, from *conning* (controlling the speed and direction of the ship). To *have the Conn* means to be in charge of directing the ship.

The point at which the hull is at the water's surface is called the WATERLINE. The DRAFT is the depth of water a ship requires to float freely, allowing for the keel. The ship will have draft marks on each side near the bow, the stern, and amidships to determine the draft. The draft is not usually the same at all points, depending on weight distribution and hull shape. The term *trim* notes the difference between the draft at the bow and at the stern.

There are several other important measurement terms: *length* refers to the distance from bow to stern over the entire ship, including any overhangs or appendages. The *beam* is the side-to-side width of the ship at its widest point. Measuring up from the same point on the waterline to the main deck (uppermost continuous deck of the hull) is the *freeboard*, a key measure of how much reserve buoyancy the vessel has.

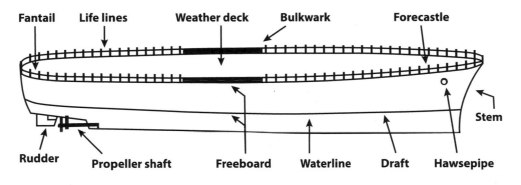

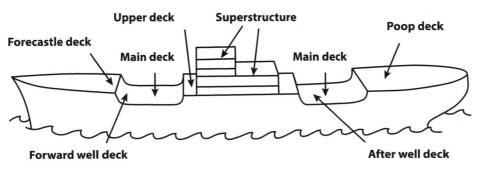

Figure 5.4. External Parts of the Hull

When a ship is MOORED (secured) to a pier (a raised structure in a body of water) or dock, a temporary bridge (with steps or a ramp) called a GANGWAY is used for passage on and off the ship. Instead of mooring at the pier, a ship can anchor in designated areas away from the shore. There are usually two **ANCHORS** at the bow used to hold the ship in the desired area, as well as anchors at the sterns of some vessels. Anchor chain stored in the chain locker connects the anchor to the ship, and a **WINDLASS** will raise or lower the anchor as required.

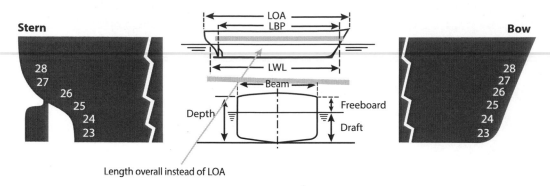

Figure 5.5. Dimensions on a Ship

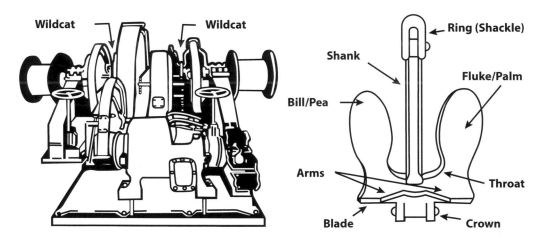

Figure 5.6. Anchor Windlass and Anchor

Example

Where is the helm located on a ship?

(A) forecastle

(B) quarterdeck

(C) cargo hold

(D) bridge

Answer:

(D) is correct. The helm is in the bridge.

TYPES OF SHIPS

Among surface combat ships, **CRUISERS** are the largest currently in service; these are multi-mission warships capable of engaging multiple simultaneous targets and employed in force support or independent action. Fast **DESTROYERS** provide multi-mission offensive and defensive capability, independently or in fleet support. **BATTLESHIPS**, while no longer in service, traditionally had large guns and comprised the main striking force of a surface warfare group. Smaller FRIGATES do not have the multi-mission capability of destroyers and serve as escorts. Some surface combatants can work independently, but most form groups based on the required task (carrier strike groups, amphibious ready groups, and surface combat groups, to name a few).

BALLISTIC MISSILE SUBMARINES are considered national strategic assets, as they carry intercontinental ballistic missiles (ICBMs) for nuclear deterrence, while ATTACK SUBMARINES are offensive vessels designed to seek out both surface and subsurface opponents. A small number of ballistic missile submarines have also been converted to carry cruise missiles and other items. Unlike surface combatants, while submarines may work in support of other units, they primarily operate independently.

Many of these ships and submarines support AIRCRAFT CARRIERS. These enormous vessels use aircraft as opposed to shipboard weapons to project power ashore as well as to control large ocean areas. While there are many types of support vessels, the COMBAT LOGISTICS SHIPS keep the fleet ready at sea by replenishing fuel, ordnance, supplies, and spare parts.

AMPHIBIOUS HELICOPTER/LANDING CRAFT CARRIERS carry combat troops and vehicles. Landing craft, helicopters, and fixed-wing aircraft are capable of landing and taking off from the decks of these ships to transport and support troops ashore. Landing craft carriers, while similar and sometimes with helicopter landing decks, do not normally have a large aviation component.

Smaller vessels such as mine warfare ships and coastal defense ships, while less capable in surface combat than cruisers, have critical specialized roles not easily accomplished by conventional surface combat ships.

Example

Which type of ship is used to hunt and attack subsurface opponents?

(A) combat logistics ship

(B) ballistic missile submarine

(C) mine warfare ship

(D) attack submarine

Answer:

(D) is correct. The attack submarine is an offensive vessel designed to seek out both surface and subsurface opponents.

NAUTICAL UNITS AND MAPS

A CHART may resemble a map, but it is a fundamentally different tool for navigation. A chart, especially a nautical chart, is a living, periodically updated document. The MERCATOR PROJECTION (the process used to translate a three-dimensional earth onto a flat paper) is well suited for most shipboard needs. It shows the nature and shape of the coast, water depths, land features, and bottom characteristics of the seafloor. Directional information, isolated points of danger, and aids to navigation are also clearly marked.

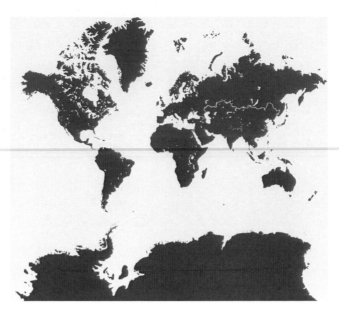

Figure 5.7. Mercator Projection

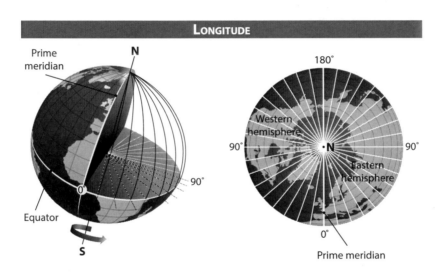

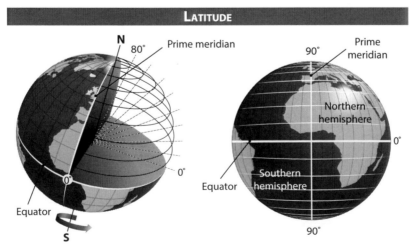

Figure 5.8. Latitude and Longitude

AIDS TO NAVIGATION (ATON) include lighthouses, lightships, beacons, and buoys, which are built specifically to help determine position, define a safe course, and highlight hazards. Channels (marked and designated "highways" for ships with established water depths), anchorages (designated areas for ships to anchor), and bottom characteristics of the seafloor are also on the chart.

LATITUDE and LONGITUDE, both angular measurements, are coordinates that determine the location of a point on the earth's surface. Lines running from east to west along the same latitude are circles on the globe and are called *parallels*. The value can range north or south from 0° at the equator to 90° at the poles. The higher the latitude, the farther one is from the equator.

A line drawn from the North Pole to the South Pole that connects points of the same longitude is called a *meridian*. A PRIME MERIDIAN is a meridian at which the longitude is defined to be 0°. The prime meridian used worldwide today is the IERS Reference Meridian, which is maintained by the International Earth Rotation and Reference Systems Service; it passes through the Royal Observatory in Greenwich, England. Longitude then ranges from +180° eastward and 180° westward from the prime meridian.

With these coordinates, there are sixty minutes in one degree, and historically one minute of latitude is equal to one nautical mile. The nautical mile (1,852 meters or 1.1508 statute miles) is the standard unit of measurement for ocean-going navigation. When using nautical miles for measuring distances, speed is expressed in knots (nautical miles per hour).

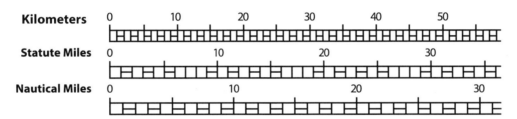

Figure 5.9. Distance Conversion

There are several terms used for directions. A *course* is the direction of travel from one point to another, either planned or actual. The *heading* is the direction the bow of the ship is facing. Due to current and winds, the heading is not always the same value as the course. A *bearing*, meanwhile, is not a direction of movement but rather is the direction one object or point is from another.

Mercator charts show north at the top of the surface of the chart with at least one compass rose for directions, measured from 0° clockwise to 359° (while a circle has 360°, the value of 360° is zero again: due north). On Mercator charts, meridians (lines from the North Pole to the South Pole connecting the same longitude) are always 0° or 180°, depending on the direction. They will be at the top and bottom on the surface of the chart.

The compass rose gives both true direction (outer circle) and magnetic (inner), with notations for magnetic variation depending on the location. When using magnetic direction, deviation (based on the magnetic field of the ship itself and changing with the ship's heading) should be accounted for in addition to the magnetic variation. When bearings are determined, they are either true (0° = true north), magnetic (0° = magnetic north), or relative (0° = the bow of the ship).

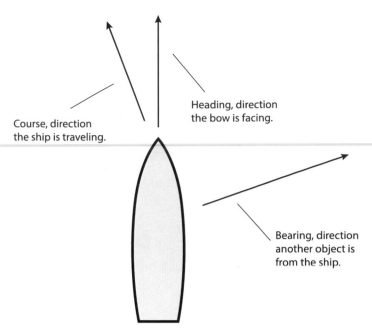

Figure 5.10. Heading, Course, and Bearing

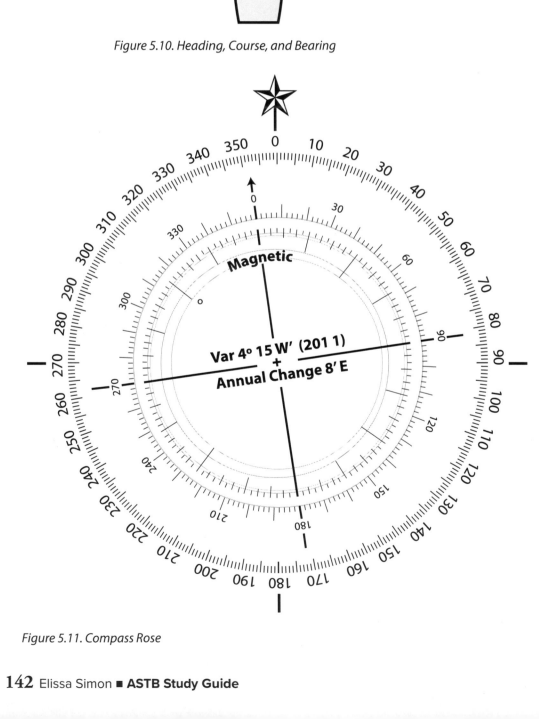

Figure 5.11. Compass Rose

Knowing the water depth (vertical distance from the water surface to the seafloor) helps determine the vertical distance between the seafloor and the lowest point on the vessel to prevent grounding of the ship. Charts have detailed and accurate depictions of coastlines that specify the sounding (water depth) and datum (starting or reference point) to which water depths refer. The chart specifies the unit of measurement for water depths. One example of measurement is fathoms and feet, a fathom being equal to six feet. Thus on such a chart is 6 fathoms and 2 feet, or 38 feet. Due to tidal action, the water level is not static. By knowing the tidal condition, or vertical distance that the water level is above or below that same datum, the actual water depth at any given time can be determined.

 Always account for the charted depth, the tide, your ship's draft at its deepest point, any underwater appendages, and a safety factor to keep from running aground.

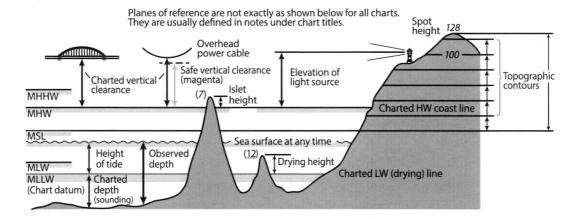

Figure 5.12 Water Depth on a Chart

Lateral aids to navigation indicate what side of the ship a buoy should be on. In the United States, the term *red, right, returning* is a good way to remember that red-colored buoys or other aids should be on the right (starboard) side of the ship when returning from sea. Other aids to navigation indicate safe water, isolated danger markers, and preferred channel markers. Each type is at a specified point on the chart and has distinct colors, shapes, and light characteristics if lit. While providing useful information, it should never be assumed that a buoy will be in the charted location.

 When returning from the sea to a harbor in the United States, keep the red to your right (starboard) so you remain in the channel.

Example

The ship's course is

(A) the direction the bow is facing.

(B) the direction an object is from the ship.

(C) the direction of travel.

(D) measured in knots.

Answer:

(C) is correct. A *course* is the direction of travel from one point to another.

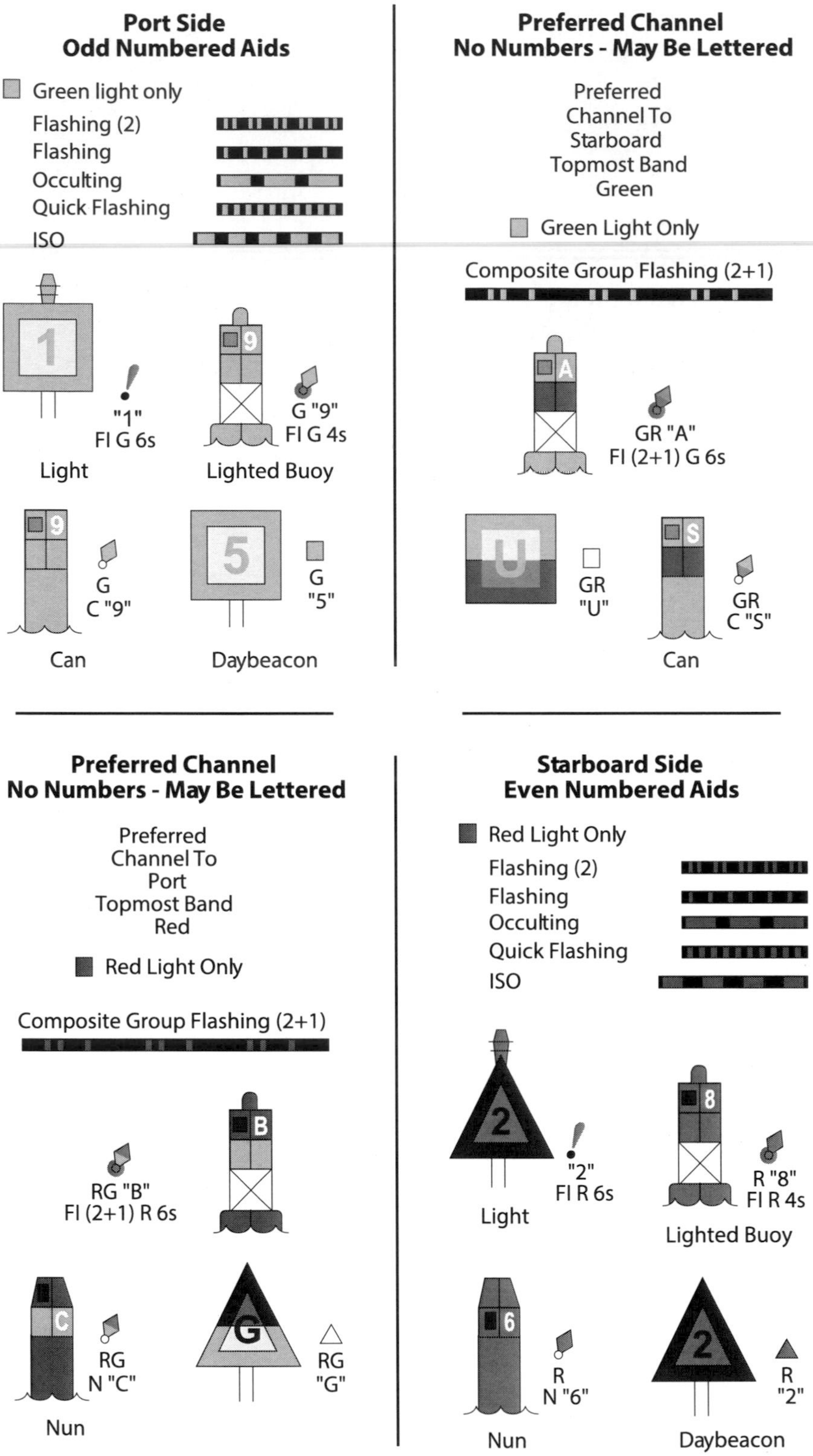

Port Side
Odd Numbered Aids

☐ Green light only

Flashing (2)
Flashing
Occulting
Quick Flashing
ISO

"1"
Fl G 6s
Light

G "9"
Fl G 4s
Lighted Buoy

G
C "9"
Can

G
"5"
Daybeacon

Preferred Channel
No Numbers - May Be Lettered

Preferred
Channel To
Starboard
Topmost Band
Green

☐ Green Light Only

Composite Group Flashing (2+1)

GR "A"
Fl (2+1) G 6s

GR
"U"

GR
C "S"
Can

Preferred Channel
No Numbers - May Be Lettered

Preferred
Channel To
Port
Topmost Band
Red

■ Red Light Only

Composite Group Flashing (2+1)

RG "B"
Fl (2+1) R 6s

RG
N "C"
Nun

RG
"G"

Starboard Side
Even Numbered Aids

■ Red Light Only

Flashing (2)
Flashing
Occulting
Quick Flashing
ISO

"2"
Fl R 6s
Light

R "8"
Fl R 4s
Lighted Buoy

R
N "6"
Nun

R
"2"
Daybeacon

Figure 5.13. Lateral Aids to Navigation

6

NAVAL AVIATION TRAIT FACET INVENTORY

The Naval Aviation Trait Facet Inventory (NATFI) is a personality test used by the military to predict an individual's success at various stages throughout his or her career in the navy. The test includes a series of paired statements that describe common situations, feelings, and behaviors. Candidates must choose which of the paired statements most accurately describes them.

Becoming a US Navy pilot requires a strong sense of motivation, confidence, self-control, persistence, and focus. The NATFI helps the military identify candidates who possess these qualities. Generally, these inventories concentrate on the Big Five personality traits: extraversion, agreeableness, conscientiousness, neuroticism, and openness to experience. A potential pilot must have a balanced portion of each trait to successfully navigate the stress, expectations, and training involved in becoming a navy pilot.

The NATFI consists of eighty-eight paired statements. Each pair of statements contains either a set of flattering or a set of unflattering descriptions. Candidates must pick which statement best applies to them. With each response, candidates establish a pattern of described behavior that will help determine their "fit" within the navy.

There are no right or wrong answers, so there is no need to waste time deciding what the answer should be. Some of the statements are unflattering or critical, so it might be uncomfortable to select one. That is okay—it is best to answer as honestly as possible. Candidates should also keep in mind that the chosen answers are not meant to be statements of fact: they don't have to select an answer that is necessarily a true statement about themselves, just the one that most generally applies to them.

Examples

1.

(A) I am confident in my abilities.

(B) I find it easy to create new ideas.

2.

(A) I let my temper get the best of me sometimes.

(B) Sometimes I say or do things to see how people react.

3.

A. I believe that people cannot be trusted.

B. People who act like my friends have betrayed me.

4.

A. I often hesitate to make choices in difficult situations.

B. I consider myself a follower rather than a leader.

5.

A. I am almost always on time.

B. I consider myself a leader.

7

PERFORMANCE BASED MEASURES BATTERY

OVERVIEW OF THE PBMB

The PBMB is a hands-on, interactive, web-based subtest of the **AVIATION SELECTION TEST BATTERY (ASTB)**. It is administered on the **AUTOMATED PILOT EXAMINATION (APEX) NETWORK**. Results from the ASTB—the PBMB, in particular—determine a candidate's eligibility for attendance in US Navy flight school. The PBMB is unique in that it assesses abilities in the specialized tasks required of an aviator, such as spatial orientation, physical dexterity, multitask management, and dichotic listening, and it measures decision-making capacity in a timed environment. A candidate utilizes a computer equipped with flight simulator software, a throttle control, and a joystick to respond to directions received through a headset. Responses directly replicate how an aircraft would react under certain situations.

The PBMB consists of seven subtests, given in the following order:
- Directional Orientation Test (DOT)
- Dichotic Listening Test (DLT)
- Vertical Tracking Test (VTT)
- Airplane Tracking Test (ATT)
- Airplane Tracking Test/Vertical Tracking Test (ATT/VTT)
- Multi-Tracking Test (MTT)
- Emergency Scenario Test (EST)

BREAKDOWN OF PBMB SUBTESTS

Directional Orientation Test (DOT)

In each of the forty-eight timed questions, or trials, in this subtest, the computer screen displays two images. The Tracker Map image shows an aircraft's orientation over a background map. The Camera View image shows the perspective of a camera mounted to that aircraft. A building is in the center of the Camera View image, which represents where the aircraft is located on the Tracker Map, and the building is surrounded by four parking lots:

north, south, east, and west. The candidate receives instructions through the headset to identify one of the parking lots (e.g., "Select the north parking lot"). To input an answer, the candidate hovers the cursor over the correct parking lot and squeezes the joystick trigger.

The candidate is evaluated by the number of correct answers and by the amount of time he or she takes to respond.

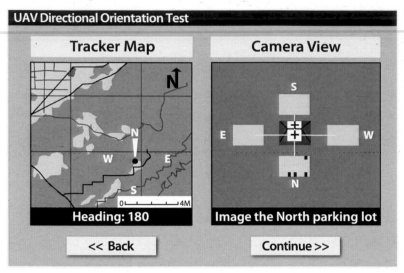

Figure 7.1. DOT Computer Display

Dichotic Listening Test (DLT)

This subtest measures aural cognition and attentiveness by evaluating a candidate's ability to differentiate audio cues and execute tasks based on those cues. Directions are provided at the beginning of the test to inform the candidate where to focus his or her attention.

Turning your target ear toward the computer may aid in concentrating on letters and numbers heard in the headset.

Through the headset, a candidate is presented with audio cues consisting of sixteen-character alphanumeric strings. The candidate must listen for odd or even numbers broadcasted through the headset to the target ear. Once the candidate hears a specific number in the target ear, he or she is instructed to correlate the audio cue by pressing either the throttle (for an odd number) or the joystick (for an even number). If the candidate presses more than one response, only the first response is recorded.

Odd and even numbers also may be broadcasted to the non-target ear, in which case if the candidate presses the throttle or the joystick, it counts as an incorrect answer. The candidate must listen to the correct target ear and ignore any simultaneous verbal sounds in the non-target ear.

The two-minute DLT, presented in four thirty-second increments, includes a total of forty alphanumeric character strings. As in the DOT, the candidate is evaluated by the number of correct answers and by the amount of time he or she takes to respond.

Vertical Tracking Test (VTT)

This one-minute subtest gauges a candidate's ability to track a yellow moving target—an airplane—as it moves vertically. The candidate moves the throttle up or down to keep the crosshair on the moving airplane. When the airplane moves toward the top of the screen, the throttle should be pulled up. When the airplane moves toward the bottom of the screen, the throttle should be pulled down. The crosshair turns green when it is locked on the airplane and red when it is not locked on the airplane. After being locked on for a brief moment, the target changes course. Also, as the test continues, the target's speed accelerates.

Scoring is based on both correct and incorrect average distances between the crosshair and the moving airplane throughout the test and the number of times the aircraft changes course (the crosshair remains on top of the aircraft for a preprogrammed amount of time). Candidates have the opportunity of a thirty-second practice session prior to the official subtest.

Aircraft speed increases as it changes course throughout this subtest, requiring quicker response times.

Airplane Tracking Test (ATT)

This subtest is identical to the VTT, except it gauges a candidate's ability to track an airplane in a two-dimensional environment. The candidate moves the joystick up, down, left, or right to keep the crosshair centered on the target.

Scoring for this one-minute subtest is similar to the scoring for the VTT. Candidates again have the opportunity of a thirty-second practice session prior to the official subtest.

Airplane Tracking Test/Vertical Tracking Test (ATT/VTT)

This two-minute subtest, presented in three forty-second increments, is a combination of the ATT and VTT. The candidate must track the vertical movement of the airplane on the left side of the screen, using the throttle in the left hand, and the freely moving airplane on the right side of the screen, using the joystick in the right hand.

The ATT/VTT and remaining subtests utilize the skills required in the previous subtests.

Scoring is based on the candidate's ability to perform these tasks simultaneously. Once more, candidates have the opportunity of a thirty-second practice session prior to the official subtest.

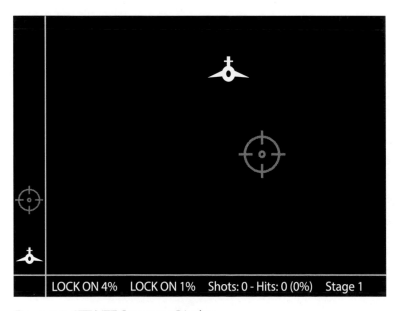

Figure 7.2. ATT/VTT Computer Display

Multi-Tracking Test (MTT)

This subtest is a combination of the DLT, ATT, and VTT, but in the dichotic listening portion of the test, the candidate should maneuver the trigger on the joystick and the RDR cursor button on the throttle when reacting to the audible numbers heard through the headset. In this three-minute test, presented in sixty-second increments, the candidate must attend to all tasks equally.

Scoring is based on the target accuracy with both vertical and freely moving airplanes, the number of redirects, and the accuracy and speed of aural responses.

Emergency Scenario Test (EST)

The **EST** evaluates a candidate's ability to recall emergency corrective actions and respond within an acceptable amount of time (twenty seconds of emergency notification). At the beginning of this subtest, the candidate is provided with written corrective instructions to perform when an emergency exists. The candidate must read the detailed instructions and memorize the associated responses for each emergency scenario. The scenarios included are fuel flow, engine power, and propeller position faults.

This three-minute subtest, presented in sixty-second increments, is a culmination of all previous subtests, measuring cognitive ability, capacity to manage stressful situations, spatial ability, multitasking skills, and dexterity levels.

PREPARING FOR THE PBMB

The best way to prepare for the PBMB is to practice using flight simulator software on a computer with a throttle and joystick set. This will help sharpen multitasking abilities. A candidate should also practice transcribing data using headphones, which helps hone listening skills and teaches how to concentrate on specific sounds—such as letters, words, and numbers—using one ear. Additionally, practicing hand and finger exercises improves dexterity. Exercises that entail processing information from mental images are helpful as well. They include mentally rotating three-dimensional shapes and pressing a key when certain shapes appear on the screen.

PRACTICE TEST

MATH SKILLS

40 minutes

This section measures your knowledge of mathematical terms and principles. Each question is followed by four possible answers. You are to decide which one of the four choices is correct.

1. Simplify: $-(3^2) + (5 - 7)^2 - 3(4 - 8)$

    (A) −17

    (B) −1

    (C) 7

    (D) 25

2. If a person reads 40 pages in 45 minutes, approximately how many minutes will it take her to read 265 pages?

    (A) 202

    (B) 236

    (C) 265

    (D) 298

3. W, X, Y, and Z lie on a circle with center A. If the diameter of the circle is 75, what is the sum of $\overline{AW}$, $\overline{AX}$, $\overline{AY}$, and $\overline{AZ}$?

    (A) 75

    (B) 300

    (C) 150

    (D) 106.5

4. A worker was paid $15,036 for 7 months of work. If he received the same amount each month, how much was he paid for the first 2 months?

    (A) $2,148

    (B) $4,296

    (C) $6,444

    (D) $8,592

5. 40% of what number is equal to 17?

    (A) 2.35

    (B) 6.8

    (C) 42.5

    (D) 680

6. The measures of two angles of a triangle are 25° and 110°. What is the measure of the third angle?

    (A) 40°

    (B) 45°

    (C) 50°

    (D) 55°

7. Michael is making cupcakes. He plans to give $\frac{1}{2}$ of the cupcakes to a friend and $\frac{1}{3}$ of the cupcakes to his coworkers. If he makes 48 cupcakes, how many will he have left over?

(A) 8

(B) 10

(C) 16

(D) 24

8. Which of the following is closest in value to 129,113 + 34,602?

(A) 162,000

(B) 163,000

(C) 164,000

(D) 165,000

9. If $j = 4$, what is the value of $2(j - 4)^4 - j + \frac{1}{2}j$?

(A) 0

(B) −2

(C) 2

(D) 4

10. Which of the following is equivalent to $(5^2 - 2)^2 + 3^3$?

(A) 25

(B) 30

(C) 556

(D) 538

11. In the fall, 425 students pass the math benchmark. In the spring, 680 students pass the same benchmark. What is the percentage increase in passing scores from fall to spring?

(A) 37.5%

(B) 55%

(C) 60%

(D) 62.5%

12. What is the area of the shape?

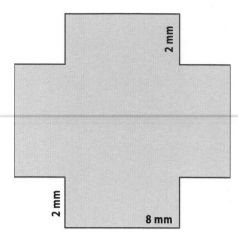

(A) 6 mm²

(B) 16 mm²

(C) 64 mm²

(D) 128 mm²

13. A fruit stand sells apples, bananas, and oranges at a ratio of 3:2:1. If the fruit stand sells 20 bananas, how many total pieces of fruit does the fruit stand sell?

(A) 10

(B) 30

(C) 40

(D) 60

14. Erica is at work for $8\frac{1}{2}$ hours a day. If she takes one 30-minute lunch break and two 15-minute breaks during the day, how many hours does she work?

(A) 6 hours, 30 minutes

(B) 6 hours, 45 minutes

(C) 7 hours, 15 minutes

(D) 7 hours, 30 minutes

15. If the value of y is between 0.0047 and 0.0162, which of the following could be the value of y?

(A) 0.0035

(B) 0.0055

(C) 0.0185

(D) 0.0238

16. A car traveled at 65 miles per hour for $1\frac{1}{2}$ hours and then traveled at 50 miles per hour for $2\frac{1}{2}$ hours. How many miles did the car travel?

    (A) 190.5 miles

    (B) 215.0 miles

    (C) 222.5 miles

    (D) 237.5 miles

17. A bike store is having a 30%-off sale, and one of the bikes is on sale for $385. What was the original price of this bike?

    (A) $253.00

    (B) $450.00

    (C) $500.50

    (D) $550.00

18. Adam is painting the outside walls of a 4-walled shed. The shed is 5 feet wide, 4 feet deep, and 7 feet high. How many square feet of paint will Adam need?

    (A) 46 square feet

    (B) 63 square feet

    (C) 126 square feet

    (D) 140 square feet

19. A grocery store sold 30% of its pears and had 455 pears remaining. How many pears did the grocery store start with?

    (A) 602

    (B) 650

    (C) 692

    (D) 700

20. A landscaping company charges 5 cents per square foot for fertilizer. How much would they charge to fertilize a 30-foot-by-50-foot lawn?

    (A) $7.50

    (B) $15.00

    (C) $75.00

    (D) $150.00

21. What is the value of the expression $0.5^x + 1$ when $x = -2$?

    (A) 0.75

    (B) 1.25

    (C) 4

    (D) 5

22. John and Ethan are working at a car wash. It takes John 1 hour to wash 3 cars. Ethan can wash 3 cars in 45 minutes. If they work together, how many cars can they wash in 1 hour?

    (A) 6

    (B) 7

    (C) 9

    (D) 12

23. Tiles are $12.51 per square yard. What will it cost to cover the floor of a room with tiles if the room is 10 feet wide and 12 feet long?

    (A) $166.80

    (B) $178.70

    (C) $184.60

    (D) $190.90

24. How many digits are in the sum $951.4 + 98.908 + 1.053$?

    (A) 4

    (B) 5

    (C) 6

    (D) 7

25. Melissa is ordering fencing to enclose a square area of 5,625 square feet. How many feet of fencing does she need?

    (A) 75 feet

    (B) 150 feet

    (C) 300 feet

    (D) 5,625 feet

READING SKILLS

30 minutes

This section measures your ability to read and understand written material. Passages are followed by a series of multiple-choice questions. You are to choose the option that best answers the question based on the passage. No additional information or specific knowledge is needed.

The Battle of Little Bighorn, commonly called Custer's Last Stand, was a battle between the Lakota, the Northern Cheyenne, the Arapaho, and the Seventh Calvary Regiment of the US Army. Led by war leaders Crazy Horse and Chief Gall and the religious leader Sitting Bull, the allied tribes of the Plains Indians decisively defeated their US foes. Two hundred and sixty-eight US soldiers were killed, including General George Armstrong Custer, two of his brothers, his nephew, his brother-in-law, and six Indian scouts.

1. What is the main idea of this passage?
    (A) Most of General Custer's family died in the Battle of Little Bighorn.
    (B) The Seventh Calvary regiment was formed to fight Native American tribes.
    (C) Sitting Bull and George Custer were fierce enemies.
    (D) The Battle of Little Bighorn was a significant victory for the Plains Indians.

In 1953, doctors surgically removed the hippocampus of patient Henry Molaison in an attempt to stop his frequent seizures. Unexpectedly, he lost the ability to form new memories, leading to the biggest breakthrough in the science of memory. Molaison's long-term memory—of events more than a year before his surgery—was unchanged as was his ability to learn physical skills. From this, scientists learned that different types of memory are handled by different parts of the brain, with the hippocampus responsible for *episodic memory,* the short-term recall of events. They have since discovered that some memories are then channeled to the cortex, the outer layers of the brain that handle higher functions, where they are gradually integrated with related information to build lasting knowledge about our world.

2. The main idea of the passage is that
    (A) Molaison's surgery posed significant risk to the functioning of his brain.
    (B) short-term and long-term memory are stored in different parts of the brain.
    (C) long-term memory forms over a longer period than short-term memory.
    (D) memories of physical skills are processed differently than memories of events.

Archaeologists have discovered the oldest known specimens of bedbugs in a cave in Oregon where humans once lived. The three different species date back to between 5,000 and 11,000 years ago. The finding gives scientists a clue as to how bedbugs became human parasites. These bedbugs, like those that plague humans today, originated as bat parasites. Scientists hypothesize that it was the co-habitation of humans and bats in the caves that encouraged the bugs to begin feeding on the humans. The three species found in the Oregon caves are actually still around today, although they continue to prefer bats. Humans only lived seasonally in the Oregon cave system, however, which might explain why these insects did not fully transfer to human hosts like bedbugs elsewhere did.

3. With which of the following claims about bedbugs would the author most likely agree?

(A) Modern bedbugs that prefer humans thrive better in areas with extensive light.

(B) Bedbugs are a relatively fragile species that has struggled to survive over time.

(C) The transition to humans significantly accelerated the growth of bedbug populations.

(D) Bedbugs that prefer humans originated in caves that humans occupied year-round.

The Bastille, Paris's famous historical prison, was originally built in 1370 as a fortification, called a *bastide* in Old French, to protect the city from English invasion during the Hundred Years' War. It rose 100 feet into the air, had eight towers, and was surrounded by a moat more than eighty feet wide. In the seventeenth century, the government converted the fortress into an elite prison for upper-class felons, political disruptors, and spies. Residents of the Bastille arrived by direct order of the king and usually were left there to languish without a trial.

4. In the first sentence, the word *fortification* most nearly means

(A) royal castle.

(B) national symbol.

(C) seat of government.

(D) defensive structure.

Taking a person's temperature is one of the most basic and common health care tasks. Everyone from nurses to emergency medical technicians to concerned parents should be able to grab a thermometer to take a patient or loved one's temperature. But what's the best way to get an accurate reading? The answer depends on the situation.

The most common way people measure body temperature is orally. A simple digital or disposable thermometer is placed under the tongue for a few minutes, and the task is done. There are many situations, however, when measuring temperature orally isn't an option. For example, when a person can't breathe through his nose, he won't be able to keep his mouth closed long enough to get an accurate reading. In these situations, it's often preferable to place the thermometer in the rectum or armpit. Using the rectum also has the added benefit of providing a much more accurate reading than other locations can provide.

It's also often the case that certain people, like agitated patients or fussy babies, won't be able to sit still long enough for an accurate reading. In these situations, it's best to use a thermometer that works much more quickly, such as one that measures temperature in the ear or at the temporal artery. No matter which method is chosen, however, it's important to check the average temperature for each region, as it can vary by several degrees.

5. Which statement is NOT a detail from the passage?

(A) Taking a temperature in the ear or at the temporal artery is more accurate than taking it orally.

(B) If an individual cannot breathe through the nose, taking his or her temperature orally will likely give an inaccurate reading.

(C) The standard human body temperature varies depending on whether it's measured in the mouth, rectum, armpit, ear, or temporal artery.

(D) The most common way to measure temperature is by placing a thermometer in the mouth.

6. What is the author's primary purpose in writing this essay?

   (A) to advocate for the use of thermometers that measure temperature in the ear or at the temporal artery

   (B) to explain the methods available to measure a person's temperature and the situation where each method is appropriate

   (C) to warn readers that the average temperature of the human body varies by region

   (D) to discuss how nurses use different types of thermometers depending on the type of patient they are examining

7. What is the meaning of the word *agitated* in the last paragraph?

   (A) obviously upset

   (B) quickly moving

   (C) violently ill

   (D) slightly dirty

8. According to the passage, why is it sometimes preferable to take a person's temperature rectally?

   (A) Rectal readings are more accurate than oral readings.

   (B) Many people cannot sit still long enough to have their temperatures taken orally.

   (C) Temperature readings can vary widely between regions of the body.

   (D) Many people do not have access to quick-acting thermometers.

One of the most dramatic acts of nonviolent resistance in India's movement for independence from Britain came in 1930, when independence leader Mahatma Gandhi organized a 240-mile march to the Arabian Sea. The goal of the march was to make salt from seawater, in defiance of British law. The British prohibited Indians from collecting or selling salt—a vital part of the Indian diet—requiring them instead to buy it from British merchants and pay a heavy salt tax. The crowd of marchers grew along the way to tens of thousands of people. In Dandi, Gandhi picked up a small chunk of salt and broke British law. Thousands in Dandi followed his lead as did millions of fellow protestors in coastal towns throughout India. In an attempt to quell the civil disobedience, authorities arrested more than 60,000 people across the country, including Gandhi himself.

9. With which of the following claims about civil disobedience would the author most likely agree?

   (A) Civil disobedience is a disorganized form of protest easily quashed by government.

   (B) Civil disobedience requires extreme violations of existing law to be effective.

   (C) Civil disobedience is an effective strategy for effecting political change.

   (D) Civil disobedience is only effective in countries that already have democracy.

The odds of success for any new restaurant are slim. Competition in the city is fierce, and the low margin of return means that aspiring restaurateurs must be exact and ruthless with their budget and pricing. The fact that The City Café has lasted as long as it has is a testament to its owners' skills.

10. Which of the following conclusions is well supported by the passage?
    (A) The City Café offers the best casual dining in town.
    (B) The City Café has a well-managed budget and prices items on its menu appropriately.
    (C) The popularity of The City Café will likely fall as new restaurants open in the city.
    (D) The City Café has a larger margin of return than other restaurants in the city.

11. Which of the following is the meaning of *testament* as used in the sentence?
    (A) story
    (B) surprise
    (C) artifact
    (D) evidence

We've been told for years that the recipe for weight loss is fewer calories in than calories out. In other words, eat less and exercise more, and your body will take care of the rest. As many of those who've tried to diet can attest, this edict doesn't always produce results. If you're one of those folks, you might have felt that you just weren't doing it right—that the failure was all your fault.

However, several new studies released this year have suggested that it might not be your fault at all. For example, a study of people who'd lost a high percentage of their body weight (>17%) in a short period of time found that they could not physically maintain their new weight. Scientists measured their resting metabolic rate and found that they'd need to consume only a few hundred calories a day to meet their metabolic needs. Basically, their bodies were in starvation mode and seemed to desperately hang on to each and every calorie. Eating even a single healthy, well-balanced meal a day would cause these subjects to start packing back on the pounds.

Other studies have shown that factors like intestinal bacteria, distribution of body fat, and hormone levels can affect the manner in which our bodies process calories. There's also the fact that it's actually quite difficult to measure the number of calories consumed during a particular meal and the number used while exercising.

12. Which of the following would be the best summary statement to conclude the passage?
    (A) It turns out that conventional dieting wisdom doesn't capture the whole picture of how our bodies function.
    (B) Still, counting calories and tracking exercise is a good idea if you want to lose weight.
    (C) In conclusion, it's important to lose weight responsibly: losing too much weight at once can negatively impact the body.
    (D) It's easy to see that diets don't work, so we should focus less on weight loss and more on overall health.

13. Which of the following would weaken the author's argument?

   (A) a new diet pill from a pharmaceutical company that promises to help patients lose weight by changing intestinal bacteria

   (B) the personal experience of a man who was able to lose a significant amount of weight by taking in fewer calories than he used

   (C) a study showing that people in different geographic locations lose different amounts of weight when on the same diet

   (D) a study showing that people often misreport their food intake when part of a scientific study on weight loss

When a fire destroyed San Francisco's American Indian Center in October of 1969, American Indian groups set their sights on the recently closed island prison of Alcatraz as a site of a new Indian cultural center and school. Ignored by the government, an activist group known as Indians of All Tribes sailed to Alcatraz in the early morning hours with eighty-nine men, women, and children. They landed on Alcatraz, claiming it for all the tribes of North America. Their demands were ignored, and so the group continued to occupy the island for the next nineteen months, its numbers swelling up to 600 as others joined. By January of 1970, many of the original protestors had left, and on June 11, 1971 federal marshals forcibly removed the last residents.

14. The main idea of this passage is that

   (A) the government refused to listen to the demands of American Indians.

   (B) American Indians occupied Alcatraz in protest of government policy.

   (C) few people joined the occupation of Alcatraz, weakening its effectiveness.

   (D) the government took violent action against protestors at Alcatraz.

In an effort to increase women's presence in government, several countries in Latin America, including Argentina, Brazil, and Mexico, have implemented legislated candidate quotas. These quotas require that at least 30 percent of a party's candidate list in any election cycle consists of women who have a legitimate chance at election. As a result, Latin America has the greatest number of female heads of government in the world, and the second highest percentage of female members of parliament after Nordic Europe. However, these trends do not carry over outside of politics. While 25 percent of legislators in Latin America are now women, less than 2 percent of CEOs in the region are female.

15. What is the main idea of the passage?

   (A) In Latin America, political parties must nominate women for office.

   (B) Latin America is the region with the greatest gender equality.

   (C) Women in Latin America have greater economic influence than political influence.

   (D) Women have a significant presence in Latin American politics.

Tourists flock to Yellowstone National Park each year to view the geysers that bubble and erupt throughout it. What most of these tourists do not know is that these geysers are formed by a caldera, a hot crater in the earth's crust, that was created by a series of three eruptions of an ancient supervolcano. These eruptions, which began 2.1 million years ago, spewed between 1,000 to 2,450 cubic kilometers of volcanic matter at such a rate that the volcano's magma chamber collapsed, creating the craters.

16. The main idea of the passage is that
    (A) Yellowstone National Park is a popular tourist destination.
    (B) The geysers in Yellowstone National Park rest on a caldera in the earth's crust.
    (C) A supervolcano once sat in the area covered by Yellowstone National Park.
    (D) The earth's crust is weaker in Yellowstone National Park.

When the Spanish-American War broke out in 1898, the US Army was small and understaffed. President William McKinley called for 1,250 volunteers primarily from the Southwest to serve in the First US Volunteer Calvary. Eager to fight, the ranks were quickly filled by a diverse group of cowboys, gold prospectors, hunters, gamblers, Native Americans, veterans, police officers, and college students looking for an adventure. The officer corps was composed of veterans of the Civil War and the Indian Wars. With more volunteers than it could accept, the army set high standards: all the recruits had to be skilled on horseback and with guns. Consequently, they became known as the Rough Riders.

17. According to the passage, all the recruits were required to
    (A) have previously fought in a war.
    (B) be American citizens.
    (C) live in the Southwest.
    (D) ride a horse well.

At first glance, the landscape of the northern end of the Rift Valley appears to be a stretch of barren land. Paleoanthropologists, however, have discovered an abundance of fossils just beneath the dusty surface. They believe this area once contained open grasslands near lakes and rivers, populated with grazing animals. Forty miles from this spot, in 1974, scientists uncovered a 3.2 million-year-old non-human hominid they nicknamed "Lucy." And, in 2013, researchers found the oldest fossil in the human ancestral line. Before this, the oldest fossil from the genus *Homo*—of which *Homo sapiens* are the only remaining species—dated only back to 2.3 million years ago, leaving a 700,000 gap between Lucy's species and the advent of humans. The new fossil dated back to 2.75 and 2.8 million years ago, pushing the appearance of humans back 400,000 years.

18. According to the passage, the discovery of Lucy
    (A) gave scientists new information about the development of humans.
    (B) provided evidence of a different ecosystem in the ancient Rift Valley.
    (C) supported the belief that other hominids existed significantly before humans.
    (D) closed the gap between the development of other hominids and humans.

→

CONTINUE

The social and political discourse of America continues to be permeated with idealism. An idealistic viewpoint asserts that the ideals of freedom, equality, justice, and human dignity are the truths that Americans must continue to aspire to. Idealists argue that truth is what should be, not necessarily what is. In general, they work to improve things and to make them as close to ideal as possible.

19.   Which of the following best captures the author's purpose?

   (A) to advocate for freedom, equality, justice, and human rights

   (B) to explain what an idealist believes in

   (C) to explain what's wrong with social and political discourse in America

   (D) to persuade readers to believe in certain truths

Alexander Hamilton and James Madison called for the Constitutional Convention to write a constitution as the foundation of a stronger federal government. Madison and other Federalists like John Adams believed in separation of powers, republicanism, and a strong federal government. Despite the separation of powers that would be provided for in the US Constitution, anti-Federalists like Thomas Jefferson called for even more limitations on the power of the federal government.

20.   In the context of the passage below, which of the following would most likely NOT support a strong federal government?

   (A) Alexander Hamilton

   (B) James Madison

   (C) John Adams

   (D) Thomas Jefferson

The cisco, a foot-long freshwater fish native to the Great Lakes, once thrived throughout the basin but had virtually disappeared by the 1950s. However, today fishermen are pulling them up by the net-load in Lake Michigan and Lake Ontario. It is highly unusual for a native species to revive, and the reason for the cisco's reemergence is even more unlikely. The cisco have an invasive species, quagga mussels, to thank for their return. Quagga mussels depleted nutrients in the lakes, harming other species highly dependent on these nutrients. Cisco, however, thrive in low-nutrient environments. As other species—many invasive—diminished, cisco flourished in their place.

21.   It can be inferred from the passage that most invasive species

   (A) support the growth of native species.

   (B) do not impact the development of native species.

   (C) struggle to survive in their new environments.

   (D) cause the decline of native species.

After looking at five houses, Robert and I have decided to buy the one on Forest Road. The first two homes we visited didn't have the space we need—the first had only one bathroom, and the second did not have a guest bedroom. The third house, on Pine Street, had enough space inside but didn't have a big enough yard for our three dogs. The fourth house we looked at, on Rice Avenue, was stunning but well above our price range. The last home, on Forest Road, wasn't in the neighborhood we wanted to live in. However, it had the right amount of space for the right price.

22. What is the author's conclusion about the house on Pine Street?

   (A) The house did not have enough bedrooms.

   (B) The house did not have a big enough yard.

   (C) The house was not in the right neighborhood.

   (D) The house was too expensive.

It could be said that the great battle between the North and South we call the Civil War was a battle for individual identity. The states of the South had their own culture, one based on farming, independence, and the rights of both man and state to determine their own paths. Similarly, the North had forged its own identity as a center of centralized commerce and manufacturing. This clash of lifestyles was bound to create tension, and this tension was bound to lead to war. But people who try to sell you this narrative are wrong. The Civil War was not a battle of cultural identities—it was a battle about slavery. All other explanations for the war are either a direct consequence of the South's desire for wealth at the expense of her fellow man or a fanciful invention to cover up this sad portion of our nation's history. And it cannot be denied that this time in our past was very sad indeed.

23. What is the meaning of the word *fanciful* in the passage?

   (A) complicated

   (B) imaginative

   (C) successful

   (D) unfortunate

24. What is the author's primary purpose in writing this essay?

   (A) to convince readers that slavery was the main cause of the Civil War

   (B) to illustrate the cultural differences between the North and the South before the Civil War

   (C) to persuade readers that the North deserved to win the Civil War

   (D) to demonstrate that the history of the Civil War is too complicated to be understood clearly

The greatest changes in sensory, motor, and perceptual development happen in the first two years of life. When babies are first born, most of their senses operate in a similar way to those of adults. For example, babies are able to hear before they are born; studies show that babies turn toward the sound of their mothers' voices just minutes after being born, indicating they recognize the mother's voice from their time in the womb.

The exception to this rule is vision. A baby's vision changes significantly in its first year of life; initially it has a range of vision of only 8 – 12 inches and no depth perception. As a result, infants rely primarily on hearing; vision does not become the dominant sense until around the age of 12 months. Babies also prefer faces to other objects. This preference, along with their limited vision range, means that their sight is initially focused on their caregiver.

25. Which of the following senses do babies primarily rely on?

   (A) vision

   (B) hearing

   (C) touch

   (D) smell

MECHANICAL COMPREHENSION

15 minutes

This section measures your understanding of basic mechanical principles. Each question is followed by three possible answers. You are to decide which one of the three choices is correct.

1.

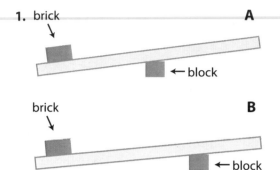

Compared to figure A above, the brick in figure B will

(A) be lifted the same height, and it will take the same amount of effort to do so.

(B) be lifted higher, and it will take more effort to do so.

(C) not be lifted as high, and it will take more effort to do so.

2. Because a crowbar has a fulcrum in the middle of the effort and the resistance, it is an example of a

(A) first-class lever.

(B) second-class lever.

(C) third-class lever.

3.

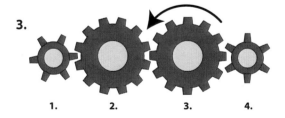

Which of the other gears is moving in the same direction as Gear 3?

(A) Gear 1 only

(B) Gear 2 only

(C) Gear 4 only

4.

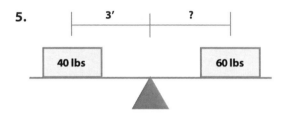

If Pulley B is the driver and turns clockwise, which pulley turns the slowest?

(A) Pulley A turns the slowest.

(B) Pulley C turns the slowest.

(C) Pulley D turns the slowest.

5.

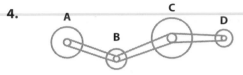

A 40-pound block and a 60-pound block are placed on a uniform board as shown above. How far to the right of the fulcrum must the 60-pound block be placed in order for the board to be balanced?

(A) 1 foot

(B) 2 feet

(C) 4 feet

6.

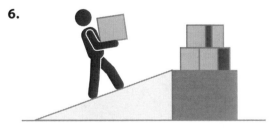

The simple machine shown above is an example of

(A) a lever.

(B) a pulley.

(C) an inclined plane.

7.

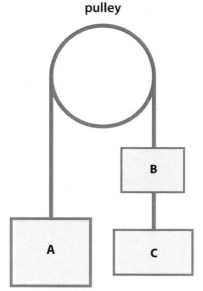

pulley

Blocks A, B, and C are hanging from a pulley as shown in the figure. If Block A weighs 70 pounds and Block B weighs 20 pounds, what must the weight of Block C be in order for the blocks to be at rest?

(A) 30 pounds

(B) 35 pounds

(C) 50 pounds

8.

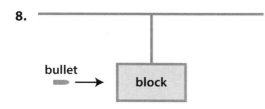

A bullet is shot at a stationary block that is hanging from the ceiling as shown. What direction will the block swing after the bullet hits the block?

(A) down and to the right

(B) down and to the left

(C) up and to the right

9. Why is it so difficult to hold a beach ball under water?

(A) The ball is full of air, which is much less dense than water.

(B) The ball expands under water, so it rises faster.

(C) The cool water will cool the air in the ball, making it rise.

10.

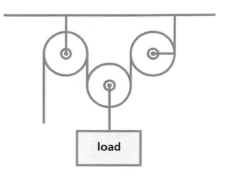

load

A block is hanging from a pulley system as shown in the figure. The theoretical mechanical advantage of the system is

(A) 1.

(B) 2.

(C) 3.

11. On Earth, Objects A and B have the same mass and weight. If Object B is moved to the moon, which of the following statements is true?

(A) Both objects have the same mass, but Object A now has the greater weight.

(B) Both objects have the same weight, but Object A now has the greater mass.

(C) Both objects still have the same mass and weight.

12.

100 lbs

An object is being carried by three people as shown above. Which person bears the most weight?

(A) A

(B) B and C

(C) All three bear the same weight.

CONTINUE

13.

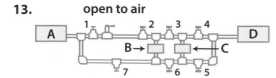

open to air

In the figure shown below, assume that all valves are closed. For the air to flow from A to D without flowing through B and C, it is necessary to open valves

(A) 1, 2, and 5.

(B) 1, 2, 3, and 4.

(C) 5, 6, and 7.

14. A steel ball with a temperature of 150°C is dropped into a liquid with a temperature of 120°C. Which of the following statements about the equilibrium temperature has to be true?

(A) The equilibrium temperature is exactly 135°C.

(B) The equilibrium temperature is between 120°C and 150°C.

(C) The equilibrium temperature is exactly 270°C.

15. Water is flowing through Pipe A, which has a diameter of 15 cm, into Pipe B, which has a diameter of 20 cm. The water will flow

(A) faster through Pipe A.

(B) faster through Pipe B.

(C) at the same speed through Pipe A and Pipe B.

16. Water flows out of a water tower at a rate of 3 gallons per minute and flows in at a rate of 140 gallons per hour. After one hour, the volume of water in the tank will be

(A) the same.

(B) 40 gallons less.

(C) 40 gallons more.

17.

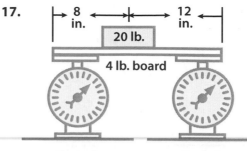

Scale A   Scale B

A weight is placed on a uniform board between two identical scales. Which of the following statements is true?

(A) Scale A will show a higher reading than Scale B because more weight is to the left of the fulcrum.

(B) Scale B will show a higher reading than Scale A because more weight is to the left of the fulcrum.

(C) The scales read the same weight.

18.

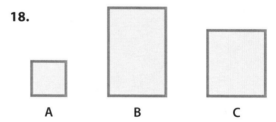

A   B   C

The three containers shown above are filled with the same gas. Which statement is true?

(A) Container A will experience the greatest pressure.

(B) Container B will experience the greatest pressure.

(C) Container C will experience the greatest pressure.

19. Two charges are held at a distance of 1 m from each other. Charge q_1 is $-2e$ and charge q_2 is $-2e$. What will happen when the charges are released and free to move?

(A) q_1 and q_2 will remain at rest and not move.

(B) q_1 and q_2 will attract and move closer together.

(C) q_1 and q_2 will repel and move farther apart.

20.

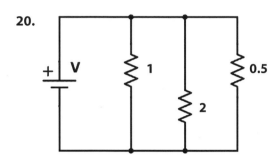

Find the equivalent resistance, R_{eq}, for the circuit in the figure above.

(A) 0.5 kΩ

(B) 1 kΩ

(C) 3.5 kΩ

21. What is the key electrical difference between a conducting material and an insulating material?

(A) A conducting material will conduct electricity, and an insulating material will not.

(B) A conducting material creates electrons, and an insulating material destroys them.

(C) An insulating material will create heat when electricity flows through it, and a conducting material will not.

24. An 80-pound object is placed on a scale inside an elevator that begins to travel upward. The scale will read that the weight of the object is

(A) 80 pounds.

(B) greater than 80 pounds.

(C) less than 80 pounds.

22. Two ropes are connected on either side of a mass of 100 kg resting on a flat surface. Each rope is pulling on the mass with 50 N of force, parallel to the ground. What can be said about the motion of the mass?

(A) The mass will accelerate to left.

(B) The mass is in equilibrium.

(C) The mass will accelerate to the right.

23.

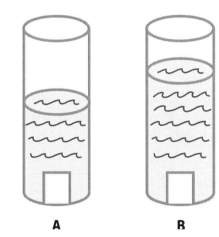

A   B

Objects A and B have the same mass and are placed in separate graduated cylinders that are each filled with 50 mL of water. If the water level rises higher in the cylinder containing Object B, which statement is true?

(A) Object A has a higher density than Object B.

(B) Object B has a higher density than Object A.

(C) Objects A and B have the same density.

25. A boat is crossing a river with a fast-moving current. If the captain aims the boat at a point of the opposite bank directly across from his starting point, where will the boat land?

(A) Downstream from his starting point

(B) Upstream from his starting point

(C) Directly across from his starting point

30 minutes

This section measures your knowledge of aviation and nautical concepts and terms. Each of the questions or incomplete statements is followed by four choices. You are to decide which one of the choices best answers the question or completes the statement.

1. When raised elevators push down on the tail of an aircraft, what effect does that have on the aircraft?

    (A) The nose of the aircraft lowers.

    (B) The nose of the aircraft rises.

    (C) The aircraft veers left.

    (D) The aircraft veers right.

2. Which aircraft component(s) affect yaw?

    (A) the ailerons

    (B) the elevators

    (C) the rudder

    (D) the spoilers

3. What part of a rotary-wing aircraft makes directional control possible?

    (A) the teeter hinge

    (B) the swashplate

    (C) the ducted fan

    (D) the tail boom

4. Which type of climb produces the most altitude in a given distance?

    (A) a best angle of climb

    (B) a best rate of climb

    (C) a normal climb

    (D) a shallow climb

5. If the cyclic or control wheel in a helicopter is moved forward

    (A) the aircraft pitch changes.

    (B) the airspeed decreases.

    (C) the airspeed increases.

    (D) the airspeed increases and the pitch changes.

6. What causes a rotary-wing aircraft to drift laterally due to tail rotor thrust?

    (A) a coaxial rotor system

    (B) translating tendency

    (C) gyroscopic precession

    (D) the tail rotor

7. If the airspeed indicator needle is in the yellow and approaching the red line during a maneuver, what would be the correct response?

    (A) change attitude by 90 degrees

    (B) decrease altitude

    (C) decrease airspeed

    (D) increase thrust

8. In aviation terminology, rate of climb is expressed as

    (A) AGL.

    (B) degrees.

    (C) fpm.

    (D) knots.

9. The lateral axis of an aircraft controls which of the following?

    (A) adverse yaw

    (B) banks

    (C) pitch

    (D) roll

10. Which component allows the rotor blades to feather?

    (A) the teeter hinge

    (B) the rotor hub

    (C) the blade grips

    (D) the skids

11. Which statement describes absolute altitude?

   (A) This is the altitude displayed on the altimeter.

   (B) This is the pressure altitude corrected for variations from standard temperature.

   (C) This is the vertical distance above MSL.

   (D) This is the vertical distance AGL.

12. Which of the following is expressed in degrees that include the area between the direction of the wind and the chord of the aircraft wing?

   (A) AOA

   (B) the artificial horizon

   (C) the lower limits of the vertical speed indicator

   (D) the pressure altitude

13. When entering and exiting Class C controlled airspace, which statement is true regarding airspace clearance?

   (A) The ATC must acknowledge the pilot by responding with the aircraft's call sign for communication to be considered established.

   (B) An ATC response of only "Standby" is enough to establish approval for entry to the controlled airspace.

   (C) No approval for clearance is needed.

   (D) Only jets flying faster than 200 mph need to request or receive approval for clearance.

14. What types of turns requires the pilot to input aileron pressure to return the aircraft to level flight?

   (A) all turns

   (B) medium and shallow turns

   (C) a shallow turn

   (D) medium and steep turns

15. If there is no increase in thrust, which action would result in an ultimate stall?

   (A) descending to a lower altitude

   (B) decreasing pitch

   (C) extending the ailerons and flaps

   (D) increasing pitch

16. What one of the acronyms for all-up weight defined as the total aircraft weight at any given moment during flight?

   (A) AGW

   (B) MLW

   (C) MRW

   (D) MTOW

17. What aerodynamic principle describes the unequal lifting forces of the rotor system due to the advancing and retreating blades?

   (A) weight, lift, thrust, and drag

   (B) translational lift

   (C) dissymmetry of lift

   (D) gyroscopic precession

18. What flight control maintains the engine within optimal flight parameters?

   (A) the cyclic

   (B) the collective

   (C) the tail rotor pedals

   (D) the throttle

24. Describe the purpose of the helm.

   (A) It controls the direction of the ship.

   (B) It stores supplies used for the crew.

   (C) It raises and lowers the anchor.

   (D) It prevents the spread of damage due to fire or flooding.

19. Which statement is true about lag and trend information?

    (A) Lag is the same as trend information.

    (B) Lag displays real-time movement of the aircraft.

    (C) Both lag and trend information display real-time movement of the aircraft.

    (D) Trend information displays real-time movement of the aircraft.

20. What is the unit of measure for airspeed?

    (A) AOA

    (B) degrees

    (C) knots

    (D) MSL

21. A ship travels 1 nautical mile in 6 minutes. What is the speed of the ship?

    (A) 10 miles per hour

    (B) 10 knots

    (C) 20 miles per hour

    (D) 5 knots

22. If you are facing the bow of a ship, which of the following is on the right-hand side?

    (A) midships

    (B) port

    (C) starboard

    (D) knuckle

23. What part of the hull is considered the backbone?

    (A) frames

    (B) rudder

    (C) longitudinal frames

    (D) keel

25. Chart soundings are in fathoms and feet, and there is a sounding of 12_4. What is the depth?

    (A) 12 feet

    (B) 36 feet

    (C) 72 feet

    (D) 76 feet

26. What part of the ship is at the water's surface?

    (A) beam

    (B) keel

    (C) waterline

    (D) draft

27. What type of ship is the largest surface combat ship currently in service?

    (A) frigate

    (B) attack submarine

    (C) cruiser

    (D) mine warfare ship

28. What item below is NOT considered an aid to navigation (ATON)?

    (A) a lighthouse on the coast

    (B) a buoy marking a river channel

    (C) a buoy marking an isolated hazard

    (D) a temporary marked tree on the riverbank

29. What is used to determine the location of a point north or south of the equator?

    (A) longitude

    (B) true north

    (C) bridge

    (D) latitude

30. When returning from sea to a harbor in the United States, a ship is traveling in a channel. A green buoy with the number 7 is sighted off the starboard bow with a relative bearing of 005°. The ship's present course will keep this buoy on the starboard side as it passes. What should be done?

(A) The ship should continue traveling on its present course.

(B) The ship's heading should be turned to port to allow more distance between the ship and the buoy.

(C) The heading should quickly be changed to starboard so the buoy will be on the port side as the ship passes.

(D) The ship should increase its speed and keep its heading the same.

ANSWER KEY

MATH SKILLS

1. **(C)**

   Simplify using PEMDAS.
   $-(3^2) + (5 - 7)^2 - 3(4 - 8)$
   $= -(3^2) + (-2)^2 - 3(-4)$
   $= -9 + 4 - 3(-4)$
   $= -9 + 4 + 12 = \mathbf{7}$

2. **(D)**

   Write a proportion and then solve for x.
   $\frac{40}{45} = \frac{265}{x}$
   $40x = 11{,}925$
   $x = 298.125 \approx \mathbf{298}$

3. **(C)**

   All the points lie on the circle, so each line segment is a radius. The sum of the 4 lines will be 4 times the radius.
   $r = \frac{75}{2} = 37.5$
   $4r = \mathbf{150}$

4. **(B)**

   Write a proportion and then solve for x.
   $\frac{15{,}036}{7} = \frac{x}{2}$
   $7x = 30{,}072$
   $x = \mathbf{4{,}296}$

5. **(C)**

   Use the equation for percentages.
   $whole = \frac{part}{percentage} = \frac{17}{0.4} = \mathbf{42.5}$

6. **(B)**

   The sum of the measures of the three angles in a triangle is 180°. Subtract the two given angle measures from 180 to find the measure of the third angle.
   $180° - 25° - 110° = \mathbf{45°}$

7. **(A)**

   Add the number of cupcakes he will give to his friend and to his coworkers, then subtract that value from 48.
   # of cupcakes for his friend:
   $\frac{1}{2} \times 48 = 24$
   # of cupcakes for his coworkers:
   $\frac{1}{3} \times 48 = 16$
   $48 - (24 + 16) = \mathbf{8}$

8. **(C)**

   Round each value and add.
   $129{,}113 \approx 129{,}000$
   $34{,}602 \approx 35{,}000$
   $129{,}000 + 35{,}000 = \mathbf{164{,}000}$

9. (B)

Plug 4 in for j and simplify.

$2(j-4)^4 - j + \frac{1}{2}j$

$2(4-4)^4 - 4 + \frac{1}{2}(4) = \mathbf{-2}$

10. (C)

Simplify using PEMDAS.

$(5^2-2)^2 + 3^3$

$(25-2)^2 + 3^3$

$(23)^2 + 3^3$

$529 + 27 = \mathbf{556}$

11. (C)

Use the formula for percent change.

$percent\ change = \frac{amount\ of\ change}{original\ amount}$

$= \frac{(680-425)}{425}$

$= \frac{255}{425} = 0.60 = \mathbf{60\%}$

12. (D)

Find the area of the square as if it did not have the corners cut out.

$12\ mm \times 12\ mm = 144\ mm^2$

Find the area of the four cut out corners.

$2\ mm \times 2\ mm = 4\ mm^2$

$4(4\ mm^2) = 16\ mm^2$

Subtract the area of the cut out corners from the large square to find the area of the shape.

$144\ mm^2 - 16\ mm^2 = \mathbf{128\ mm^2}$

13. (D)

Assign variables and write the ratios as fractions. Then, cross multiply to solve for the number of apples and oranges sold.

x = apples

$\frac{apples}{bananas} = \frac{3}{2} = \frac{x}{20}$

$60 = 2x$

$x = 30$ apples

y = oranges

$\frac{oranges}{bananas} = \frac{1}{2} = \frac{y}{20}$

$2y = 20$

$y = 10$ oranges

To find the total, add the number of apples, oranges, and bananas

together. $30 + 20 + 10 = \mathbf{60\ pieces}$ **of fruit**

14. (D)

Find the time that Erica spends on break and subtract this from her total time at work.

$30 + 2(15) = 1$ hour

$8\frac{1}{2} - 1 = 7\frac{1}{2} = \mathbf{7\ hours,\ 30\ minutes}$

15. (B)

All of the decimal numbers are expressed in ten-thousandths. 55 is between 47 and 162, so **0.0055** is between 0.0047 and 0.0162.

16. (C)

Multiply the car's speed by the time traveled to find the distance.

$1.5(65) = 97.5$ miles

$2.5(50) = 125$ miles

$97.5 + 125 = \mathbf{222.5\ miles}$

17. (D)

Set up an equation. The original price (p) minus 30% of the original price is $385.

$p - 0.3p = 385$

$p = \frac{385}{0.7} = \mathbf{\$550}$

18. (C)

Two of the walls are 5 feet by 7 feet. The other two walls are 4 feet by 7 feet. Therefore, the total area of the four walls is:

$2(5)(7) + 2(4)(7) = 70 + 56 =$ **126 square feet**

19. (B)

Set up an equation. If p is the original number of pears, the store has sold $0.30p$ pears. The original number minus the number sold will equal 455.

$p - 0.30p = 455$

$p = \frac{455}{0.7} = \mathbf{650\ pears}$

20. (C)

Multiply the area by the charge per square foot.

Area = 50 × 30 = 1,500 square feet

1,500 × 0.05 = **$75.00**

21. **(D)**

Substitute −2 for x and evaluate.

$0.5x^{-2} + 1 = 4 + 1 = \textbf{5}$

22. **(B)**

Use a proportion to find the number of cars that Ethan can wash in 1 hour (60 minutes). Then add to answer the question.

$\frac{3}{45} = \frac{x}{60}$

$3(60) = x(45)$

$180 = 45x$

$4 = x$

$3 + 4 = \textbf{7}$

23. **(A)**

Find the area of the room in square feet and convert it to square yards (1 square yard = 9 square feet). Then multiply by the cost per square yard.

Area = 10 × 12 = 120 square feet

$\frac{120}{9} = \frac{40}{3}$ square yards

$\frac{40}{3} \times \$12.51 = \frac{\$500.40}{3} = \textbf{\$166.80}$

24. **(D)**

Add zeros as needed so that each number is expressed in thousandths; then add the numbers.

951.400 + 98.908 + 1.053 =

1,051.361 → **7 digits**

25. **(C)**

Use the area to find the length of a side of the square. Then find the perimeter of the square.

$x^2 = 5{,}625$

$x = \sqrt{5{,}625} = 75$

Perimeter = $4x = 4(75) = $ **300 feet**

READING SKILLS

1. (A) is incorrect. While the text does list several family members of Custer who died in the battle, this is not the main idea.

    (B) is incorrect. The author does not explain why the cavalry was formed.

    (C) is incorrect. The author does not describe the personal relationship between Sitting Bull and Custer.

    (D) is correct. The author writes, "the allied tribes decisively defeated their US foes."

2. (A) is incorrect. While the author does describe his memory loss, this is not the main idea of the passage.

    (B) is correct. The author writes, "From this, scientists learned that different types of memory are handled by different parts of the brain."

    (C) is incorrect. The author does explain the differences in long-term and short-term memory formation, but not until the end of the passage.

    (D) is incorrect. While it is implied that memories of physical skills are processed differently than memories of events, this is not the main idea of the passage.

3. (A) is incorrect. The author does not address the impact of light on bedbugs.

    (B) is incorrect. The author explains that the three discovered species still exist today.

    (C) is incorrect. The author does not address the growth rate of bedbug populations.

    (D) is correct. The author writes, "Humans only lived seasonally in the Oregon cave system, however, which might explain why these insects did not fully transfer to human hosts like bedbugs elsewhere did."

4. (A) is incorrect. There is no indication that the Bastille was occupied by royalty.

    (B) is incorrect. There is no indication that the structure was intended to represent anything.

    (C) is incorrect. There is no indication that the Bastille was used for governing.

    (D) is correct. The author writes that the Bastille was originally built "to protect the city from English invasion during the Hundred Years' War."

5. **(A) is correct.** This detail is not stated in the passage.

    (B) is incorrect. The second paragraph states that "when a person can't breathe through his nose, he won't be able to keep his mouth closed long enough to get an accurate reading."

    (C) is incorrect. The final paragraph states that "no matter which method [of taking a temperature] is chosen, however, it's important to check the average temperature for each region, as it can vary by several degrees."

    (D) is incorrect. The second paragraph states that "the most common way people measure body temperature is orally."

6. (A) is incorrect. Thermometers that measure temperature in the ear and temporal artery are mentioned in the passage; however, they are a supporting detail for the author's primary purpose.

    (B) is correct. In the first paragraph, the author writes, "But what's the best way to get an accurate reading? The answer depends on the situation." She then goes on to describe various options and their applications.

    (C) is incorrect. Though this detail is mentioned, it is not the author's primary focus.

    (D) is incorrect. The author writes about how many people—not only nurses—use different types of thermometers in different situations.

7. **(A) is correct.** The final paragraph states that "agitated patients...won't be able to sit still long enough for an accurate reading[.]" The reader can infer that an agitated patient is a patient who is visibly upset, annoyed, or uncomfortable.

(B) is incorrect. While some agitated patients may move quickly, this is not necessarily the meaning of the word in context.

(C) is incorrect. The term *violently ill* does not necessarily explain why a patient would have a difficult time sitting still.

(D) is incorrect. The team *slightly dirty* does not explain why a patient would have a difficult time sitting still.

8. **(A) is correct.** The second paragraph of the passage states that "[u]sing the rectum also has the added benefit of providing a much more accurate reading than other locations can provide."

(B) is incorrect. In the final paragraph, the author suggests that "certain people, like agitated patients or fussy babies" might have a difficult time sitting still but does not suggest that this is a problem for "many" people.

(C) is incorrect. In the final paragraph, the author writes that "it's important to check the average temperature for each region, as it can vary by several degrees" but does not cite this as a reason to use a rectal thermometer.

(D) is incorrect. The author does not mention access to thermometers as a consideration.

9. (A) is incorrect. The author writes that the protest spread in spite of government attempts to end it.

(B) is incorrect. The author writes, "In Dandi, Gandhi picked up a small chunk of salt and broke British law." Picking up a piece of salt is not itself an extreme act; Gandhi was able to make a big statement with a small action.

(C) is correct. The author describes a situation in which civil disobedience had an enormous impact.

(D) is incorrect. The action the author describes occurred in India when it was controlled by Britain, a colonial and nondemocratic power.

10. (A) is incorrect. The author points to the skills of the owner as the reason for The City Café's long-term success, not the quality of the dining experience.

(B) is correct. The passage states that restaurateurs must be "exact and ruthless with their budget and pricing." The success of The City Café implies that its owners have done that.

(C) is incorrect. The passage suggests that most new restaurants struggle but does not discuss how new restaurants affect the popularity of existing restaurants.

(D) is incorrect. The passage implies that all restaurateurs must work with the low margin of return and simply suggests that the owners of The City Café have made the most of it, not that they have any advantage in this respect.

11. (A) is incorrect. This answer choice does not fit in the context of the sentence; the author has not told a story about The City Café's success.

(B) is incorrect. This answer choice does not fit in the context of the sentence; the author does not indicate surprise.

(C) is incorrect. This answer choice does not fit in the context of the sentence.

(D) is correct. *Evidence* best describes the idea that The City Café's longevity is proof of its owners' skills.

12. **(A) is correct.** The bulk of the passage is dedicated to showing that conventional wisdom about "fewer calories in than calories out" isn't true for many people and is more complicated than previously believed.

(B) is incorrect. The author indicates that calorie counting is not an effective way to lose weight.

(C) is incorrect. Though the author indicates that this may be the case, the negative impacts of losing weight quickly are not the main point of the passage; a more inclusive sentence is needed to conclude the passage successfully.

(D) is incorrect. The author does not indicate that diets don't work at all, simply that the scientific understanding of dieting is still limited.

13. (A) is incorrect. A new diet pill would have no effect on the existing studies and would not prove anything about conventional dieting wisdom.

(B) is incorrect. A single anecdotal example would not be enough to contradict the results of well-designed studies; if anything, the account would provide another example of how complex the topics of dieting and weight loss are.

(C) is incorrect. This answer choice would strengthen the author's argument by highlighting the complexity of the topic of dieting.

(D) is correct. People misreporting the amount of food they ate would introduce error into studies on weight loss and might make the studies the author cites unreliable.

14. (A) is incorrect. While the author states this, it is not the main idea.

(B) is correct. The author states, "Ignored by the government, an activist group known as Indians of All Tribes sailed to Alcatraz in the early morning hours with eighty-nine men, women, and children." The author goes on to describe the nineteen-month occupation of the island.

(C) is incorrect. The author states that up to 600 people joined the occupation.

(D) is incorrect. The author does not describe any violent action towards protestors.

15. (A) is incorrect. While this fact is stated in the passage, it is not the main idea.

(B) is incorrect. The author writes, "However, these trends do not carry over outside of politics."

(C) is incorrect. The author explains that women have a large amount of political influence but less economic influence.

(D) is correct. The passage discusses the large number of women in political positions in Latin America.

16. (A) is incorrect. While this is stated in the first sentence, it is not the main idea.

(B) is correct. The passage describes the origin of Yellowstone's geysers.

(C) is incorrect. While the author states this in the passage, it is not the main idea.

(D) is incorrect. This is not stated in the passage.

17. (A) is incorrect. The author writes that the officers, not the volunteers, were veterans.

(B) is incorrect. There passage does not mention a citizenship requirement.

(C) is incorrect. While most of the volunteers were indeed from the Southwest, the passage does not say this was a requirement.

(D) is correct. The author writes, "the army set high standards: all of the recruits had to be skilled on horseback…"

18. (A) is incorrect. The author writes, "scientists uncovered a 3.2 million-year-old non-human hominid they nicknamed 'Lucy.'"

(B) is incorrect. The author does not connect Lucy's discovery with the knowledge about the area's past ecosystem.

(C) is correct. The author writes that before Lucy's discovery, the oldest known fossil from the genus Homo "dated only back to 2.3 million years ago, leaving a 700,000 gap between Lucy's species and the advent of humans."

(D) is incorrect. The author explains it was the 2013 discovery that narrowed the gap.

19. (A) is incorrect. The author identifies the ideals associated with idealism but does not offer an opinion on or advocate for them.

    (B) is correct. The purpose of the passage is to explain what an idealist believes in. The author does not offer any opinions or try to persuade readers about the importance of certain values.

    (C) is incorrect. The author states that social and political discourse are "permeated with idealism" but does not suggest that this is destructive or wrong.

    (D) is incorrect. The author provides the reader with information but does not seek to change the reader's opinions or behaviors.

20. (A) is incorrect. The author states that "Alexander Hamilton…called for the Constitutional Convention to write a constitution as the foundation of a stronger federal government."

    (B) is incorrect. The author states that "James Madison called for the Constitutional Convention to write a constitution as the foundation of a stronger federal government."

    (C) is incorrect. The author states that "Federalists like John Adams believed in... a strong federal government."

    (D) is correct. In the passage, Thomas Jefferson is defined as an anti-Federalist, in contrast with Federalists who believed in a strong federal government.

21. (A) is incorrect. The author provides no evidence that invasive species typically help native species.

    (B) is incorrect. The author writes that the quagga mussels, an invasive species, harmed native species.

    (C) is incorrect. The author implies that quagga mussels are thriving.

    (D) is correct. The author writes that "the reason for the cisco's reemergence is even more unlikely. The cisco have an invasive species, quagga mussels, to thank for their return."

22. (A) is incorrect. The author indicates that the house on Pine Street "had enough space inside[.]"

    (B) is correct. The author says that the house on Pine Street "had enough space inside but didn't have a big enough yard for [their] three dogs."

    (C) is incorrect. The author does not mention the neighborhood of the Pine Street house.

    (D) is incorrect. The author does not mention the price of the Pine Street house.

23. (A) is incorrect. The author does not suggest that the narrative of the Civil War as "a battle for individual identity" is a complicated one, only that it is untrue.

    (B) is correct. The author writes, "All other explanations for the war are either a direct consequence of the South's desire for wealth at the expense of her fellow man or a fanciful invention to cover up this sad portion of our nation's history."

    (C) is incorrect. The author does not discuss the extent to which the attempt to "cover up this sad portion of our nation's history" was successful or unsuccessful.

    (D) is incorrect. Though the author may agree that the invention of the identity narrative is unfortunate, this is not the best answer choice to highlight her main assertion that it is untrue.

24. **(A) is correct.** The author writes, "But people who try to sell you this narrative are wrong. The Civil War was not a battle of cultural identities—it was a battle about slavery."

(B) is incorrect. Though the author describes the cultural differences between the North and South in the first half of the passage, her primary purpose is revealed when she states, "But people who try to sell you this narrative are wrong."

(C) is incorrect. The author makes no comment on the outcome of the Civil War.

(D) is incorrect. The author asserts that, despite the popular identity narrative, the cause of the Civil War was actually very clear: "The Civil War was not a battle of cultural identities—it was a battle about slavery."

25. (A) is incorrect. The passage states that "vision does not become the dominant sense until around the age of 12 months."

(B) is correct. The passage states that "infants rely primarily on hearing."

(C) is incorrect. The sense of touch in not mentioned in the passage.

(D) is incorrect. The sense of smell is not mentioned in the passage.

1. **(B) is correct.** Moving the block farther from the brick changes the location of the fulcrum. The weight of the brick will have more torque since it is farther from the fulcrum; therefore it is going to take more force to lift. The increase in distance also will lift the board higher than before.

2. **(A) is correct.** Levers with a fulcrum that is between the effort and the resistance are always first-class levers.

3. **(A) is correct.** Adjacent gears rotate in the opposite directions. Gears 2 and 4 will move in the same direction, and Gears 1 and 3 will both move in the direction that is opposite to Gears 2 and 4.

4. **(B) is correct.** The larger the radius of a pulley, the slower it will turn. Because Pulley C has the largest radius, it will turn the slowest.

5. **(B) is correct.** The board is balanced when the net torque is zero, meaning the torque from each block is equal.

$$T_1 = T_2$$
$$F_1 l_1 = F_2 l_2$$
$$40(3) = 60 l_2$$
$$l_2 = \frac{120}{60} = \textbf{2 ft.}$$

6. **(C) is correct.** The figure shows a ramp acting as an inclined plane.

7. **(C) is correct.** The blocks will be at rest when the net force on the system is zero, meaning the total weight on the left side of the pulley must be equal to the weight on the right side. Block C needs to be 50 pounds so that there are 70 pounds on both sides of the pulley.

8. **(C) is correct.** When the bullet moves right and collides with the block, it will move the block the same direction. Since the block is attached to the string, it will also swing up.

9. **(A) is correct.** The weight of the air in the ball is much less than the same volume of water that was displaced. Therefore, the buoyant upward force is very large.

10. **(B) is correct.** The theoretical mechanical advantage is the total number of ropes that are in contact with the load, so the advantage is 2.

11. **(A) is correct.** The mass of an object is constant. The weight of an object depends on the force of gravity that the object experiences. The gravity of the moon is less than Earth's, so Object B will have the same mass but a smaller weight.

12. **(A) is correct.** The weight is evenly distributed on both sides of the object. Because B and C are helping each other carry the weight on the right side, A is bearing the most weight.

13. **(C) is correct.** To make air flow in the desired direction, open a valve on the opposite path. This causes a difference in pressure that will keep the air flowing on the desired path. To make the air flow through the top path, open all the valves on the bottom: 5, 6, and 7.

14. **(B) is correct.** Heat will transfer from the steel ball to the liquid. The equilibrium temperature depends on the masses of the objects and the specific heat of each object. Without knowing these values, the only guarantee is that the temperatures of the objects will be somewhere between 120°C and 150°C.

15. **(A) is correct.** The velocity of a fluid through a pipe is inversely related to the size of the pipe, so the water's velocity will go down when the diameter of the pipe goes up.

16. **(B) is correct.** Water flows into the tower at a rate of 140 gallons per hour and out at a rate of 3 gallons per minute, or 180 gallons per hour. The tower is losing 180 – 140 = 40 gallons of water per hour.

17. **(A) is correct.** The weight is closer to Scale A than it is to Scale B, so Scale A will have a higher reading. The fulcrum in this case is the center of the rod, so there is more weight on the left side of the fulcrum.

18. **(A) is correct.** The gas that is compressed into the smallest space will have the greatest pressure. Container A has the smallest volume, so it has the greatest pressure.

19. **(C) is correct.** The two charges are the same type, negative, and will therefore repel and move farther apart.

20. **(C) is correct.** Plug in the values for the resistors to get the equivalent resistance.

$$R_{eq} = R_1 + R_2 + ... + R_n$$
$$R_{eq} = 1 \text{ k}\Omega + 2 \text{ k}\Omega + 0.5 \text{ k}\Omega = 3.5 \text{ k}\Omega$$

21. **(A) is correct.** A conductor has free electrons that easily move current, while an insulator has restricted electrons that do not allow current to flow.

(B) is incorrect. Electrons are not created or destroyed by electronics materials. (They can be created or destroyed in nuclear reactions, like in the sun.)

(C) is incorrect. All materials will have heat created when electricity flows through them.

22. **(B) is correct.** A scale gives the weight of an object, not its mass. The scale reading is the same as the normal force that the object experiences. The object is moving upward, so the normal force has to be greater than the downward force of the weight. Thus, the scale will read a weight that is greater than 80 pounds.

23. **(B) is correct.** The net force on the object will be zero, so the mass is in equilibrium and will not accelerate.

24. **(A) is correct.** The height of the water moves up relative to the volume the object displaces, so the object with the higher volume will raise the water level higher. Density is the ratio of mass to volume, so if Objects A and B have the same mass, Object B must have a larger volume and thus a lower density.

25. **(A) is correct.** The current in the river will carry the boat downstream.

1. (A) is incorrect. The nose of the aircraft rises when the tail is pushed down.

   (B) is correct. When the elevators are raised, the tail of the aircraft is pushed down, which increases the pitch and raises the nose of the aircraft.

   (C) is incorrect. The elevators do not control left turns.

   (D) is incorrect. The elevators do not control right turns.

2. (A) is incorrect. The ailerons affect the longitudinal axis of the aircraft during turns.

   (B) is incorrect. The elevators affect pitch.

   (C) is correct. The rudder affects yaw; it controls the vertical axis of the aircraft.

   (D) is incorrect. The spoilers reduce lift, increase drag, and control speed.

3. (A) is incorrect. The teeter hinge allows the blades to flap.

   (B) is correct. The swashplate allows for directions movement of the aircraft.

   (C) is incorrect. The ducted fan is a component of the NOTAR aircraft design.

   (D) is incorrect. The tail boom is a structural component that supports the tail rotor assembly.

4. **(A) is correct.** This climb is used to clear obstacles that may be in the flight path.

   (B) is incorrect. This climb is used to cover the most distance, not the most altitude.

   (C) is incorrect. This climb will not produce the greatest altitude.

   (D) is incorrect. This is not a type of climb.

5. (A) is incorrect. The aircraft pitch would indeed change; however, this is not the best complete answer.

   (B) is incorrect. The airspeed would increase and the nose of the aircraft would pitch downward.

   (C) is incorrect. The airspeed would indeed increase due to the change of airflow around the wings caused by the cyclic or control wheel; however, this is not the best answer.

   (D) is correct. This is the best answer because it describes the combination of changes to the aircraft.

6. (A) is incorrect. A coaxial rotor system cancels torque effect by using counter rotating rotor heads.

   (B) is correct. Translating tendency causes a rotary-wing aircraft to drift laterally due to tail rotor thrust.

   (C) is incorrect. Gyroscopic precession is when a force input is applied yet the force output is felt 90 degrees later in the plane of rotation.

   (D) is incorrect. The tail rotor cancels out the torque effect.

7. (A) is incorrect. A change of heading would not reduce airspeed.

   (B) is incorrect. Decreasing altitude will result in an initial higher airspeed.

   (C) is correct. Approaching the red line means the aircraft is reaching the maximum airspeed for the aircraft.

   (D) is incorrect. Increasing thrust will increase airspeed to an excess level if all other forces remain the same.

8. (A) is incorrect. Above ground level (AGL) is an altitude measurement.

   (B) is incorrect. Degrees are used in directional headings.

   (C) is correct. Feet per minute (fpm) describes a rate of climb.

   (D) is incorrect. Airspeed is measured in knots.

9. (A) is incorrect. The rudder controls adverse yaw.

(B) is incorrect. The wings and ailerons control bank.

(C) is correct. The lateral axis controls pitch when the nose moves up and down.

(D) is incorrect. The longitudinal axis controls roll.

10. (A) is incorrect. The teeter hinge allows the blades to flap.

(B) is incorrect. The rotor hub is the center attachment point for the rotor head components.

(C) is correct. The blade grips allow the main rotor blades to feather.

(D) is incorrect. The skids are used as landing gear for rotary-wing aircraft.

11. (A) is incorrect. This describes indicated altitude.

(B) is incorrect. This describes density altitude.

(C) is incorrect. This describes true altitude.

(D) is correct. Absolute altitude is indeed the height above ground level (AGL).

12. **(A) is correct.** The angle of attack (AOA) is the angle between the chord (pitch) of the aircraft wing and the direction of relative wind.

(B) is incorrect. The artificial horizon is the line that represents the horizon of the earth and the aircraft attitude on the attitude indicator.

(C) is incorrect. The minimum limits of aircraft performance are shown on the vertical speed indicator.

(D) is incorrect. The pressure altitude is displayed on the altimeter when the setting window is adjusted to 29.92 Hg.

13. **(A) is correct.** The pilot must be acknowledged with the aircraft call sign to establish communications.

(B) is incorrect. This is true for Class C and D controlled airspaces but not true for Class B airspace.

(C) is incorrect. Approval for clearance is required for Class A through D controlled airspaces.

(D) is incorrect. When aircraft clearances are required, it applies to all types of aircraft.

14. (A) is incorrect. A shallow turn is less than 20 degrees and does not need aileron pressure to return the aircraft to level flight, unlike medium and steep turns.

(B) is incorrect. While medium turns do require aileron pressure to return the aircraft to level flight, a shallow turn is less than 20 degrees and does not need aileron pressure to return the aircraft to level flight.

(C) is incorrect. A shallow turn is less than 20 degrees and does not need aileron pressure to return the aircraft to level flight.

(D) is correct. These turns are between 20 and 45 degrees and greater than a 45-degree bank. The pilot inputs aileron pressure to return the aircraft to level flight for both of these types of turns.

15. (A) is incorrect. This would increase airspeed.

(B) is incorrect. This would increase airspeed.

(C) is incorrect. Extending the ailerons and flaps would decrease thrust, but this is done during landing to slow the aircraft.

(D) is correct. When increasing pitch, thrust must be increased to provide lift and maintain vertical speed or a stall will result.

16. **(A) is correct.** This is the acronym for aircraft gross weight, also known as all-up weight (AUW). This weight changes during the flight due to consumables (i.e., oil and fuel).

(B) is incorrect. This is the acronym for maximum landing weight.

(C) is incorrect. This is maximum ramp weight.

(D) is incorrect. This is maximum takeoff weight.

17. (A) is incorrect. Weight, lift, thrust, and drag must be in balance in order to hover.

(B) is incorrect. An effective translational lift results from increased efficiency of the main rotor system as directional flight is established.

(C) is correct. Advancing and retreating blades of the rotor system generate unequal lifting forces: a dissymmetry of lift.

(D) is incorrect. Gyroscopic precession is when a force input is applied yet the force output is felt 90 degrees later in the plane of rotation.

18. (A) is incorrect. The cyclic controls the pitch and roll axis of the aircraft.

(B) is incorrect. The collective changes the pitch of the blades simultaneously.

(C) is incorrect. The tail rotor pedals control the yaw axis of the aircraft.

(D) is correct. The throttle maintains the engine within optimal flight parameters.

19. **(A) is correct.** The helm is the apparatus used to control the direction of the ship. An associated term is the Conn, as in conning (controlling the direction and speed of the ship).

20. (A) is incorrect. Lag has a delay of 6 to 9 seconds; trend information is in real time.

(B) is incorrect. Lag has a delay of 6 to 9 seconds.

(C) is incorrect. Although trend information is in real time, lag is not.

(D) is correct. Trend information displays in real time in relation to the movement of the cyclic.

21. (A) is incorrect. AOA is the angle between the direction of the airflow and the chord on a wing—the imaginary reference line that extends from the leading edge to the trailing edge.

(B) is incorrect. A degree is the directional measurement for an aircraft.

(C) is correct. Airspeed is measured in knots.

(D) is incorrect. Mean sea level (MSL) is an altitude measurement.

22. **(B) is correct.** Time multiplied by speed equals distance. When using nautical miles for measuring distances, speed is expressed in knots (nautical miles per hour). Six minutes is 1/10th of an hour, so shifting the decimal point to the right determines speed (i.e., 1.0 miles in 1/10th of an hour is 10 knots).

23. **(C) is correct.** Starboard is the term for the right-hand side of a ship when facing forward.

24. **(D) is correct.** The keel is the backbone of the ship and runs along the centerline of the hull from bow to stern.

25. **(D) is correct.** When soundings are in fathoms and feet, the first number is fathoms and the second number is feet. One fathom is 6 feet; thus 2 fathoms is equal to 12 feet. So is 12 fathoms and 4 feet, and 12 fathoms multiplied by 6 feet per fathom is 72 feet. Add the extra 4 feet to get 76 feet.

26. **(C) is correct.** The point at which the hull is at the water's surface is the waterline.

27. **(C) is correct.** The cruiser is the largest ship in service.

28. **(D) is correct.** Aids to navigation (lighthouses, lightships, beacons, and buoys) are built specifically to help determine position, define a safe course, and highlight hazards.

29. **(D) is correct.** The higher the latitude, the farther one is from the equator.

30. **(C) is correct.** When returning from sea to a harbor in the United States, red buoys indicate the right-hand (starboard) side of the channel, and green buoys indicate the left-hand (port) side of the channel. A green buoy on a ship's starboard side indicates that it is outside and to the port side of the safe channel. It is critical that the ship turns to return to the channel promptly.

Made in United States
North Haven, CT
28 July 2023